Drugs and Crime

Drugs and Crime
Second edition

Philip Bean

WILLAN
PUBLISHING

Published by

Willan Publishing
Culmcott House
Mill Street, Uffculme
Cullompton, Devon
EX15 3AT, UK
Tel: +44(0)1884 840337
Fax: +44(0)1884 840251
e-mail: info@willanpublishing.co.uk
website: www.willanpublishing.co.uk

Published simultaneously in the USA and Canada by

Willan Publishing
c/o ISBS, 920 NE 58th Ave, Suite 300,
Portland, Oregon 97213-3786, USA
Tel: +001(0)503 287 3093
Fax: +001(0)503 280 8832
e-mail: info@isbs.com
website: www.isbs.com

First edition 2001
Second edition 2004
Reprinted 2006

ISBN-10 1-84392-097-2
ISBN-13 978-1-84392-097-7

British Library Cataloguing-in-Publication Data

A catalogue record for this book is available from the British Library

Typeset by GCS, Leighton Buzzard, Bedfordshire, LU7 1AR
Project managed by Deer Park Productions, Tavistock, Devon
Printed and bound by TJI Digital, Padstow, Cornwall

Contents

List of figures and tables

Figures

Tables

For
Charlotte, Stacie, Celina, Jade
and Charlie

Preface

Writing in the late 1960s on drug taking and crime, I thought any link (such as there was) would be complex and full of pitfalls for the unwary. I little realised how true this was, nor how many and deep were the pitfalls. Nor was I able to see that drugs and crime would dominate government thinking. In the 1960s questions were rarely about crime but of over-prescribing, about the role of the medical profession and how best to explain drug taking within the context of the social attitudes of the time.

In the last 40 years or so things have changed. Then drug users were rare; now they are commonplace. Then they were pitied; now they are likely to be scorned. Then there was no supply system except through over-prescribing doctors; today cocaine comes from the Andes, heroin from Afghanistan, Turkey or South East Asia, and amphetamines, ecstasy and similar drugs are manufactured in Britain or on the continent. In the last five years or so the government has reacted to the drug problem – but whether always with the appropriate vision or in the right direction remains a matter for debate. Some of the policies seem right, but others (which have led to the Drug Treatment and Testing Order) and the dominant role given to drug action teams are surely not. In addition, government-funded research is scanty, often promoting short-term, small, atheoretical, epidemiological studies. Large-scale longitudinal studies that would provide detailed information about the natural history of the phenomena have not been forthcoming. Nor do non-governmental agencies fare better for they, too, rarely promote high-quality research.

I offer this book as a way of assessing what is broadly known about drugs and crime and related matters such as policing, drug testing and treatment. I have also made suggestions about how best to proceed. Inevitably the topics selected represent a personal interest, and no claim is made to suggest they produce a compendium of the drugs–crime debate. None the less, it is hoped enough areas have been covered to sustain the claim that this book includes most of what we mean when we talk of drugs and crime, especially as these affect Britain.

It is nearly three years since I wrote the first edition. Things have moved on since then. In some ways not as fast as one would have liked, for we are still a long way from meeting and dealing with some of the more obvious structural difficulties. There has been no attempt to replace the Drug Treatment and Testing Orders, and nothing has been done about trying to get treatment and criminal justice agencies to work together more closely. Nor has there been an evaluation of the way the 149 Drug Action Teams operate, with their budget of about £400 million per year (*Guardian* 22 May 2003). Might all this be an indication that inertia or the like is the dominating force? Perhaps so. Let us hope someone somewhere will provide the necessary political drive to move things forward.

In this second edition, major changes have been introduced. Chapters 1, 2 and 3 have been recast, with some of the material in Chapter 2 being transferred to Chapter 1, and Chapter 2 extended considerably. In Chapter 2, I have tried to develop the drugs–crime debate more fully and to try to 'unpack' it, to use the modern terminology. Chapter 2 is therefore a much enlarged theoretical chapter which shows that the matter is both more and less complicated than imagined. Chapter 3 has been changed largely to bring it up to date with recent developments, including recent data and information. In this and the first chapter I have drawn heavily on the work of John Corkery, whose assistance I want to acknowledge. John has not only given freely of his time but generously granted permission to use a great deal of his data. My thanks to him for all the help given, which was more than anyone should expect or hope for.

Chapter 4 has been left largely unchanged, albeit with a few amendments. Chapter 5 has been extended to take account of a number of developments, mainly in drug courts in Scotland and Ireland. Chapter 6 remains largely the same, but there have been changes to Chapter 7. Whilst Chapters 8 and 9 are largely as before, the last chapter has also been extended to take account of recent developments. Hopefully, the book has been strengthened, providing a more up-to-date account of the position.

I want to thank others who have assisted (too numerous to mention) and especially those colleagues in the Midlands Centre for Criminology and the Department of Social Sciences, University of Loughborough, who have provided help and encouragement throughout. I want to take this opportunity to acknowledge the help given by so many, including friends and immediate family. That this book is dedicated to five of my grandchildren is a further indication of their importance.

Philip Bean
September 2004

Publisher's acknowledgements

We are grateful to the Home Office for permission to reproduce Figures 3.2 and 3.3 and to John Corkery to reproduce Tables 1.1 to 1.8, 1.10, 3.1 and 3.2 and Figures 1.1, 3.1.

Chapter 1

Drugs and crime: an overview

A great deal has been said about the links between drugs and crime and, in Britain, an increasing amount of resources is given to drug-crime prevention programmes. For example, the Criminal Justice and Court Services Act 2001 involves estimated costs for national implementation of the new drug-testing proposals of approximately £45.5 million (House of Commons 2000: 24). This is a small part of an ever-increasing spiral of expenditure aimed at reducing drug use – rightly described as the scourge of our age – and the corresponding social and economic problems it brings.

For our purposes, 'drugs' are defined as those substances controlled by the Drugs Prevention of Misuse of Drugs Act 1971 (henceforth the 1971 Act), of which there are a number. (The terms 'drug misuse', 'substance misuse' or 'drug abuse' will be used interchangeably.) Cannabis, amphetamines, heroin, cocaine, 'crack', LSD and ecstasy are, for these purposes, the most important, as they tend to be the most widely used illegally. Debates about what constitutes a drug, the moral connotations attached to the term and about how or under what circumstances certain substances are selected for control are important but not considered here. These are topics in their own right warranting more consideration than space permits. The task here is different: it is to examine some of the major criminological implications of the drugs–crime nexus, to determine how drugs and crime are linked and to assess the responses made to those links.

It is not just the 1971 Act which is under scrutiny: in the 1990s, major pieces of legislation were introduced dealing with drug offences and drug trafficking. For example, the Criminal Justice Act 1993 and the Drug

Trafficking Act 1994 dealt with drug offenders and trafficking, and the Criminal Justice and Public Order Act 1994, the Crime and Disorder Act 1998 and the Criminal Justice and Court Services Act 2001 dealt with similar matters. These will be considered where necessary. The drugs–crime debate also extends beyond the legislation to include, *inter alia*, policing (whether on matters of interdiction – i.e. before drugs enter Britain – or local procedures, including the use of informers) and the sentencing of drug offenders involving treatment programmes, whether as part of a sentence of the court or not. It can and, indeed, should, include the impact of drug use on local communities – not least because of the deleterious effect drugs have upon them.

To complicate things further, many of the substances controlled by the 1971 Act can be prescribed by selected physicians to substance misusers. Maintenance prescribing has a long tradition in British drug policy, going back at least to the Rolleston Committee in 1926 (Bean 1974; Spear 2002). Without going into the merits or defects of maintenance prescribing, one of its critics defined it as 'producing a maladaptive pattern of use manifested by recurrent and significant adverse consequences related to the repeated use of substances with clinically significant impairment or distress' (Ghodse 1995: 162). This should alert us to some of the complexities. If substances can be prescribed, the question must be: for what reason? Are they to assist the offender or to reduce crime? And what, after all, is a 'maladaptive pattern'? Or, how are we to talk of dangerous drugs when some prohibited substances are not dangerous, whilst others not included are? Moreover, what are the boundaries of the debate? Hopefully some of these questions will be answered here, but some remain elusive and difficult to unravel. We can begin, however, with a workable definition of what we mean by 'drugs'. For these purposes, and to avoid a lengthy and acrimonious debate, a pragmatic, circular definition has been used – 'drugs' are what are usually included in the debate about drugs.

Extent of drug use

Who, and how many, are the users? Drug misuse is largely an illegal activity, making it difficult to measure. Traditionally, national estimates have been based on a set of indicators which have included convictions for possession or supply, drug seizures by police and HM Customs and Excise, and notification to the Addicts Index where notification was required under the Misuse of Drug (Notification of and Supply to

Addicts) Regulations 1973. Taken together they provided some evidence of trends of use throughout Britain. These standard indicators are still used, although to what effect remains unclear. The Addicts Index has been replaced by what is now called a 'starting agency episode'. This is where users are recorded when they first attend a selected drug treatment agency or reattend after a break of six months or more. Unfortunately, data from these starting agency episodes are not comparable with those of the older Addicts Index and, of course, seizures or possession offences of themselves are uncertain indicators, reflecting the activities of the police and HM Customs rather than measuring the extent of use.

In this section I want to give a general overview of the extent of drug abuse, bearing in mind that, at best, the results will give only a crude estimate – which to some critics is so poor as to be virtually worthless. To others, including myself, the results are indicators that illustrate trends and developments. Accordingly, I have selected one or two key indicators which, in their way, provide insights into the current position. Most of the data come from large-scale self-report surveys (such as the British Crime Survey) and from government data on reported addict notifications (what are called starting agency episodes).

The British Crime Survey (BCS) is a large-scale household survey representative of the general public in England and Wales where, although the main focus is on victims of crime, drug taking has been included. As a self-report study the limitations are clear: drug users under-report the drugs taken (Carver 2004). Hence there is a need for drug testing and close objective monitoring through independent means. The 'best estimates' (as listed below) are also taken from the BCS, whilst the data on seizures come from the police and HM Customs. But, defective though they are, taken together they offer something worth while.

First, the surveys. The Home Office and Scottish Office (now the Scottish Executive) conduct regular surveys of people's experience of crime (see, in particular, Corkery 2003 for an excellent summary of this data). The most recently published fully detailed report covers the 2000 survey in England and Wales (Ramsay et al. 2001). These surveys provide a measure of prevalence of drug misuse in Great Britain on the part of the general population. (For a review of how survey methodology in this field has developed, see Ramsay and Percy 1997.) John Corkery (2003) has summarised the main points emerging from the 2000 BCS as follows:

- Young people aged 16–29 years reported the highest level of drug misuse: 50% indicated they had taken a prohibited drug at some time. Only 25% of 16–29-year-olds had taken drugs within the last year, with just 16% having done so within the last month.

- Levels of drug misuse were relatively stable across England and Wales between 1994 and 1996. This stability generally persisted between 1996 and 1998. The overall level of drug use did not change between 1998 and 2000. However, there were some changes in the use of individual drugs.

- Cannabis was still the most widely consumed prohibited drug. There was a significant increase between 1996 and 1998 in the use of this drug by young men aged 16–29 years, whose prevalence rate for the last year rose from 25 to 29%. However, this fell to 23% in 2000. The equivalent rate for females rose from 10 to 12%.

- There has been continued (but possibly decelerating) growth in the use of cocaine across all age groups, including 16–19-year-olds. Amongst this group, last-year use increased from 1% in 1994 to 4% in 2000.

- The use of amphetamines, LSD and 'poppers' fell in 2000. Use of any drug by 16–19-year-olds fell from about one third in 1994 to just over a quarter in 2000.

- Levels of use have remained fairly stable, except amongst males aged 25–29 years, for whom there was a significant rise in 2000.

Comparisons over the BCS years 1994–2002/3 are given in Figure 1.1. The data show a steady, albeit slow, increase in the eight-year period. From 2001/2 the BCS became an annual survey, with respondents interviewed continuously throughout the year. The main points as noted by Aust *et al.* (2002; Condon and Smith 2003 cited in Corkery 2003; pers. com.) are as follows:

- In 2001/2, 34% of 16–59-year-olds reported they had used an illicit drug at some time, and 12% in the last year (equating to around 4 million users). Last-year use remained at this level in 2002/3. Cannabis was the most frequently used drug in the last year (11%) for this age group in both these survey years. Last-year use of amphetamines, LSD, magic mushrooms and steroids had decreased significantly since 1998. Cocaine and crack use had increased significantly over the same time period, whilst ecstasy use had risen significantly to 2001/2 but had fallen slightly in 2002/3.

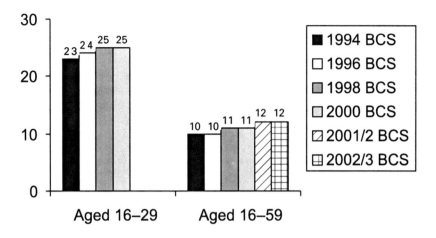

Figure 1.1 Use of drugs in previous year, BCS 1994–2002/3 expressed as a percentage
Source: Corkery 2003

- People aged 16–24 years are significantly more likely to have used drugs in the last year and the last month than older people. The use of Class A drugs by this age group has not changed significantly since 1994. Last-year use of amphetamines, LSD, magic mushrooms, methadone and solvents had decreased significantly since 1998 but cocaine and crack use had risen significantly. A fall in the use of ecstasy was noted in 2002/3.

- In 2001/2 the mean age of first use of cannabis was 15.5 years compared with heroin at 17.4 and cocaine at 18.2.

- The 16–24 age group reported that cannabis was the easiest drug to obtain, followed by ecstasy, amphetamines and cocaine.

- The 2002/3 BCS estimated that 62% of 16–24-year-old drug users had used only one drug in the last year and nearly three quarters had used just one drug in the last month. This is slightly lower than the rates for the survey sample as a whole.

In 1994 the BCS came up with what it called the 'best estimates' (see Table 1.1) of the number of people aged 16–59 years in England and Wales who had tried four specific substances (Ramsay and Percy 1996: Table 4.5). Five years later, the 1999 BCS provided best estimates for 16–24-year-olds using a different set of drugs in the last year and month in England and Wales in 1998. These are given in Table 1.2 (Ramsay and

Table 1.1 Best estimates of those who had tried four specific substances (England and Wales and in the last month, 1994)

	Ever	Last month
Cannabis	6,307,000	1,486,000
Amphetamine	2,486,000	303,000
LSD	1,324,000	152,000
Ecstasy	728,000	121,000

Source: Ramsay and Percy 1996, cited in Corkery 2003.

Table 1.2 Best estimates for selected drugs (for last year and last month, 1999)

	Last year	Last month
Any drug	1,865,000	1,220,000
Cannabis	1,735,000	1,095,000
Cocaine	195,000	65,000
'Opiates+'	195,000	65,000

Source: Ramsay and Partridge 1999, cited in Corkery 2003.

Partridge 1999: Table B16). Table 1.3 covers later years. It shows the best estimates for use by 16–24-year-olds in the last year (2000, 2001/2 and 2002/3) and last month (2000) (Ramsay *et al.* 2001: Table B11; Aust *et al.* 2002: Table 4; Condon and Smith 2002: Table 4).

Comparisons between Tables 1.2 and 1.3 are interesting. They suggest that cannabis remained the most widely used illicit drug but, interestingly enough, the use of cocaine, crack and heroin appeared to decline, as did the use of 'any drug'. Dare one believe that there has been a decline in drug use? Perhaps, although of course the data are 'estimates' and should be seen in those terms. Moreover, whilst there may have been a general overall decline in the use of some drugs, there will be 'hotspots' where drug use remains heavy and may be increasing. Large-scale surveys do not pick up hotspots that might be local and, hence, confined to small geographical areas.

The picture in Scotland during 1996 was similar to that in England and Wales. John Corkery (2003) reports that the Scottish Crime Survey (Anderson and Frischer 1997) estimated that between 600,000 and 750,000 individuals in the 16–59 years age group had ever tried illicit drugs. It would appear from the Scottish Crime Survey that, in Scotland,

Table 1.3 Best estimates for 16–24-year-olds for selected drugs for the last year and last month.

	Last year 2000	2001/2	2002/3	Last month (2000)
Cocaine	285,000	275,000	270,000	103,000
Crack	50,000	26,000	27,000	11,000
Heroin	46,000	18,000	12,000	18,000
Class A	533,000	499,000	474,000	275,000
Cannabis	1,503,000	1,525,000	1,497,000	959,000
Any drug	1,649,000	1,678,000	1,629,000	1,036,000

Source: Ramsay *et al.* 2001; Aust *et al.* 2002; Condon and Smith 2002, cited in Corkery 2003.

heroin, crack and methadone are rarely used, whereas cannabis is widely used. However, Corkery says that, in reality, these drugs are also widely used – as shown by the comparatively high numbers of deaths involving these substances in Scotland. Between 1993 and 1996 there were statistically significant increases in the use of cannabis and also for cocaine and valium. This contrasts with a fairly stable picture in England and Wales between 1994 and 1996. It appears that females in Scotland are less likely to continue using drugs on a regular basis after initial experimentation (Corkery 2003).

The results of the 2000 Scottish Crime Survey show that life-time use of any drug was significantly higher for males (at 22.4%) than for females (at 16.1%) (Fraser 2002). Overall, life-time use fell from 22.5% in 1996 to 19.2% in 2000. The most important falls were in the use of temazepam and valium (down by 1.9%), followed by cannabis, magic mushrooms and amphetamines. Life-time use rose for heroin (from 0.8 to 1.2%) and for crack (from 0.7 to 1.0%) between 1996 and 2000. However, it should be noted that the sample size of this survey is not very large, and that it is a survey of general households rather than of problematic users (Corkery 2003).

These patterns are also replicated in last-year use, where the overall rate fell from 9% to 7%. Whilst overall rates remained stable amongst 16–25-year-old females (20% in 1996; 19% in 2000), use amongst males fell from 33 to 18%. More than a third (37%) of 16–29-year-olds had ever tried drugs compared with 13% of those aged 30 or over. Those in low-income households (under £15,000 p.a.) or who were unemployed or in full-time education, and those who spend most evenings away from home, are more likely to have used drugs in the previous year. The general impression from the 2000 survey results is that the previous increases in

7

drug use noted amongst the general population in Scotland may be tailing-off (Corkery 2003).

The Northern Ireland Omnibus Surveys for 1996 and 1997 indicate a slight fall (from 28% to 24%) in the proportion of respondents aged 16–59 years admitting to taking at least one illegal drug (Northern Ireland Office 1999). The most commonly used drug at any time in the past was cannabis (20% in 1996; 16% in 1997). The next most popular drugs were tranquillisers (falling from 8% in 1996 to 6% a year later), but there was very little experience of crack, cocaine, heroin, methadone and anabolic steroids. After cannabis, males were more likely to use LSD, whilst females were more likely to use tranquillisers. In 1997, 27% of males and 20% of females had ever taken drugs. There was a statistically significant fall in the percentage of men who had ever taken drugs – down from 37% in 1996. Drug misuse in Northern Ireland is low compared with other parts of the UK (Corkery 2003).

These results are broadly in agreement with findings from the 1998 Northern Ireland Crime Survey (Hague *et al.* 2000). This also gives life-time drug use as 24% in 1998. However, this is a rise from the 20% recorded in 1995. Life-time use of cannabis also increased during this period from 12% to 18%. Male use of any illicit drug in 1998 was higher than that of female use, no matter which period of recall was involved: life-time rates were 30% and 19% respectively (last year 13% and 5%; and last month 7% and 3%). The most common drugs ever used by males were cannabis (24%), amphetamines and magic mushrooms (both 9%). However, for last-year use, the rates were cannabis 11%, ecstasy 4% and amphetamines 2% (the corresponding rates for last-month use were 6%, 2% and 1%). Those aged 16–29 years are significantly more likely to use illicit drugs than 30–59-year-olds. Males in the younger age group are one and a half times more likely to have used drugs than females. Males are also more likely to have used drugs such opiates, cocaine or crack – again, especially those in the younger age group and particularly in relation to cocaine and heroin (Corkery pers. comm.).

The results of the 2001 Northern Ireland Crime Survey are still awaited. However, the results of the first all-Ireland survey were recently released. They give figures for both the Republic of Ireland and Northern Ireland separately and combined (NACD and DAIRU 2003). The results for Northern Ireland show that 20% of people aged 15–64 years had used drugs at some time. Last-year use was 6% and recent (last-month) use was 3.3%. Life-time use of cannabis was 17% and last month 3%. Other life-time use rates were ecstasy 6%, LSD 5%, cocaine 2% and heroin 0.2%.

The highest level of life-time illegal drug use was amongst 15–34-year-olds (31%), compared with 10% for 45–54-year-olds and 4% of those aged

55–64 years. Six per cent of males reported last-month use of drugs, compared with 1% of females. Women and older age groups have higher levels of use of tranquillisers, sedatives and antidepressants. These findings are in line with those of other recent surveys and suggest that drug use patterns in Northern Ireland remain fairly stable.

Table 1.4 sets out details of age and gender in the six-month period ending 31 March 2001 of those users classified as 'starting agency episodes' in Great Britain. Table 1.5 gives the data for England, Wales and Scotland. To repeat the point made earlier, these figures replace those derived from the old Home Office Addicts Index but they are not a complete replacement. Notification to the Addicts Index was compulsory, even if often flouted, but, even so, the data were better than those currently collected using the 'starting agency episode'. These new data are collected by anonymous reports, and there may be duplication in reporting. Also from 1987 onwards, the index recorded 'renotifications' but this is not used in the data for Table 1.4, which gives episodes not persons. Table 1.4, therefore, shows little more than a set of general trends. None the less, the figures confirm what has been shown before – that males users outnumber females, in this case by just under 3 to 1, and that the peak age for seeking treatment for problematic drug use is 20–24 years for females and 25–29 years for males. After the age of 29, the decline is steady and dramatic (at least after the age of 35).

Table 1.4 Age and gender of users starting agency episodes in the six months ending 31 March 2001 (Great Britain)

Age group	Male	Female	All persons
<15	287	109	396
15–19	3,161	1,574	4,735
20–24	7,311	2,919	10,230
25–29	7,604	2,417	10,021
30–34	5,772	1,736	7,508
35–39	3,177	976	4,153
40–44	1,297	432	1,729
45–49	659	216	875
50–54	268	77	345
55–59	94	24	118
60–64	21	20	41
>64	18	12	30
All ages	29,669	10,512	40,181

Source: Derived from DH (2002: Table D2), cited in Corkery 2003.

Table 1.5 shows that the figures for England and Scotland have more than doubled from 30 September 1993 to 31 March 2001 but rather less so for Wales. However, it is not easy to link these figures to other indicators (such as drug seizures or drug offenders) which point to a rise in use, but this has not always been the case: there were drops in both the number of seizures and offenders dealt with in 1999 and 2000, although there was a rise in seizures in 2001. Sadly, there are few good longitudinal studies in Britain to provide better data, and this is another serious failing. That by Aldridge *et al.* (1999) is an exception.

HIV/AIDS and the mortality of drug users

What, then, are some of the health problems common to drug users (especially those concerning HIV/AIDS), and what are the death rates associated with that drug use? For reasons which are obvious, drug users have special health problems, in addition to any psychological or social problems they may exhibit. Some of these concern mental health matters – i.e. the problem of what is often known as dual diagnosis. Drug offenders or, rather, drug users, also have high rates for HIV/AIDS, alongside a high death rate.

Table 1.5 Users starting agency episodes by period and country

Six months ending	England	Wales	Scotland	Great Britain
30-9-93	16,810	1,204	2,207	20,221
31-3-94	17,864	1,261	2,457	21,582
30-9-94	19,331	1,159	3,217	23,707
31-3-95	20,733	1,320	3,387	25,440
30-9-95	22,848	1,211	3,876	27,935
31-3-96	23,313	1,288	4,255	28,856
30-9-96	24,879	1,220	4,193	30,292
31-3-97	25,925	1,141	4,618	31,684
30-9-97	21,996	1,107	4,159	27,262
31-3-98	23,916	1,068	4,781	29,765
30-9-98	28,599	1,270	5,006	34,875
31-3-99	28,499	1,412	4,891	34,802
30-9-99	30,545	1,837	5,299	37,681
31-3-00	31,815	1,913	5,327	39,055
30-9-00	33,093	1,776	4,789	39,658
31-3-01	33,234	1,954	4,993	40,181

Source: Derived from DH (2002: Table D1), cited in Corkery 2003.

Consider first HIV / AIDS – again the data are taken from the report by John Corkery (2003). Table 1.6 reports the HIV and AIDS statistics obtained from the Communicable Disease Surveillance Centre (CDSC) and the Scottish Centre for Infection and Environmental Health (SCIEH). A quarterly bulletin published in July 2003 gives details for the quarter ending June 2003. This shows that some 3,987 of AIDS and some 1,176 of HIV cases were contracted by heterosexual injecting drug users. There were a further 707 cases concerning homosexual injecting drug users (Corkery 2003), but these are not included in Table 1.6 as it is not clear whether the AIDS or HIV was directly attributable to drug use or homosexuality. The table gives details of HIV and AIDS cases by gender and age, as well as breaking the data down by country and region. Not surprisingly, the largest concentration of HIV or AIDS was in London. Wales had 10 AIDS cases and 36 HIV cases, whereas Northern Ireland had 4 AIDS cases and 8 HIV. Scotland had 404 AIDS cases and 1,200 HIV. It is surprising that the figures for Wales and Northern Ireland are low (as are those for the West Midlands) – especially when compared with the East Midlands. Those for the North East are also low; those for Scotland are almost as high as London.

John Corkery (2003) reports that the prevalence data for hepatitis B and C antibody (HBV and HCV) are available for England and Wales from the Unlinked Anonymous Prevalence Monitoring Programme survey of injecting drug users (DH 2001). There has been no consistent trend over recent years in the proportion of cases reported as being hepatitis B or antibody positive. However, laboratory reports of acute hepatitis B infection show an upward trend between 1994 and 1998, more than doubling in that period but declining in 1999. The level of hepatitis C antibodies has been screened for since 1998. These screenings have demonstrated considerably higher levels of hepatitis C antibodies than those of hepatitis B, and have shown an increase amongst those aged under 25.

Corkery also reports that, up to the end of June 2002, 8,719 (60.6%) of a total of 14,390 known cases in Scotland of hepatitis C antibody positive were injecting drug users. Ninety-five per cent (8,281 cases) of these were aged between 15 and 44 years at the time of testing – the age range within which most injecting drug users are found. Up to 1993, the proportion of persons acquiring the infection through injecting drug use rose sharply, peaking at 63.4%. Since that time the proportion has varied between 54.3% and 60.5% (ibid.). However, since 1999 the rate has risen to about 65% or 66%.

Taking the UK as a whole, Table 1.7 presents the data in terms of age and gender. Table 1.8 presents the data in terms of ethnicity and gender.

Table 1.6 HIV and AIDS rates per 100,00 population by region of report (UK, June 2003)

| | Number of cases | | | | Pop. est. 2002 (thousands) | | Rates per 100,000 population | | | |
| | AIDS | | HIV | | | | AIDS | | HIV | |
	Male	Female	Male	Female	Male	Female	Male	Female	Male	Female
England										
North East	7	4	37	16	1,200.0	1,269.9	0.58	0.31	3.08	1.26
Yorkshire & Humberside	36	9	111	44	2,384.5	2,512.4	1.51	0.36	4.66	1.75
East Midlands	31	14	73	24	2,036.9	2,099.9	1.52	0.67	3.58	1.14
Eastern	23	7	111	35	2,614.3	2,713.3	0.88	0.26	4.25	1.29
London	310	126	1,069	533	3,587.5	3,671.6	8.64	3.43	29.80	14.52
South East	63	18	211	78	3,836.5	4,007.9	1.64	0.45	5.50	1.95
South West	23	13	87	36	2,357.8	2,483.8	0.98	0.52	3.69	1.45
West Midlands	10	6	65	27	2,564.9	2,656.5	0.39	0.23	2.53	1.02
North West	42	16	127	59	3,226.5	3,406.3	1.30	0.47	3.94	1.73
Total	545	213	1,891	852	23,808.9	24,821.6	2.29	0.86	7.94	3.43
Wales	6	4	28	8	1,393.5	1,480.7	0.43	0.27	2.01	0.54
Northern Ireland	2	2	5	3	828.9	867.8	0.24	0.23	0.60	0.35
Scotland	292	112	831	369	2,431.8	2,623.0	12.01	4.27	34.17	14.07
UK	845	331	2,755	1,232	28,463.1	29,793.1	2.97	1.11	9.68	4.14
CI/IOM*	0	0	6	4	110.3	115.7	0.00	0.00	5.44	3.46

Notes: Excludes sex between men and Intraveneous Drug Users

*2001 census figures for Channel Islands and Isle of Man.

Source: Derived from CDSC and SCIEH (2003: Tables 5a and 5b), cited in Corkery 2003.

The tables show that, not surprisingly, males outnumber females, and the 15–34 age group is at the greatest risk. Most (1,068 out of 1,176 cases) were of white ethnic origin.

Looking next at death rates, again the data presented by John Corkery are the best available (2003). He reports that the Office of National Statistics (ONS) has the responsibility for the registration and compilation of official statistics on all deaths in England and Wales, including drug-related deaths (DRDs). Until the beginning of 2001 they coded all causes of death on the death registration forms according to the International Classification of Diseases (ninth revision – ICD 9). More details of the coding and of the problems associated with defining a drug-related death are given in Christophersen *et al.* (1998) and the ACMD report (2000). Their 'standard' definitions for DRDs comprises the codes given in Table 1.9.

Corkery (2003) reports that a database was developed by ONS in 1999 to facilitate research into deaths caused by drug poisoning, and to help in the identification of specific substances involved in such cases (see also Christophersen *et al.* 1998). Information is taken from death certificates and the coroners' inquisition forms (ONS 2000a, 2000b, 2001; Griffiths *et al.* 2002; Griffiths 2003). The ONS database of drug-related poisoning

Table 1.7 AIDS and HIV cases by age group at diagnosis by gender (injecting drug users, UK, June 2003)

	AIDS		HIV	
	Male	Female	Male	Female
15–19	1	1	135	96
20–24	34	21	522	342
25–29	171	80	748	346
30–34	288	127	656	255
35–39	196	65	390	122
40–44	109	30	175	40
45 and over	46	7	93	19
Total	845	331	2,719	1,120
Not known	0	0	42	16

Note: Excludes sex between men and IDU.
Source: Derived from CDSC and SCIEH (2003: Tables 10a and 10b), cited in Corkery 2003.

Table 1.8 Ethnicity and gender of AIDS cases (injecting drug users, UK, June 2003)

	Male	Female
White	773	295
Black-African	7	6
Black-Caribbean	6	3
Black-other	8	1
Asian	1	3
Other/mixed	9	3
Not known	42	16
Total	845	331

Note: Excludes sex between men and IDU.
Source: Derived from CDSC and SCIEH (2003: Table 12a), cited in Corkery 2003.

Table 1.9 ONS definitions of drug-related deaths

ICD9	
292	Drug psychoses
304	Drug dependence
305.2–9	Non-dependent abuse of drugs
E850–E858	Accidental poisoning by solid or liquid substances – drugs, medicaments and biologicals
E950.0–5	Suicide and self-inflicted poisoning by solid or liquid substances – drugs and medicaments
E980.0–5	Poisoning by solid or liquid substances, undetermined whether accidentally or purposely inflicted – drugs and medicaments
E962.0	Assault by poisoning – drugs and medicaments
ICD 10	
F11-F16, F18–F19	Mental and behavioural disorders due to drug use (excluding alcohol and tobacco)
X40–X44	Accidental poisoning by drugs, medicaments and biological substances
X60–X64	Intentional self-poisoning by drugs, medicaments and biological substances
Y10–Y14	Poisonings by drugs, medicaments and biological substances, undetermined intent
X85	Assault by drugs, medicaments and biological substances

Source: Griffiths 2003.

deaths covers accidents and suicides (including undetermined cases) involving drugs, in addition to poisonings due to drug dependence and abuse of drugs. The range of substances it records is wide, including licit and illicit substances, prescribed substances and over-the-counter medications. The database includes, for each death, every mention of a substance recorded on the death certificate or mentioned by the coroner. The underlying cause of death is recorded as well as other information about the deceased, including age, gender, marital status, occupation and usual place of residence. There is also an indicator to show if alcohol was mentioned.

Table 1.10 shows that the overall numbers of drug-related poisonings in England and Wales rose by 32% from 2,252 in 1993 to 2,968 in 2000, before falling to 2,898 in 2001. The number of males who died in 2001 was 2,019, a fall of 39 on the previous year. The number of female deaths fell by 31 to 879 in 2001. The male/female ratio increased from 1.29:1 in 1990 to 2.30:1 in 2001. The number of males dying rose by about 50% during the period 1993–2000 (48% for 1993–2001), compared with an increase for females of 10% to 1998 but with an overall fall of 1% over the whole nine-year period (Corkery 2003).

Whilst the average age of those dying in 1999 was 39.9 years, there was a difference of nearly a decade in the average ages of males (37.0) and females (46.5). The distribution of ages is skewed to the younger age groups in the male population, in contrast to that for females which is more evenly distributed – except for a significant proportion in the 65 and over age group.[1] The modal five-year age group for both genders combined during the period 1990–8 was 25–29 years, whilst in 1999 it was 30–34 years. There have been falls in the numbers of those dying aged between 15 and 19 and between 20 and 24 in the period 1997–9 (Corkery 2003).

Table 1.10 translates the data into causes of death. In 2001 there were 1,248 deaths as a result of suicide/undetermined poisonings; the next largest group were as a result of accidents, closely followed by drug dependence (798). Over the period as a whole (i.e. from 1993 to 2001), most deaths were attributed to an underlying cause of suicide/un-determined poisoning. This proportion was highest for females. More male deaths were ascribed to drug dependence/non-dependent abuse of drugs and also to accidental poisonings. The total for 2001 shows a slight fall on that from 2000, i.e 2,969 as opposed to 2,898. Although the numbers of deaths are disappointingly high it is interesting that, in spite of a rather dramatic increase in drug use from 1993, the deaths appear not to have risen in proportion. For 1993 there were 2,252 deaths, rising to 2,898 in 2001, a small percentage rise overall.

Table 1.10 Numbers of deaths from drug-related poisoning by underlying cause (England and Wales, 1993–2001)

Cause ICD 9 (ICD 10)		1993	1994	1995	1996	1997	1998	1999	2000	2001	1993–2001	% of Total
Drug dependence/non-dependent abuse 304, 305.2–9 (F11-F16, F18-F19)	Male	245	301	375	432	491	599	681	714	685	4,523	27.7
	Female	45	48	70	96	84	120	85	124	113	785	9.6
Accident E850-E858 (X40–X44)	Male	425	507	537	612	612	595	595	609	610	5,102	31.2
	Female	209	215	187	225	209	246	217	227	222	1,957	23.9
Suicide and undetermined E950.0–5, E980.0–5 (X60–X64, Y10–Y14)	Male	690	718	725	757	826	746	755	723	712	6,652	40.7
	Female	631	608	661	582	629	609	597	555	536	5,409	66.0
Drug pyschoses/assault 292, E962.0 (X85)	Male	5	3	6	10	3	4	12	12	12	67	0.4
	Female	2	4	2	7	4	3	1	4	8	35	0.4
Total	Male	1,365	1,529	1,643	1,811	1,932	1,944	2,043	2,058	2,019	16,344	100.0
	Female	887	875	920	910	926	978	900	910	879	8,185	100.0

Source: Derived from Griffiths et al. (2002); Griffiths (2003), cited in Corkery 2003.

Corkery (2003) reports that, from 1993 to 2001, more than one drug was mentioned on the death certificate in 19% (4,639/24,529) of cases, and alcohol listed in 23% (5,533/24,529) of drug-related deaths. Most deaths are associated with opiates (chiefly heroin/morphine and methadone), often in combination with other drugs and/or alcohol. Large numbers of deaths also involve benzodiazepines, such as temazepam and diazepam.[2] However, the non-opiate types of drug most often mentioned are antidepressants – especially dothiepin and amitriptyline – and paracetamol (which is not a controlled drug) – either on its own or in compound preparations such as distalgesic. By comparison, aspirin was implicated in only one tenth of the cases involving paracetamol compounds.

The numbers of deaths where heroin/morphine was mentioned were five times higher in 2000 (at 926) than in 1993, but fell to 889 in 2001.[3] The number of cases in which methadone was implicated rose steadily from 232 in 1993 to peak at 421 in 1997, since which time it has fallen (to 207 in 2001). Mentions of cocaine, although still low when compared with heroin/morphine, rose more than seven-fold between 1993 and 1999 and eight-fold over the period 1993–2001 as a whole (Corkery 2000).

Although much media attention has been paid to deaths involving ecstasy, they account for only 0.8% of drug-related deaths. Corkery (*ibid.*) reports on a study of 81 deaths where ecstasy was recorded on the death certificate. This showed that 59% of cases had also consumed opiates and 38% had been prescribed medication, whilst just 7% had consumed ecstasy only (Schifano *et al.* 2003a). However, a recent study by the National Programme on Substance Abuse Deaths (NP-SAD) of 202 deaths in England and Wales between August 1996 and April 2002 where ecstasy was recorded on the death certificate found that 34 (16.83%) had involved ecstasy only (Schifano *et al.* 2003b).

Clearly the problem is serious. A total number of deaths associated with substance abuse of over 2,000 per year, where about 80% of those were under the age of 35, is little short of a tragedy. This is clearly a waste of life. As far back as 1968, Bewley *et al.* showed that the death rate for heroin addicts was 28 times that for the commensurate age group, so we ought not to be surprised at the current figures. Drug taking has always been a high-risk exercise, and these figures confirm it.

How, then, to assess the overall state of things? What we have is a mass of data, some of doubtful quality, acquired via a variety of different methodologies. The self-report data are widely quoted but should be regarded with considerable scepticism. A priority in my view is to seek ways of improving existing methods of acquiring information. This means thinking of fresh techniques to achieve this goal and, if necessary, of taking existing data and analysing them in a new way (Corkery 2003). So far as official sources of information are concerned, Corkery believes the situation was given a much-needed fillip by the government's drug strategy, published in April 1998 (CDCU 1998). One of its underlying principles states that 'Learning about an illicit activity can be difficult but our strategy must be based on accurate, independent research, approached in a level-headed analytical fashion'. Corkery (2003) sees this as proof that policies are to be underpinned by solid factual foundations and anchored to the bedrock of objective knowledge. Let's hope so, for we have still a long way to go.[4]

A historical approach to theories linking drugs to crime

Michael Tonry (Tonry and Wilson 1990) says of American drug research that 'the literature is scant, much of it fugitive, the research community fragmented, and too much of the research is poor in quality and weak in design' (p. 2). He adds that, for a number of central questions very little systematic knowledge is available from methodologically rigorous research (*ibid*. p. 2). If so of America, how much more so in Britain?

Here I want to provide a brief overview of some of the major theoretical developments in the drugs crime scene before looking at some of the research in more detail in the next chapter. I want to do this by relating the theories to the period from about the mid-1960s to the present.

Early British literature on drugs and crime was dominated by epidemiological considerations aimed at establishing the extent of drug use in a particular cohort, or at showing that drug taking and crime go together, whether before or after the user is arrested. There was little by way of theoretical development. The literature was mainly concerned with trying to determine what drug users were up to – establishing links with existing sociological theory or with other theoretical propositions was much too heady. Occasionally the odd theory was offered: I remember in 1965 being particularly taken by one which linked drug taking to the aristocrats of eighteenth-century France. This was founded on the presumption that a lack of social obligation led to experimentation. So in eighteenth-century France the nobility were financially independent; they eschewed responsibilities for the less fortunate. During that time there was also experimentation with sexual practices, in the form of sado-masochism. Parallels were made with the drug users in Britain in the 1960s: they were economically independent, with few social obligations, and they likewise experimented, but this time with drugs, not sex. I do not know how much credence I would now give to such a theory as it fails to account for experimentation with drugs rather than elsewhere, but it was interesting, none the less. However, it was one of the few attempts to explain the sudden increase in drug use, and then as now try to account for its continued use.

Throughout the period under review and speaking very generally, it is possible to see a number of stages, each stage being dominated by a certain set of paradigms and each lasting about a decade. We begin with the 1960s, when drug taking first became recognised as a problem (although, of course, the Rolleston Committee had debated the matter in the 1920s), although drug use as we now know it began in about 1957 when some London clubs were frequented by cannabis users who openly proselytised its use (see Bean 1974). Joy Mott (1994) described the established London heroin addicts of the late 1950s and early 1960s as 'jazz junkies', often from comfortable middle class homes who belonged to a drug using subculture sharing interest in jazz (many were musicians), art and poetry and identifying with the United States addict subculture using U.S. drug argot. By the late 1960s London's heroin addicts wheedled, cheated and extorted excessive supplies of heroin from their physicians and sold the surplus to supplement unemployment benefits to maintain a style of life without work consistent with the values of the subculture (Young 1971).

Explanations were then mainly concerned with the pathologies of the users, and they concentrated on heroin addicts. Here, the psychiatric paradigm dominated, which is not surprising as this was the period of psychiatric dominance generally, and psychiatric explanations were offered for all new and existing problems. (Britain was not alone in this. Other countries appear to have followed a similar pattern – that is, in the first stages of a drug epidemic psychiatric explanations overshadow all others.) Sociological explanations were rare in or around the late 1960s, and economic ones unheard of. Amongst psychiatrists, psychoanalytical explanations often held sway (Freudian), linking drug use to nascent experiences, to narcissism (through the process of injecting), or to other ontogenetic factors – this was, after all, the time when that type of psychiatric influence was at its greatest.

By the mid-1970s, drug taking or, rather, heroin addiction, began to arouse less attention, although the number of users continued to increase. For example, the number of new addicts notified to the Home Office was 663 in 1967 and rose slightly to 984 in 1976. By 1986 this figure had risen five-fold to 5,325 and was to increase significantly again during the following decade to 18,281. This represents a 28-fold increase in 30 years. In spite of this mammoth increase, the 1970s were the latency period, or simply the second period where little attention was given to the problems of drugs, sociologically or otherwise. If anything the drug taker was seen increasingly as the product of the deprivation of inner-city poverty – drug taking was being transferred from psychopathology to a form of social pathology. Sometimes there was concern about alcohol use and glue sniffing, but the heroin addict remained the major preoccupation. Also, there was a continuing debate about the role of cannabis and amphetamines as gateway drugs – that is, as drugs leading to heroin use. The other preoccupation, however, was with the over-prescribing physician as a supplier of drugs, especially of heroin. Treatment centres had just been opened in 1968, and the 'British system', which earlier allowed any physician to prescribe maintenance doses to addicts, was amended. Only licensed doctors/physicians could now prescribe heroin as a maintenance drug (Spear 2002).

By the 1990s the emphasis had shifted again. Theoretical interest broadened, and a wider range of models began to emerge. Economic explanations also began to be offered. Slowly a socioeconomic model emerged underpinned by the premise that drugs were commodities bought and sold in markets and, like other commodities, governed by laws of supply and demand. This economic market model emphasised the centrality of drug prices (Wagstaff and Maynard 1988). That is to say, it was recognised that price affects consumption, whether in terms of the quantity consumed, who uses the drugs or how the drugs are used (Reuter and Kleiman 1986; Caulkins and Reuter 1996). Price was also seen to affect entry into treatment (i.e. the user enters treatment when he or she can no longer afford the drugs). Similarly, the incentive to remain in treatment may weaken if the price declines.

It was recognised that the extent of use is also affected by price – e.g. reductions in the price of heroin in Britain have almost always led to a sharp increase in the numbers of users. Clearly this model can also be used to explain other forms of criminality. For example, drugs have an enormous valuable per-unit weight, allowing ease of transportation. If transactions are huge, the incentives to protect those markets will like-wise be huge. Caulkins and Reuter (1996) show how price also affects levels of corruption, whether of police or other authorities; high prices provide the incentive for corruption, and the incentives for organised crime are also affected by price and quantity (*ibid.*: 1262).

The economic model is not a single model – in fact, it is not a model at all, more a paradigm of the type suggested above. There are numerous subdivisions within this model – for example there are Marxist, neo-Marxist, sociodemographic and *laissez faire* market (such as that offered by the Rand Corporation – *ibid.*) subdivisions within this model. More recently others have emerged. Mike Hough (1996: 8) has identified three models which, he says, now dominate current thinking:

1 The *coping* model or self-medication model which tries to explain why drug misuse goes hand in hand with social deprivation. Drug taking is seen as a palliative to the poor quality of economic and social life.

2 The *structure* model which emphasises that those denied legitimate opportunity to achieve society's economic and social goals do so by achieving them through illegitimate routes.

3 The *status* model develops opportunity theory, identifying status and identity associated with economic exclusion. It identifies the positive social payoffs from drug use in subcultures which respect anti-authoritarian macho, risk-taking and entrepreneurial activities.

These three models are neither mutually exclusive nor exhaustive. In the few years since Hough described them, they have become largely redundant, having been superseded by new theories (of which eco-systems theory and social capital are but two), alongside integrated theory, general theory and life-course transitions theory. Briefly, eco-systems theory (which, incidentally, is more of an organising framework than a theory) calls for an active awareness that the interaction of biology, entrepreneurial relationships, culture and legal economic organisational and political forces affects an individual's behaviour (McBride *et al.* 2002: 14). Social capital theory is defined 'as the quality and depth of relationships between people in a family and community, or the stock of networks (relationships between individuals) that are used to produce goods and services in society' (*ibid.*: 15). These new theories are in the early stages of development, with the social capital theory likely to emerge as the dominant one.

Returning to the three models described by Hough, it is interesting that they have developed outside the main theories of the sociology of deviance, almost as if earlier theories had never existed. For example, control theory is not mentioned, nor is labelling or differential association. Nor is anomie which, for many years (at least up to the late 1960s) was the dominant theory of deviance (Merton 1957). In anomie theory, drug taking was a deviant adaptation to anomie, itself created as a mismatch between culture goals and legitimate means. That adaptation was described by Merton as retreatism, where the substance misuser (then it was mainly alcoholism) no longer accepted or strove for the cultural goals of success, nor accepted the legitimate means to achieve them. Anomie theory depicts the user as an escapist, a passive respondent to the world around him or her. It gave way to subcultural theory which, in turn, gave way to labelling theory where the user was labelled either as a drug user (the important factor being the manner in which the label was applied) or responded to, and took on board the effect of the label. As noted earlier, it is surprising that none of these is mentioned in the theories listed above.[5]

Why should this be so? I suspect this is because those earlier sociological theories fail to consider the social reality of the drug user. Take, for example, the first model – the coping model. It emphasises the social and economic poverty that so often mars and blights drug users' earlier lives. It shows how drug use is heavily concentrated in the deprived areas of cities and although not exclusively so, is often enough located there to be more than coincidental. That community is invariably a poor neighbourhood (Advisory Council on the Misuse of Drugs 1998). In her description of Bladon in northeast England, Janet Foster (2000) describes this place as containing 'drug abuse and crime combined with a debilitating range of other social problems, high levels of truancy, poor health and pervasive unemployment (about 50%) where exclusion and deprivation are very much in evidence'. Her thesis is to link social exclusion and social deprivation to drug taking, a view that echoes other British studies but does not appear to resonate with those earlier sociological theories of deviance. Her solution is a more inclusive society but in this she is pessimistic; she fears that many of Bladon's residents did not dare to hope for a better tomorrow and, for those accustomed to living on the margins, it is a long and impossible path back (*ibid.*: 327). Coping in this environment requires strength of character and, for those who fail, drug taking is the palliative they need in order to survive.

Or consider the third model which is closely associated with *structure* in that it emphasises the use of entrepreneurial skills and adds the positive payoffs associated with dealing. This model draws heavily on some carefully focused ethnographic descriptions of drug users which do not show the drug user as 'a man on his back'. Rather they see him or her as an active participant in the life of the community who, if not a 'mover and shaker', then at least is someone who acquires status from drug dealing. The descriptions of local outbreaks of heroin use (users starting by smoking illicitly imported supplies which had not previously been available) in the early to mid-1980s in some towns and cities in North West England provided strong evidence that economic factors rather than ideology, or the attractions of the addict subculture, played a large part in their development and for a stronger link with acquisitive crime. Heroin use was found to be most prevalent in the most socially and economically deprived areas with high rates of youthful unemployment where the busy life style of 'thieving and scoring' provided occupation during the long workless days and user-dealers enjoyed considerable status (Pearson 1987; Parker 1988).

The defining American research on this came from Preble and Casey (1969: 14):

> Their behaviour is anything but an escape from life. They are actively engaged in meaningful activities and relationships seven days a week. The brief moments of euphoria after each administration of a small amount of heroin constitute a small fraction of their daily lives. The rest of the time they are aggressively pursuing a career that is exciting, challenging, adventurous, and rewarding. They are always on the move and must be alert, flexible, and resourceful. The surest way to identify heroin users in a slum neighbourhood is to observe the way people walk. The heroin user walks with a fast, purposeful stride, as if late for an important appointment – indeed he is. He is hustling trying to sell stolen goods, avoiding the police looking for a heroin dealer. He is in short taking care of business.

The key phrase is 'taking care of business'. The heroin user, according to Preble and Casey, is busy and purposeful and an important figure to those who live in the drug areas of our cities. He or she has status, power and influence, certainly not a 'double failure' nor someone to be ignored. There is empirical evidence to support this view, for the highest concentrations of drug abuse tend to be in run-down derelict inner-city areas. Blotting out the awfulness and hopelessness is an understandable reaction, and trying to assert and claim status, albeit through drug dealing, is an obvious reaction.

That, however, is only one side of the problem. How do we explain the drug use of the more successful middle classes whose lives have not been economically and socially blighted? What of them? (See the ACMD report on drugs and the environment 1998 and Ramsay and Spiller 1997.) Clearly, drug taking is not a palliative to them nor to the never ending stream of celebrities who daily appear at expensive treatment centres. Their lives are as different as could be. Must we then have different explanations based on class or status? Presumably yes, in which case we are back to that age-old problem in criminology: how to account for middle-class delinquency? There are no satisfactory theories for that.

Creating distance from mainstream sociological theory may turn out to be an error; control theory, alongside others in the sociology of deviance, has much to contribute. Centring the debate on ethnography is too narrow, but that is the currently fashionable direction for research. In my view we can take much from small ethnographic studies, but they need to be set against others which take account of the natural history of the problem (i.e. longitudinal studies or those which are concerned with the users' social development). I am thinking here of that earlier, and now much neglected, theory of Alfred Lindesmith who began with the central premise that addiction means the addict recognises his or her addiction. Recognition comes from an earlier acceptance that there are cravings for the drug (Lindesmith 1965). Lindesmith anchors his theory firmly in sociological territory, having no time for the fashion nowadays to expand the definition of addiction to include dependency or habituation – or to include such matters as excessive gambling in a definition of addiction.

In the next chapter I want to look more closely at the links with crime, giving more attention to research which has tried to unravel the various strands of the drugs/crime nexus.

Notes

1 An examination by ONS, for the Advisory Council on the Misuse of Drugs (ACMD 2000), of deaths for 1994–6 showed that men in their 20s and early 30s are more likely to die than men in other age groups and females. This peak is largely attributable to higher death rates from accidental overdoses. Death rates for females are more consistent and at a lower level than males. Deaths from drug dependence/non-dependent abuse in women occur most commonly amongst young adults. Both men and women in their 80s or older exhibit higher rates of suicidal poisonings.

2 The involvement of temazepam had been falling since 1993, and this movement was assisted by the imposition of controls on jelly-filled capsules from 1 January 1996. However, temazepam is typically used in combination with other drugs. Diazepam, also prescribed for treating drug dependence, is often implicated in DRDs. Antidepressants and prescribed analgesics feature very highly, as do non-controlled drugs such as paracetamol and aspirin. However, there are signs that the involvement of the latter two substances may be reducing, following the introduction in September 1998 of tighter restrictions on the number of tablets that can be sold at any one time (Hawton et al. 2001).

3 Nearly half the DRDs amongst young men in 1994–6 were accounted for by opiates. Between 1995 and 2000, the male death rate for heroin/morphine rose from 11 per million population to 29, the greatest increases occurring in 1997–9. Male deaths involving amphetamines doubled between 1995 and 1999, although numbers are still very low. By contrast, deaths mentioning methadone fell by 47% in 1997–2000. Death rates for opiates fall off at older ages. Amongst elderly men, there has been an increase in deaths due to barbiturates and tranquillisers, and a decline in antidepressants.

4 Corkery (2003) reports on the government's strategy to improve the data on drug-related deaths and to devise a strategy to reduce them. He says that in November 1997 the Advisory Council on the Misuse of Drugs (ACMD) decided to investigate the issue of DRDs. The ACMD's Prevention Working Group published its report, *Reducing Drug-related Deaths* in June 2000. The report made some 65 recommendations covering all aspects of DRDs, including data collection and analysis; issues relating to methadone, viral diseases, road accidents, and prisons; and drug services' practices. The government's response was published in April 2001 (DH 2001). This covered all aspects except data collection. A Technical Working Group (TWG), composed of cross-government officials, the devolved administrations and external experts, was set up following the publication of the ACMD report to consider data collection aspects. The government's action plan was announced by Health Minister, Hazel Blears, on 15 November 2001. The 3–5 year programme is aimed at playing a key role in achieving the government's objective of reducing such deaths by 20% by 2004. The programme for England and Wales comprises three strands (DH 2001): campaign work will provide training to drug treatment staff on reducing injecting and syringe sharing and on overdose prevention; first-aid training to reduce overdose risk; and support for a poster and information campaign. Surveillance work will establish a baseline for monitoring the success of action plan activities; will increase the analysis of information from coroners' reports; will provide guidance and training to coroners; and will provide guidance to DATs (drug action teams) on running local inquiries into drug-related deaths. The action plan is required under the drugs strategy and will help to set targets for agencies and government departments under the strategy's key aim iii. The target for reducing DRDs requires a baseline from 2000–1 data. One of the key proposals made by the TWG was a definition of what constitutes a DRD that can be used for this target. The ACMD defined a drug-related death as 'Deaths where the underlying cause is poisoning, drug abuse or drug dependence and where any of the substances scheduled under the Misuse of Drugs Act 1971 were involved'.

5 The second of Hough's models (the structure model) can be said to be based loosely on an earlier theory derived from the Cloward and Ohlin thesis but in an amended form. It modifies or, rather, removes one of the main features of Cloward and Ohlin's argument – that of the emergence of the retreatist subculture. Cloward and Ohlin (1961) posited the user as facing two opportunity structures, the legitimate and illegitimate. In their terms, the drug user fails at both; he or she is a double failure having failed as a non-offender and as an offender. Drug abuse is the retreat from both opportunity structures. However, the structure model does not see the drug user as a double failure but one who is still striving to achieve success goals, albeit by illegitimate means. He or she has not retreated; he or she may not be a successful entrepreneur in the legitimate sense but is still trying to make it illegitimately. Indeed, the very nature of modern drug markets is that buying and selling, along with 'hustling' in all its forms, are a *sina qua non* of contemporary existence.

25

Chapter 2

Drugs and crime: theoretical assumptions

Introduction

Crime is one of, if not *the* major, attendant problems of drug misuse. At one level drugs and crime are linked if only because it is an offence to possess certain substances unlawfully. However, at another level, where drugs are said to cause, influence or be associated with crime, matters are less clear. For whilst there is considerable anecdotal evidence, aided by some research that drug use causes crime, the closer we get to establishing a causal connection, the more difficult things become.

If we are to make progress towards solving the drugs–crime problem we need to determine effective responses (Brownstein and Crossland 2002). That means developing an appropriate research agenda, and tackling the central issues of the drugs–crime link – or 'unpacking' it, to use the modern phrase. Is the link a matter of cause and effect or is it something more complex (*ibid.*: 1)? And in which direction does it go? Do drugs lead to crime, or crime to drugs? Or perhaps there is no connection after all and the one remains separate from the other?[1]

Confusion arises where there is a tendency to explain the drugs–crime nexus using terms that are too wide or that include a range of behaviours, some of which are criminal, some not. Or sometimes we simply settle for supposed commonsense explanations offered by the media. Consider two psychological explanations: one suggests criminality is as much a product of the drugs as the need for the drugs; and the other that drugs change the drug user's personality. In the first users are said to be 'enslaved' by the drug and, in the second, act in ways that are 'out of character' – i.e. behave in ways unlike anything before.

Where drug users are said to be 'enslaved', the assumption is of users being unable to offset the impact of the drug. Offences are committed with little or no control over actions or consideration for anyone, let alone the victim. 'Enslavement' means behaving in ways which satisfy the craving – which is close to a mild version of the economic necessity model. The second, the 'out of character' model, overlaps with the 'enslavement' model, for being 'out of character' means behaving in a different way than hitherto. It might involve abusing close family members, not showing concern about personal appearance or hygiene or committing offences to satisfy a habit. In extreme circumstances these offences may be over and above that needed to pay for the drugs (i.e. the user may become violent or damage property in a way alien to his or her erstwhile character).

In both models similar psychological mechanisms seem to be at work, except that the 'enslaved' users are more powerfully driven by the demand for the drug, whilst the 'out of character' user behaves in ways that may be highly unusual (this may or may not include crime). Unfortunately, being 'enslaved' or acting 'out of character' merely offers a series of character statements which permit only wide generalisations to be made. If 'enslaved', then is the drug user unable to exercise control over his or her behaviour and thus caught in an unwinding pattern as a prisoner of the drug? Or similarly for the 'out of character' drug user, how many crimes are committed as a direct result of this condition? Even if that could be established, will they always be of the same order, of the same amount and type irrespective of the drug user's previous experiences? How is there a causal (sufficient) connection between the drug and the criminality in these two models? And the answer is that it is difficult, almost impossible, to determine or establish such contingent influences. MacCoun *et al.* (2002) say that there is little evidence that drug use per se causes people to commit crime in some direct and un-conditional manner, or that criminality per se causes someone to use drugs: 'The drug crime link varies across individuals, over time within an individual's development, across situations, and possibly over time periods (as a function of the dynamics of drug epidemics and, possibly drug control policies)' (p. 2).

Or consider the view, often portrayed by the media, that drug users commit crimes to fund their habit – not an unreasonable position and one with considerably more strength than being enslaved or acting out of character. Support for this comes from a number of studies. Ethnographic and longitudinal studies of drug-abusing criminals, many in the USA, show that high levels of drug use are associated with high levels of crime; similarly, low levels of drug use are associated with low levels of crime (Chaiken and Chaiken 1990: 235). Heroin users, more than any others, conform to this pattern; less so for those using other drugs – except perhaps cocaine (*ibid.*). Moreover, predatory offenders persistently and frequently use large amounts of multiple types of drugs – i.e. polyaddicts or polyusers – and commit crimes at significantly higher rates over longer periods than less drug-involved criminals. Predatory offenders commit fewer crimes during periods in which they use no heroin (*ibid.*). An out-of-control male drug user is likely to commit between 80 and 100 serious property offences per year, or a female may resort to prostitution to pay for the drugs (*ibid.*).

Similarly in Britain, the National Criminal Intelligence Service (NCIS) estimate that, in 2001, the street market in crack cocaine was worth £1.8 billion. Users fund at least 48% of that (£864 million) by stealing goods which are sold on the black market for between 20 and 25% of their real value (i.e crack users are stealing at least £3.45 billion of property each year) (*Guardian* 22 May 2003). Other British studies give a similar picture. Studies of heroin users in Merseyside show how burglary rates increase when heroin use increases (Parker and Newcombe 1987). The Shadow Home Secretary in 1996 produced evidence which he subsequently used to introduce the Drug Treatment and Testing Order (or DTTO), showing that the growth in the rate of crime was accompanied by a similar growth in the rate of substance abuse (Labour Party 1996).

Yet matters are not so clear cut. Most drug users are not otherwise criminally active, and the vast majority of drug-using incidents neither cause nor accompany other forms of criminality (MacCoun *et al.* 2002). Large numbers of drug users do not commit property offences and have no convictions except perhaps for illegal possession. The use of illicit drugs does not appear to cause (sufficient condition) participation in predatory crime. Moreover, that some drug users *are* criminal should not lead to the conclusion that they are criminal because of their drug use. Some offenders might commit more crimes as a result of their drug use – and this would be a reasonable conclusion to draw – but how many and which offences are causally (sufficiently) linked cannot be known (see particularly Hammersley *et al.* 1989 for a useful discussion on this). Similarly, some otherwise non-offenders might be drawn into committing offences, and some offenders drawn to non-offending. It is reasonable to infer there are links with drug taking and crime (necessary conditions) but what they are, how they affect crime rates and how offending might be reduced are not always easy to establish.

One of the many problems is that self-report studies support the idea that crime is committed to fund a habit. Offenders will often say they committed their crime to feed their habit, implying that, were they not drug users, they would not be offenders. But many were burglars anyway. The question is how to disaggregate the crimes committed *qua* offending and the crimes committed because of drug taking. What is required, and almost impossible to achieve, is a means by which those offences committed as a result of drug taking could be separated from those which would have been committed anyway. Drug users might believe, or want us to believe, their claims that they were somehow forced into criminality to fund their habit. This might produce a less serious condemnation. They might even suggest the fault lies elsewhere – e.g. with the government for not making drugs legal or with the dealer for raising the prices. (This incidentally might turn out to be a risky strategy which could backfire with an unsympathetic judge or magistrate and lead to a longer spell in prison. None the less, some offenders might see this as a useful ploy.) Their aim would be to convince all and sundry that they committed offences only because of their habit, not because they were burglars or whatever.

Also, most studies go no further than establishing a correlation or say that drug use is *associated* with criminality. For example, in Trevor Bennett's research offenders seen at the police station often tested positive for drugs (Bennett 1998). Or as with Chaiken and Chaiken (1990: 231), drug addicts who have entered treatment commit fewer crimes during the period of treatment than when they were addicted. In both cases there is a statistical correlation which, in the latter study, is rather more pronounced than in the former, but even so it is not a causal connection.

To establish a cause, or to say an event has a cause, is to establish that there are universal laws which, together with statements about initial conditions prevailing at particular times, will, when taken together, allow a prediction to be made. That prediction will be of an event called an effect. So, under certain conditions water will freeze and, given that those conditions exist, we can predict the effect of temperature upon water. Here we have a typical causal relationship and those conditions are regarded as sufficient to explain the event. It is also a causal explanation (Benn and Peters 1975: 199).

Social scientists talk of 'links' with crime or create the impression of the user being trapped in certain social or psychological circumstances so that no other course is open, either to become a drug user or, when that is so, to become an offender. It is better to offer something less deterministic – that is, use the term 'cause' in its weakest sense where there are no sufficient conditions but there may be necessary ones. So to say drugs cause crime would be to say drug use is associated with criminal behaviour.

Little has been said of some of the methodological problems within drug research which should lead to even greater levels of caution when it comes to interpreting results. For example, rarely do the studies have a control group of non-drug users to make comparisons. A lack of a control group is a common failing in drug research, linked incidentally to another failing – the small sample size. Studies involving interviews with 20 or 30 drug users are commonplace. Too often samples are taken from offender populations, so it is likely that criminality features heavily in the results and equally likely that criminality could be seen as being caused by the drug abuse. Were the samples to be taken from a non-offender group, say 'clubbers', then criminality would be less prominent (Release 1998).

There is evidence to suggest that some types of drugs are more associated with crime than others, but that might have more to do with the background and personal circumstances of the user than anything else. For example, whilst there are links with alcohol and crime (Mott 1987), ecstasy (MDMA) use is not usually associated with crime. This may be due to the sociodemographic features of the population taking it – i.e. ecstasy users are more likely to be occasional drug users, to be employed, of higher social class and are not multiple drug users (i.e. taking similar types of drugs but not the heavy end of the drug scene). Nor are they likely to have a criminal history or a subsequent criminal career. This in contrast to the heroin user, who is usually working class, unemployed (probably unemployable having never had a job), homeless and a polyaddict (taking heavy amounts of all drugs, including cocaine). Drugs and crime are strongly associated with this group, especially if a street user, but, again, their sociodemographic background puts them at a higher risk of criminality in the first place.

To summarise: all this suggests that we should be wary of trying to establish causal (sufficient) links of the type which state that those who take drugs are compelled in some way to commit crime. At best the term 'cause' can be used as a necessary condition offering a weak form of explanation, which does not imply much more than a statistical correlation or association. Moreover, extracting causal explanations (of whatever sort) from the available data is a risky business given that we know so little about the types of behaviour we are examining, whether before or after drug taking. The general conclusion, therefore, of over four decades of research on the relationship between drugs and crime is that, whilst there is a clear and significant statistical relationship, causal connections are more difficult to establish (McBride 2002).

The three major explanatory models

There are three major models that examine the drugs–crime link. That:

1 drug use leads to crime;
2 crime leads to drug use; and
3 drug use and crimes have a common aetiology.

Although of interest academically these models also have important practical consequences. If drugs cause crime (or lead to crime, for these purposes the distinction is of less importance) then treatment for drug abuse should be expected to lead to a reduction in crime rates. Conversely if crime causes drug abuse then drug treatment will not affect crime rates, in which case the appropriate response is to treat the criminality. And if drugs and crime are not linked then treatment (or punishment) will not necessarily result in a reduction of the other as neither addresses the behaviours.

1. *Drugs cause crime*

This first model (i.e. that drugs cause crime) is the most popular, whether in the media or elsewhere. Sometimes the relationship is presented in direct causal terms, sometimes more by association. MacCoun *et al.* (2002) argue that the link is now so strong in the public mind it will be difficult to dislodge it. They say there is considerable research evidence in the USA, Britain and Europe to support it but no conclusive evidence of a direct causal link and, as will be shown later, other explanatory models retain their influence.

Four major studies have been selected here from the USA to provide a background to this model:

1 In 1998 across 35 US cities, between 40 and 80% of all male arrestees in the ADAM programme (Arrestee Drug Abuse Monitoring) tested positive for at least one drug at arrest (US Department of Justice 1999).

2 The Bureau of Justice Statistics show that 22% of all federal prison inmates and 33% of state prison inmates convicted of robbery, burglary or motor vehicle theft reported being under the influence of drugs at the time of arrest (Bureau of Justice Statistics 1991).

3 Among state and federal prison inmates, 27% of those serving offences for robbery and 30–32% of those for burglary said they

committed their offence to buy drugs (Bureau of Justice Statistics 1991).

4 In the 70% of cases in which the victim had an opinion, 31% said the offender was under the influence of drugs or alcohol (National Crime Victimisation Survey 2000).

From Britain there are the following:

1 The Criminal Justice and Court Services Act 2000 gave the police the power to test detainees in police custody and courts the power to order the drug testing of offenders under the supervision of the probation service. The testing was restricted to heroin and cocaine and in three sites throughout the UK. In total 1,835 tests were undertaken: the positive test results were London (Hackney) 63%; Nottingham 58%; Stafford and Cannock 47%. For those on probation (106 individuals), over half tested positive (Mallender *et al.* 2002).

2 The study by Trevor Bennett and Rae Sibbitt between 1997 and 1999 in two sites in England entitled *Drug Use among Arrestees* (2000) showed that 69% tested positive for at least one drug (excluding alcohol), with 29% testing positive for opiates and 20% for cocaine.

3 A later study, the NEW-ADAM programme (New English and Welsh Drug Abuse Monitoring), was designed to investigate drug use among arrestees currently held in police custody sites in 16 locations in England and Wales. It showed similar results.

4 Joy Mott for the Home Office (1991) examined the proportion of acquisitive crimes which could be attributed to dependent heroin users in England and Wales in 1987; she said this was between 6 and 24% of all burglaries; between 6 and 22% of all thefts; and between 0.8 and 8% of all shoplifting offences. Using this methodology, the government estimated that the costs of all acquisitive crime committed by drug users was, for 1992, between £58 million and £864 million (Mott 1991).

Other studies elsewhere show roughly similar results. For example, in the Drug Use Monitoring programme (DUMA) in Australia, Makkai and McGregor (2002) looked at those users detained and brought to a police station. The data taken from four sites refer to about 2,000 detainees. These show that 57% had a prior arrest in the past 12 months, excluding the current arrest and, of those, 52% tested positive for heroin, amphetamine or cocaine. In terms of imprisonment, 20% had been in prison in the last 12 months and of these 59% tested positive to heroin, amphetamine or cocaine.

However, when one looks more closely at these studies, or most others for that matter, the position is less clear cut. In a later survey with a sample size of 5,440 (males 4,472; females 421), 3,141 provided a urine sample. Toni Makkai (2002) found that the extent of drug use varied enormously for, whilst over two thirds had tried a 'hard' drug, around 60% had not used any drug in the past 30 days, nor did they test positive, and 70% said they were not dependent. The initial conclusions of the study (analysis is not yet complete) are that not all offenders use illicit drugs, not all offenders who use illicit drugs are dependent, not all dependent offenders necessarily commit crime to support a drug habit and illicit use varies by location (i.e. by drug markets across different sites) and across time (Makkai 2002 pers. comm.).

These factors have implications for an evidence-based policy and drug/crime prevention strategies. To have prevention strategies, it is necessary to know who is the target and what is to be achieved. Is the aim to reduce all crime or specific crime? Or just drug-related crime? Targets may be different in different places; they may change, and new ones may emerge.

Paul Goldstein (1985) has provided a tripartite framework for analysing the drugs–violence connection, but it can be adapted to fit other crimes. It has been described as 'a boon to research reviewers – it is invaluable as an organising scheme' (MacCoun *et al.* 2002: 4). Even so, the number of studies using this framework is small: 'We are struck by the relative rarity of actual empirical applications' (*ibid.*). None the less, the Goldstein framework provides a taxonomic scheme, which can be expanded and refined without changing the basic elements. The three features are as follows:

1 *Psychopharmacological*: crime due to the direct acute effects of a psychoactive drug on the user.

2 *Economic-compulsive*: crime committed intermittently to generate money to purchase drugs.

3 *Systemic*: crime associated with the marketing of illicit drugs, such as disputes over contracts, territory, markets, etc.

Goldstein *et al.* (1992) applied the framework to homicides in New York in 1984 and 1988. In 1984, before the onset of the crack epidemic, they found that 42% of homicides were drug related. After the crack epidemic it had risen to 53% (out of 414). In terms of the features listed above,

Goldstein *et al.* found in 1984 that 59% of the homicides were classified as psychopharmacological, 3% were economic-compulsive and 21% systemic. In 1988 this had changed to 14% psychopharmacological, 4% economic-compulsive and a massive 74% systemic. Almost certainly changes in the nature and composition of the markets account for the differences – but so too might the geography, as the study area changed from New York State to New York City. Some critics have complained that the Goldstein categories are not mutually exclusive (Parker and Auerhahn 1998), and say the framework is 'not … a set of testable propositions but … a set of assumptions about the nature of drug and drug related [crime]'. Others see it as providing one of the most useful ways of analysing the 'drugs leads to crime' model (Bean 2001).

The Goldstein model is not free of notions of causality – there is an implication that drugs lead to crime. It none the less allows assessments to be made of varying crimes and provides guidance for future research. There are three parts to the framework or, in Goldstein's terms, there are three possible ways in which drugs and crime are related: the psychopharmacological, the economically compulsive and the systemic. These are ideal types and, whilst recognising that they may overlap, Goldstein believes this does not detract from their heuristic value. These ideal types are largely derived from role theory, although not acknowledged by Goldstein as such, and presumably are not exhaustive; others could be added as and when required.

Psychopharmacological crime
Looking at the three features in turn and dealing first with psychopharmacological crime (which accounted for 59% of homicides in 1984 and 14% in 1988 in New York), this category covers those crimes which result from the ingestion of specific substances where the user may become excitable, irrational or exhibit criminal (violent) behaviour. For homicides, Goldstein regards the most relevant substances as alcohol, stimulants, barbiturates and PCP, recognising too that heroin or cocaine may also be relevant.

Whilst it is important to include these psychopharmacological effects, it is not easy to determine their impact. The drugs, the need to raise money to buy drugs or the nature of illicit markets may stimulate or augment a great deal of criminal behaviour. But this is a long way from saying the drug causes the crime. The prevailing view, according to MacCoun *et al.* (2002), is that, where crimes exist, and we are talking mostly of violence, violence is attributable more to alcohol than illicit drugs. They note that Goldstein rated only 14% of drug-related homicides as psychopharmacological in 1988, but add that even so 'one in seven is hardly a trivial fraction' (p. 6).

Again, the question centres on the term 'cause'. Whilst MacCoun *et al.* (2002) say that 'no drug may be sufficient to produce aggression in isolation from psychological and situational factors, [none the less] some drugs such as alcohol can amplify the psychological and situational facilitators of aggression' (p. 6). Others, however, are more circumspect. Jeffrey Fagan (1990: 243) noted that the link between intoxication and aggression is less certain:

> Research on the nexus of aggression and substance use has consistently found a complex relationship mediated by personality and expectancy factors, situational factors and socio-cultural factors that channel the arousal effects of substance use into behaviour types which may or may not involve personal aggression ... Accordingly, there is only a limited evidence that consumption of alcohol, cocaine, heroin or other substances is a direct pharmacologically based cause of crime.

Others agree. Parker and Auerhahn (1998: 306) say that 'Our review of the literature finds a great deal of evidence that the social environment is a much more powerful contributor to the outcome of violent behaviour than are pharmacological factors'. Brownstein and Goldstein (1990), however, list case histories where they claim the connection is more certain. These include domestic disputes, such as a boyfriend/husband killing a girlfriend/wife or vice versa where the assailant had been high on cannabis or cocaine. Others, such as family members or neighbours, may also be part of that dispute. A few involved killing a complete stranger as with the case of 'a 38 year old white man who was causing problems in a bar. He had been kicked out repeatedly. After the fourth time he returned with a handgun and fired shots into the bar. A 27 year old white man, an innocent bystander, was shot and killed' (*ibid.*: 180).

A major problem in identifying the impact of a single drug is that multiple use is common. It is clear, too, that the extent of violence is affected by the amounts consumed, the patterns of use, the length of use and the psychological condition of the user (Bean 2001a: 226). With alcohol, those with a history of violence will need only small amounts for high levels of violence to occur. Stimulant drugs (such as amphetamines) produce different effects according to different doses. Low-level doses, often found in ecstasy users (MDMA), tend not to produce violent or aggressive behaviour but, with other amphetamines, low-level doses produce increased levels of competition. High-level doses, on the other hand, can produce psychosis and violence but, again, this depends on the user's personal history: those with a violent history or unstable personality tend to be more violent after chronic stimulant use (see also Fagan 1990).[2]

Cocaine is often taken with heroin, making its effects difficult to determine. None the less its impact has been the subject of much debate. It was noticed in Nottingham in 1993 whilst conducting research into cocaine supply systems that the researchers were often told that some local 'pimps' had given up using cocaine as it made them too violent (Bean 1995a). Goldstein (1985) says users describe the cocaine 'crash' (going down from the high) as a period of anxiety and depression in which external stimuli may be reacted to in a violent form. However, other studies (Reiss and Roth 1993: 194) report no difference in the frequency of violent acts between institutionalised cocaine users and violent patients.

The hallucinogenic group, which includes cannabis and LSD, is clinically diverse. These drugs have received considerable attention. Five major reviews of the research literature on cannabis concluded that violent behaviour either decreased or was unaffected by use. In animal studies, acute doses promote submissiveness or flight, and large doses inhibit attack or threatening behaviour (Reiss and Roth 1993). LSD does not appear to trigger violent behaviour but it can aggravate the effects of a pre-existing pathology, which can promote violent outbursts in those already prone to violence (Bean 2001: 227).

Morphine, heroin and other opiates appear to reduce aggression and violent behaviour, albeit temporarily and in the early stages of use. Again, it is difficult to identify the impact of a single drug such as heroin, which is often taken with others such as cocaine. Users who are in various stages of withdrawal are, however, prone to violence and are demanding and threatening. They seek money or drugs to ward off withdrawal symptoms.

Goldstein (1995) says that violence occurs as a result of the short or long-term injection of specific substances, when the user becomes excitable and/or irrational and may exhibit violent behaviour. Others (Fagan 1993) see violence as occurring when the substances produce change or impair cognition, when they intensify states or when they disrupt hormonal or psychological functions that motivate or restrain violence. However, these studies cannot be considered in isolation. Some of the violence is ritualistic; where alcohol is consumed in settings that give approval to male violence, violent incidents become part of a considered demonstration of masculine authority. Moreover, not all who take alcohol become violent, even in those settings where violence is approved. Most alcohol consumption is socially functional, achieving the desired convivial non-criminal results. The research emphasis should be on locations and contexts: 'This analytical focus shifts attention from persons to events, and emphasises locations as the critical intervening construct in the occurrence of violence' (*ibid.:* 76).

Teasing out the situational and social factors – examining the events in which crimes occur (which may involve ways in which some people turn away from a potentially violent situation while others do not) – is one way forward (Mott 1987). Psychopharmacological effects may turn out to be less important; violence and other crimes may be contrived and not the result of the drug's effects. Some researchers believe that the evidence for the psychopharmacological effects of alcohol on crime is much higher than for other drugs (Pihl and Peterson 1995 cited in McBride *et al.* 2002: 8), but this may be an artefact, as this type of research has been more extensive. Goldstein (1995) says that the psycho-pharmacological model suggests that some individuals, as a result of short or long-term ingestion of specific substances, may become excitable and irrational and may exhibit violent behaviour. He regards the most relevant substances as alcohol, stimulants, barbiturates and PCP – although he recognises that others (such as cocaine and heroin) could be added, heroin being of relevance during the period of withdrawal. Goldstein (*ibid.*) says it is impossible to assess the extent of psychological violence because most cases go unreported or, if reported, then no record is made of the physical or psychological state of the offender. He believes that victims 'can be just about anybody' as this type of violence 'occurs in the home, on the streets, in the workplace, in bars and so on' (*ibid.:* 257).

Although Goldstein restricts this model to the study of violence, it can include other offences. For example, the psychopharmacological impact of a substance can presumably lead to offences such as vandalism or to other property offences. Or it could lead to a mental disorder (the problem of dual diagnosis is a real one; see Bean 1998) which, in turn, could lead to other deviant activities, including crime.

Interestingly, Goldstein (1995: 256) sees drug use as 'having a reverse psychopharmacological effect by being able to ameliorate violent tendencies'; that is, acting as a crime reduction agent. Heroin and other tranquillisers dampen down violent impulses or make it difficult to commit property offences whilst under the influence of the drugs. Heroin typically produces a soporific effect – 'going on the nod' is how the users describe it. It removes aggressive impulses and takes away initiatives. Goldstein does not give examples or cite evidence of the impact of drugs on crime rates or how often the so-called reverse psychopharmacological effect operates, but its impact is likely to be small. It is also likely to be offset by the violence commonly associated with the withdrawal stage of addiction where the urgency to obtain supplies can easily lead to further crime – e.g. property offences or violence, domestic or otherwise. (Goldstein (*ibid.*) gives examples of prostitutes in the withdrawal stage robbing potential clients of their money to purchase sufficient heroin to 'get straight'.)

Goldstein also talks of victim-precipitated psychopharmacological crime: drug use may alter a person's behaviour in such a manner as to bring about victimisation. For example, the alcohol-intoxicated man or woman may have his or her wallet or purse stolen by being an easy target for street property offenders, the drugged pedestrian may become a victim of the dangerous driver or the drugged/drunken householder may leave his or her property unattended, thereby encouraging or assisting the burglar. These and numerous other examples illustrate the general point that drugs or alcohol can promote high rates of victimisation.

Economic-compulsive crime
The more common and publicly accepted feature of the 'drugs lead to crime' link is the so-called economic-compulsive model. Here drug users are said to engage in economically motivated crime in order to support an expensive drug habit (Goldstein 1995: 257). As heroin and cocaine are the most expensive drugs, so they produce the greatest pressure on the users – one of them, heroin, is addictive, and the other (cocaine) produces intense pleasure that adds to that pressure.

Popular perceptions of the links between drugs and crime support Goldstein's thesis. Evidence from the British Crime Survey (BCS) shows that more people see drugs as the main cause of crime; poor parental discipline came second. The Home Office requested the Office for National Statistics to include questions on perceptions of illegal drug misuse and drug-related crime in their February 1997 Omnibus Survey (Charles 1998). Random samples of 1,585 people aged 16 years or over were interviewed in England. They were asked how much of a problem they felt illegal drug use and drug-related crime to be, whether locally or nationally. Drug-related crime included stealing to buy drugs, offering drugs for sale and committing crimes under the influence of drugs. In the sample, 23% saw drugs as the main cause of crime – slightly higher for those living in the north of England (25%) than in the south (21%) (Ramsey and Percy 1996).

The Home Office findings (*ibid.*) show that a third of those questioned said they or a number of their household had been the victim of a property crime in the previous two years. Of those who had been victimised, 15% believed they were the victims of a drug-related crime, but 26% were not sure. It is not clear how victims came to this conclusion as few could have had direct contact with an offender or could have known of his or her drug habits, but this was the general perception of the causes of crime. Moreover, about a third of respondents felt that stealing for drugs was a 'very big' or 'fairly high' problem in their local area (*ibid.*: 3) – but, again, how could they know this? Perceptions of the causes of property crime remained steady: 29% in 1997 compared with 28% in 1996.

These perceptions find support in research. For example, what we know of property offences generally and burglary in particular is that the offenders rarely move out of their own neighbourhood. Areas with high drug abuse will mean that the drug users who commit offences do so against those living in their immediate locality – and that includes other drug users. In our Nottingham study we found that drug users were active burglars, but were just as often victims of burglary (Bean and Wilkinson 1988). They stole from others and were stolen from. Similarly, Trevor Bennett (1998) found that nearly half the arrestees who reported taking drugs within the last year said their drug use was connected to their offending. Amongst the various factors emphasised was the need for money to buy drugs, where an estimated 32% of all income was spent on purchasing heroin or crack cocaine. Coid *et al.* (2000) also note that most subjects in their study (85%) reported that they committed offences to buy drugs, the most common offences being shoplifting, fraud, deception and drug dealing. Following treatment, theft decreased by 52% and those who spent longest in treatment showed the greatest reduction in daily expenditure on illicit drugs.

Joy Mott for the Home Office (1987) estimated the proportion of various types of acquisitive crime attributed to heroin users in England and Wales in 1987 to be between 6 and 24% of all burglaries, between 6 and 23% of thefts from the person and between 0.6 and 8% of all shoplifting. These calculations were based on a tentative set of assumptions – for example, about the number of heroin users at the time, the frequency of offending, the extent of their habit, etc. Small changes to these parameters would affect substantially the final figures – if the extent of the drugs used is greater or less than estimated, the rate of burglaries will change accordingly. Mott kept the confidence intervals wide, and rightly so (1987; see also ACMD 1994).

Some authorities (MacCoun *et al.* 2002) suggest that the commonsense understanding and interpretation of economic compulsive crime ought to evolve as a greater level of understanding develops. They think the simple notion that the demand for the drug automatically leads to a property crime is at last being challenged. For example, Lesner (1997: 45–6 cited in MacCoun *et al.*) puts the assumptions this way: 'The more dramatic the physical withdrawal symptoms, the more serious or dangerous the drug must be. This thinking is outdated.' Lesner goes on to say that many of the addictive and dangerous drugs do not produce severe physical symptoms upon withdrawal. What is important is whether the drug promotes compulsive drug seeking and use, even in the face of negative health and consequences. Yet, even so, users of a drug such as heroin which, on the face of it, would appear to promote 'compulsive drug seeking and use, etc.' are not insensitive to price and are not wholly enslaved by the drug. Peter Reuter and Mark Kleiman have shown that heroin use is not subject to an inelastic demand – that is, price increases can reduce daily consumption and lead to a proportionate reduction in intake (1986: 300). If addicts were relatively insensitive to price, price increases would expect to produce increased levels of economic–compulsive crime. Yet Reuter and Kleiman show that the elasticity of demand for heroin is about −1 for heavy users, and even then some heavy users cease consumption with a change in price.

The quotation above emphasises the importance of heroin addiction – which includes other narcotics. Research results suggest that crime rates, including those for robbery, are higher once the offender is a regular user or is addicted to heroin. Data supporting this version of the drug–crime link are conclusive, especially for street heroin users. The crime rate drops dramatically once the user enters treatment. Chaiken and Chaiken (1990) report that crime rates are strongly related to addiction; non-addicted users commit fewer crimes, yet street heroin users commit the most. Inciardi's study of drug-abusing populations (1990) also shows that narcotic users commit more robberies per year than other drug users. If we include crack dealing, Inciardi says that 'those more proximal to the crack distribution were more involved in violent crime, especially the dealers'. Anglin and Hser (1990) reviewed the literature and showed that the frequency of criminal activity tends to vary with periods of intense use. Addicts significantly reduce their criminality during periods of methadone maintenance.

Goldstein *et al.* (1991), however, produce much lower figures. They see economic crime as consisting of only about 2% of the drug-related crimes. In their study of 414 homicides in New York, 8% were classified as psychopharmacological and only 2% economic. However, the criteria used were more stringent than most. For example, they did not include a robbery of drugs from a dealer in which the user and dealer were killed.

This was seen as systemic crime (i.e. about crimes within drug markets). This low rate of economic crime is extraordinary, although Reiss and Roth (1993: 200) report that there were differences between the assessment by the police and the researchers in this study, the police regarding more crime as economic.

Almost certainly offenders help to promote the view that they commit offences to buy drugs, and their explanation (or excuse, depending on how one sees it) has been largely accepted. Differences, however, are not just of passing interest: if criminal justice policy is based on the assumption that economic factors are the major driving force, and they are not, then resources will be directed inappropriately. These perceptions have been bolstered by the media – and media comments have often been copied by the drug users themselves to justify their own activities. MacCoun *et al.* (2002: 10) put it this way: 'Arrested and incarcerated offenders report that they committed their offences to raise money to purchase drugs. Of course this might be a convenient rationalisation or excuse for anti-social behaviour.' They go on to ask 'Should we believe them?' And the reply is that 'At least for heroin addiction the answer is probably yes' (p. 10).

Linking drugs to crime through an economic necessity model would appear to be rather more difficult than it seems. It is all too easy to slip into the criminal addict paradigm and accept media-type interpretations of behaviour. As Korf *et al.* say (1998: 4), 'The familiar theory that addiction to illicit drugs inevitably leads to property crime therefore does not hold water'. Many drug users do not have a history of criminal behaviour prior to drug use and many do not commit crimes after drug use, and after heroin use. Future studies may reveal the amount of crimes committed by drug users (other than drug dealing or illicit use), and may find it is lower than described in conventional and popular media circles. More likely, research will show a normal distribution with a bell-shaped curve where a few users at one end commit many crimes – almost certainly the street heroin addicts – and an equal number at the other end who commit none. Those in the middle, comprising the bulk of the users, commit relatively few crimes. This bell-shaped curve could, it is hypothesised, be for all drugs, not just heroin.

Systemic crime

Systemic crime arises out of drug markets and drug distribution networks. It occurs mainly between dealers and users but extends into other areas such as police corruption. Goldstein (1985) regards systemic crime as the most common. He refers to systemic crime in a narrow way, interpreting it as involving struggles for competitive advantage. In contrast, MacCoun *et al.* (2002) see it more generally, as the way markets generate crime which, they say, occurs in a variety of ways and over time and place (p. 12). The wider definition seems more appropriate: it opens up new ways of thinking and a corresponding range of new opportunities for research on the pervasive impact of the drug problem. An interesting avenue would be to determine how and why systemic crime varies between drug markets, and between drug markets for different drugs and in different cities (cannabis markets, for example, tend to be less violent).

Reiss and Roth (1993: 202) say systemic crime can take three distinct paths, but to these might be added a fourth which can include money laundering, or what can be called secondary forms of systemic crime. These are as follows:

1 Organisational crime, which involves territorial disputes over drug distribution rights, the enforcement of organisation rules, informers and battles with police.

2 Transaction-related crime, which involves theft of drugs or monies from the buyer or seller, debt collection and the resolution of disputes over the quality of drugs.

3 Third-party-related crime, which involves bystanders to drug disputes in related markets such as prostitution, protection or firearms.

4 Secondary forms, which are a consequence of the development and growth of drug markets.

Studies of organisational crime are rare, especially outside the USA. Organisational crime involves territorial disputes over drug distribution rights, the enforcement of organisational rules (such as prohibitions against drug use whilst selling or trafficking), battles with the police and the punishment of informers or anti-drug vigilantes (questions surrounding informers are dealt with below). Crime in drugs markets where the high profit levels are where few skills are required to enter as an entrepreneur and where the ease of transportation of a commodity that has an enormously valuable per-unit weight is likely to be attractive at whatever level. The protection of those markets requires high levels of corruption, whether of senior politicians, business people or low-level bank tellers. It also requires organisational skills to hold on to that part of the market in which they operate. The tensions within that market are always likely to make it unstable. One senior British police officer notes how the drug scene is imbued with treachery; the problem for the police is not to obtain information but to cope with the enormous amount given to them by dealers informing on other dealers (Grieve 1992). Levels of violence associated with the cocaine market greatly exceed those for other drug markets. Whether this is a result of a tradition of violence emanating from South America no one knows.

Secondly there is transaction crime. This refers to crime involving interpersonal relationships between dealer and dealer, or dealer and user. Drugs, like any other commodity, are bought and sold in markets (Bean 2002: 124). There are, of course, differences: unlike most other commodities, drug markets are characterised by a high degree of immeasurable risk, by the inability to enforce contracts in a court of law and by a lack of quality control of the product (Rydell 1996). Drugs markets operate without the usual protections offered by the civil tort or court system. The state, instead of attempting to facilitate transactions, aims to disrupt them. Yet within those markets debts need to be collected and property rights need to be established, alongside countless other arrangements that need to be undertaken in any business transaction. Dealers have to secure financial transactions in an otherwise crooked world, with no one else to enforce the contracts. Protecting these transactions takes up most of their time.

Most will find it necessary to employ those familiar with intimidation or violence in order to collect debts and enforce discipline. Dorn *et al.* (1990) describe how a new breed of criminal was attracted to the drugs world. Whether this was a new breed or an old breed attracted by the possibility of offering their services is not known. Whatever the reason, the overall effect is to make drugs markets violent places where dealers become more frightened of other dealers than of the police. Dealers collect debts in a number of ways: one is to use violence; another is by burglary, where they take from other dealers or users to pay off their debts (Bean and Wilkinson 1988). The easy recourse to violence was a *sine qua non* of all dealings, for disciplines had to be asserted and debts collected – the system ran on some sort of credit which needed to be overhauled at regular intervals.

Third-party-related crime is less common. There are also very few studies of this type of crime, but prostitution and protection rackets, etc.. are common to all drugs markets without necessarily being part of them. How and under what circumstances they mesh into the system is far from understood, but it is thought that they operate at the perimeter and may well be more important in the scheme of things than is believed.

The fourth type of systemic crime is less directly concerned with the operation of the drugs trade but remains dependent on it. Important forms of this type of crime include police corruption, especially when associated with informers (Clarke 2001). Police corruption may take many forms and develop in different ways, but it always includes personal gain for the officers. It may occur when the police decide not to enforce drugs laws or not prosecute drug offenders. Or it may occur where police officers become dealers or assist other dealers. Police corruption is likely to flourish where the police work with informers, where quantities of drugs are available and where informers are granted 'a licence to deal' in return for information (Skolnick 1967; Bean 2001). Skolnick (1967) reminds us that, whilst the police can arrest drug users by cruising in unmarked cars looking for those tell tale signs of dealing, the apprehension of one small-time dealer does not constitute a good 'bust' (pp. 120–1). The police officer wants Mr Big and for that he or she needs the help of informers. These informers come from the addict populations, consume large quantities of heroin and are invariably unstable. The best informers are paradoxically the most heavily involved in crime, for they then know the local drugs scene. Handling these informers is a skilful operation requiring delicate judgement. It requires the police officer to know how far the informers should be allowed to go, criminally speaking, and at what point the informer should be 'busted'.

Money laundering is part of this secondary crime. It is defined as the concealment of illicit income and its conversion to other assets to disguise its source or use (Bean 2001: 112). Drugs and money are but two sides of the same coin – a point increasingly recognised by governments. Money laundering and the police use of informers are discussed elsewhere; they are mentioned here for completeness sake.

A note on violence

Goldstein (1995) was particularly concerned with violent offenders where, he says, research has consistently found strong connections between drugs and violence (p. 255). For these purposes, violence can be defined as behaviour by persons against others that intentionally threatens, attempts or actually inflicts physical harm (Reiss and Roth 1993: 35). It does not include self-inflicted harm as in suicide, unintentional harm, or harassment or psychological humiliation in which trauma may occur. In Britain as elsewhere, the introduction of drugs such as crack cocaine in the late 1980s and early 1990s made people realise that drugs markets could be violent places where death was increasingly commonplace and violence a standard feature of drug dealing (Bean 2001a).

Violent people involved in drug misuse are neither a subset of violent offenders nor a specific subset of offenders generally. The evidence suggests a measure of convergence has occurred – that is, substance misusers and other criminals have become one and the same. Drug-selling organisations frequently recruit those with previous histories of violence, or those who are comfortable with violence, and ask them to fulfil roles within the organisation (Johnson *et al.* 1990: 35). These roles can include intimidating ordinary citizens who may refuse to co-operate with their demands (*ibid.*: 35–6).

As with other forms of crime, there has been much research linking the ingestion of drugs with violence, especially alcohol. Jeffrey Fagan (1990) concludes that there is no empirical evidence for asserting a strong causal relationship between intoxication and aggression, regardless of the type of substances, and, in any case, conditional factors make causal connections difficult to demonstrate. For example, interpersonal violence occurs more frequently in some bars than others, and violence in sports stadiums occurs more frequently in some than in others. In Britain violence is more likely at football matches than cricket or rugby matches, yet more alcohol is consumed at cricket or rugby matches than at football matches.

As a general rule, violence is greater when drug dealing takes place at street level, and is even greater where the seller has less control over access to the purchaser. For example, Reiss and Roth (1993) confirm that call-girl operations are less violent than open-air street walking: 'Similarly in drug markets, runner-beeper delivery systems may entail less violence than open air markets, while heavily fortified crack houses experience still less risk' (p. 18). In our Nottingham study we thought that levels of street violence decreased in amount and changed in form and quality once control of the profits was taken over by an outside organisation, thereby making the financial system more organised. Then, as with high-level dealing, violence becomes more focused and instrumental and is used to enforce discipline and collect debts (Bean and Wilkinson 1988). Violence is not likely to be random or haphazard. At the very highest level of dealing, violence is entirely instrumental and focused, aimed at taking out the opposition or removing internal disagreements. It occurs according to a prearranged set of signals which almost always involve co-offending (i.e. with two or more offenders against one victim), based on a scale of punishments determined in advance.

Male violence in domestic situations is often ritualised – that is alcohol is consumed in settings which give approval to male violence where violent incidents occur as part of a considered demonstration of masculine authority. In contrast, female violence in domestic settings does not have the association with alcohol found with male violence. Nor is female violence associated with other drugs, as is common with male violence. In our Nottingham study we found that female drug dealers were prepared to use violence and did so as often as their male counterparts, either to enforce discipline or to collect, but they tended not to do it themselves; male partners had to do it for them. Incidentally, they changed partners regularly when existing partners failed to deliver as required (Bean and Wilkinson 1988). Similarly, Incardi *et al.* (1993), in their study of women heroin and cocaine users in Miami, found that, like their male counterparts, female users offended in similar ways – except that over half (54%) of their offences were for prostitution – and the heavier the drug use, the more likely was the use of violence.

Fagan (1990: 261) shows that male violence associated with substance misuse is no different from other forms of criminality in the sense that it has the same antecedents, i.e. family pathology and early childhood victimisation experiences. Early childhood aggressiveness and alcoholism as an adult were found to interact and predict the highest levels of interpersonal violence. Violent men under the influence of a substance (including alcohol) were violent men when not under the influence of those substances.

Sadly, one of the most important changes in the British drugs scene has been the increasing use of firearms on the streets, where low-level crack dealers display firearms openly in areas where firearms were hitherto unknown. No one knows now many homicides in Britain are drug related but the police believe they are increasing annually. McBride and Swartz (1991) in America note that, in addition to the willingness to use lethal weapons, there has been a significant increase in the lethality of the weapons used: machine-guns and semi-automatic weapons had significantly increased in use and scope in the 1980s during the increase in crack cocaine use (p. 160). The large profits and the way in which coca growing and distribution in Central and South America have become increasingly intertwined with political revolutionary groups (*ibid.*: 161) may help to explain the growing levels of violence associated with drugs. So too must be the recruitment of violent individuals to drug trafficking, and the approval given to violence in those situations.

2. *Crime leads to drug use*

The research literature surrounding and providing support to this model is scanty by comparison. Conversely, speculation is greater. Moreover, as stated earlier, the debate is more than of academic interest. If crime leads to drugs there will be no reduction in criminality even with the successful treatment of the drugs problem. If crime leads to drugs then treatment should be directed at reducing the criminality, and the drug problem will be correspondingly reduced (Hammersley *et al.* 1989).

As with all models, there are problems with the quality of the data. At the simplest level, researchers have been interested in determining which came first: the drug abuse or the criminality. The results are equivocal. Early British studies found that about 50% of heroin addicts were antecedently delinquent but, of course, 50% were not (Bean 1971). Later studies have shown similar findings, but to what extent they point to evidence of directionality is difficult to say.

The problem is also a methodological one; it depends on the subset or where one takes the sample. As noted above, if the sample is taken from an offender group it is likely that criminality would feature heavily in the results – and in this case equally likely that criminality would be first. If, however, the sample was taken from a non-offender group (say, a group of young middle-class ecstasy 'clubbers'), criminality would be less prominent (Release 1998). And, of course, it is the presence of those drug users who are not criminals and not likely to be so that poses so many of the problems for this debate (Hammersley *et al.* 1989).

Some researchers are more certain than others. Korf *et al.* (1998) say there is empirical support for the theory that prior criminal involvement increases one's chances of getting into drugs. They say that 'Many current addicts have set out on a criminal path at an early age and *before* their first dose of heroin. These pre-drug criminals turn out to be the group most likely to generate their income from property crime' (p. 4, emphasis in original).

Those supporting this model usually explain it in one of three ways: either in terms of a subcultural theory, by using a situational crime model perspective or as a form of self-medication.

Subcultural theory

Criminal activity in subcultures provides 'the content, the reference group and the definitions of a situation that are conclusive to subsequent involvement in drugs' (White 1990: 223). The evidence for this comes from a small number of studies, quoted by White, where she says the individual is placed in an environment which is supportive of drug use. It is the desire for subcultural status rather than a need for a drug which leads the individual to commit crimes. Drug use arises and flourishes within the deprived ghetto areas of inner cities, where subcultural values sustain it and, if not actually promoting it, then they do not resist it. Drug use provides status in an otherwise low-status society. It identifies the positive payoffs where respect, anti-authoritarianism, macho lifestyles, risk taking and entrepreneuralism are given esteem (Hough 1995: 8). In Chapter 1, Janet Foster's (2000) discussion of Bladon in northeast

England was outlined. Coping in this environment requires strength of character – drug use is both a palliative and a status-promoting mechanism. However, White (1990) concludes that the evidence for this is not conclusive. Whilst it is likely that crime leads to drug use under these conditions, a direct causal path from crime to drugs using this type of subcultural explanation is not likely to reflect the dominant patterns of behaviour (*ibid.*: 223).

Situational control theory

A second form of explanation is through situational crime control theory, whose earliest and most important exponent is Ron Clarke. Clarke (1980: 136) sets out the basis of his position as follows:

> Criminological theories have been little concerned with the situational determinants of crime. Instead the main object of these theories (whether biological, psychological or sociological in orientation) has been to show that some people are born with or come to acquire a 'disposition' to behave in a consistently criminal manner. This 'dispositional' bias of theory has been identified as a defining characteristic of 'positivist' criminology. In fact a dispositional bias is presented through the social sciences.

Situational crime theory concentrates on the opportunities to commit crime and the risks attached to criminal activity. Essentially, the offender is seen as exercising a rational choice – that is, working out the cost-benefits of offending. This would be so for the addicted drug user as for the recreational user. In popular fiction the addicted offender might be portrayed as 'enslaved' by the drug but, to the situational theorist, this is over-dramatic. Rational choice theory (which, incidentally, is being increasingly accepted within criminological circles) has three main strands or subtheories:

1 Routine activities theory, which relates criminal opportunities to the routine activities of suitable victims and the characteristics and locations of suitable targets.

2 Environmental criminology, which explores spatial and temporal aspects of offending, such as crime hotspots and other policies of crime, as well as the routine activities of offenders.

3 Defensible space, crime prevention through environmental design, strategic crime analyses and situational crime prevention where the aim is to prevent crime by modifying the physical environment itself

or by changing the activities of people inhabiting the settings within which crimes are likely to occur (Cornish 2001: 306).

The development of situational crime prevention has been such as to lead its exponents to develop a new branch of criminology (or perhaps a new subject altogether) which they call 'crime science'. They subject all types of crime to this analysis. Drug taking and its associated criminality can be made subject to the same cost-benefit analysis as other drugs. Supporters of situational crime prevention would say that crime leads to drug taking so that, by modifying crime 'hotspots' and the environment, and by dealing with the characteristics and location of suitable targets, drug taking can be reduced.

In a celebrated essay entitled '*Broken windows*', James Wilson and George Kelling (1982) identified what they saw as the visible signs of an area in decay. These broken windows were accompanied by graffiti, malicious damage to property and litter, all linked in the public mind to disorder, crime and fear of crime (Downes and Rock 1998: 254). Wilson and Kelling (cited in *ibid.*) described the situation thus: 'Families move out, unattached adults move in. Teenagers gather in front of the corner store. The merchants ask them to move; they refuse. Fights occur, litter accumulates.' 'Broken windows' is a phase in the natural history of communal disorganisation (*ibid.*). The links with drug abuse centre on the manner in which the police and others deal with the broken windows environment and the associated hotspots that develop. Policing these hotspots means dealing with the accompanying incivilities: the beggars, the squeegee artists, those producing litter and graffiti. Intervening in the cycle of deterioration is expected to reverse neighbourhood decline and bring about a reduction in the rates of crime. Successes include the reclamation of the New York subway system and neighbourhood improvements elsewhere.

Critics talk of the displacement of crime to other areas of cities and suggest that crimes committed by drug users are more likely to be displaced. The evidence for displacement is, however, limited: drug users do not always displace. In the King's Cross project in London (using a situational crime prevention approach), rates of novice drug users were certainly reduced, and not displaced as a result of increased police activity (nor were some dealers). Of course some were, but the strength of situational crime prevention is paradoxically that it does not claim to be able to eliminate all crime but to regulate it (Downes and Rock 1998: 257). Moreover, to invoke a displacement argument is to assume forms and types of motivation which the situational crime theorists would eschew.

49

Cornish again:

> Claims that offences prevented will inevitably result in displace-
> ment or escalation, that technological advances in crime prevention
> will create 'arms races', or that so called 'expressive' crimes such as
> sex and violence cannot be prevented by situational strategies often
> draw their persuasiveness from hidden assumptions about
> offenders as essentially pathologically motivated and hence
> undeterrable (2001: 306).

(*Note*: 'expressive' crimes include drug taking.)

There is little doubt that situational crime prevention has much to
offer, and will continue to offer an explanation of the links between crime
and drugs. It promotes a new perspective and a new way of thinking. Its
message is straightforward; reducing crime leads to a reduction in drug
use, and policing hotspots has an impact on the quality of life in a
neighbourhood – including reducing incivilities, prostitution and drug
dealing.

Self-medication

The third way in which crime leads to drugs is through self-medication.
Again, there are not many data for this model but there is some evidence
to suggest that individuals with deviant lifestyles or personalities may
also use substances for the purposes of self-medication. These include
the so-called 'dual diagnoses' patients – i.e. where drug users also suffer
from forms of mental disorder. ('Dual diagnosis' is not a satisfactory
term; some drug users have been found to have a number of morbidities
including AIDS/HIV, but the term has now been accepted in general
usage and has acquired a measure of general recognition.)

It is thought that about 50% of drug users have dual conditions, with a
smaller number having multiple conditions including alcohol addiction
and HIV (Swanson *et al.* 1994). It has been suggested that dual diagnosis
patients are more violent than those with a single diagnosis, but the data
are not straightforward. Although respondents with dual diagnosis had
a greater risk, it was only slightly greater than that for single diagnosis
respondents – i.e. among drug users the presence of mental disorder
increased the risk of violence but not significantly (*ibid.*: 113).

Diagnosing these patients is complex and misdiagnosis common: one
condition may mask or mimic the others; hence the difficulty in
obtaining data. In this model, the link between drug abuse and mental
disorder operates as follows:

- Mental Illness* → Chemical Abuse (MICA).
- Chemical Abuse → Mental Illness* (CAMI).

(*Note:* *The term 'mental illness' has been substituted for 'mental disorder')

With MICAs the mental illness leads to chemical abuse; with CAMIs the reverse is so. In the first, those with mental illness may find themselves accepted within the drugs community in a way they had not been accepted elsewhere, although this acceptance may be superficial. It is more likely that they are being exploited by drug users, who ask them to 'stash' and 'run' for them. None the less, their deviant lifestyle (mental disorder) and/or personality lead them into a drugs subculture. Once attached to this they may begin to self-medicate, either to dampen down their symptoms of mental illness or to use substances to offset the unpleasant side-effects of their psychiatric treatment. In most cases of self-medication the drug of choice seems to be heroin, although for some inexplicable reason schizophrenics will also use cocaine, which has the opposite effect of damping down their condition. (There is much speculation why this should be so. One theory is that schizophrenia produces a cold, detached feeling. At least with cocaine the opposite is true.) None the less, self-medication seems to be a fairly common activity amongst MICAs.

For CAMIs there is a much less clear-cut relationship but there is evidence to suggest they, too, self-medicate. Long-term heroin use leads to depression (as does long-term alcohol use), and the relief of depression through stimulants is one possibility. The use of LSD, cannabis and other hallucinogenics may also produce mental disorders (amphetamine or other stimulants such as cocaine produce psychosis), and self-medication may be a way of relieving symptoms.

These activities provide further examples of the confusing and con-fused patterns or directions of the links between substance abuse and crime (or vice versa). The clinical evidence, however, alongside in-creasing research evidence on dual diagnosis, points to an important avenue for future research where the links with crime become blurred by the additional complexity of the mental disorder.

3. *A common aetiology*

White and Gorman (2000: 151) concluded that 'one single model cannot account for the drug crime relationship. Rather the drug using ... population is heterogeneous, and there are multiple paths that lead to drug use and crime'. Others have rejected the simple causal explanatory model where one (drugs or crime) leads to the other (crime or drugs). The relationship is said to be too complex (McBride 2002: 11).

Within this 'coincidental' or 'common cause' model there are a number of different sub-models:

1 Common origin – that is drug taking and crime have the same antecedent history of behaviours where there is a behaviour syndrome (or clusters) which, in this case is deviant.

2 Reciprocal model – that is, the relationship is bi-directional.

3 Spurious model or co-morbidity model – that is, both morbidities occur simultaneously.

4 Policy and prohibition model – that is, public policy shapes the drugs – crime link.

Common origin

One approach is to talk of a common origin – that is, drugs and crime may emerge from the same contextual milieu. They may share the same anecdotal variables, such as poor social support systems with difficulties at school and membership of a deviant peer group (McBride 2000: 11). As will be shown later, much of the research on juvenile drug users emphasises these features, especially that of poor parenting alongside family and domestic violence. Another approach is less certain; it is simply to talk of a set of co-morbidities – i.e. simply occurring alongside and without pointing to any causal link. In the former the family or social environment is seen as the unifying factor; in the latter, no attempts are made to believe or suggest a unifying factor exists.

The search for a common origin has tended to centre on the background of the drug user, especially where there is an early dysfunctional lifestyle, or what David Farrington (1997: 363) calls the 'anti-social syndrome' and Charles Murray (1990) refers to as an 'underclass'. Farrington argues that, whilst acts might be defined as heterogeneous, nevertheless it still makes sense to investigate the characteristics of the offenders. He cites evidence to suggest that people who commit one type of offence have a significant tendency to commit other types – i.e. to display an anti-social syndrome (1997: 363). That anti-social syndrome is linked to low social class or socioeconomic deprivation. Charles Murray, in his research on low-class welfare-dependent families, argues that new divisions are appearing in the traditional social classes, especially in Social Class 5. Traditional two-parent families are increasingly leaving working-class housing estates, which are being populated by an underclass predominantly consisting of dysfunctional single-parent families, and where unemployment, child neglect and crime and, most importantly, alcohol and drug use are prevalent (Murray 1990). Farrington, however, using a 'criminal career' model, concludes that 'offending is one element of a larger syndrome of anti-social behaviour that arises in childhood and tends to persist in adulthood with numerous different behavioural manifestations' (1997: 399). One such manifestation would be crime; another would be drug taking, but all stem from the common origin of a dysfunctional lifestyle.

Reciprocal

The reciprocal model postulates that the relationship between the drug user and crime is bi-directional (White 1990: 223) – that is, drug abuse and crime are causally linked and mutually reinforcing. White quotes Goldstein (1981) who, she says, offered some support for the reciprocity model (even though in this review Goldstein has been seen to support a drugs-cause-crime link) when he suggested that the relationship moves in both directions even for the same individuals. When a heroin addict can easily obtain money illegally, he or she will engage in crime and then buy drugs, not out of compulsion but out of consumer expenditure. Conversely when the need for drugs is great, users will commit crime to buy drugs (White: 223). White argues that, whilst reciprocity is only a recently developed area, it may hold a promise for clarifying causal relationships.

There is other evidence for reciprocity. Chaiken and Chaiken (1990) say that high-frequency drug users are also likely to be high-rate predators and to commit many different types of crimes, including violent crimes, and to use many different types of drugs (p. 213). They say this is true for adolescents and adults, independent of race and across countries. The exception are females who use drugs frequently but are less likely to commit violent crimes than males, and are more likely to resort to shoplifting, prostitution and similar covert non-violent crimes (*ibid.*). They add that, although sustained drug use cannot be considered a key variable in predatory crime, none the less serious forms of drug use enhance the continuation and seriousness of a predatory career (*ibid.*).

A major difficulty with the reciprocity model is that it can easily become nothing more than a drugs-cause-crime model (or vice versa) in that it may be saying nothing more than one (drugs or crime) moves in the same direction as the other (crime or drugs). For the model to be effective, it needs to be established that the two are 'mutually reinforcing', and this is difficult.

Spurious or co-morbidity

This model centres on the proposition that drugs and crime are simply two features of a person's life: they may be connected but there is no reason to believe this is so. The link, such as there is, may be coincidental but, more likely, features are simply clustered together – perhaps as a result of a wide range of behaviour that developed during adolescence, but perhaps not.

Too often, the spurious model merges with the common cause model so that a 'behaviour syndrome' is presented as the explanation. Klein (1989 cited in White 1990: 228) avoids this and offers support for the spurious model when he says that the relationship between drug use and crime is the result of patterns of simultaneous activity described as 'cafeteria-style delinquency'. That is to say, adolescents engage in a variety of delinquent behaviours, of which drug use and crime are but two. Cafeteria-style delinquency is dominated by fashion, peer group influences and a general dislike of all authority symbols; that which is illegal will be taken. If a 'common cause' exists, it is peer influences (Fagan 1990) which remain one of the strongest predictors of delinquency, and of which drug use is a part. White (1990: 238) looked at groups of adolescents who were delinquents and compared those who used drugs and those who did not. She found that serious drug users and delinquents were not necessarily concentrated in a homogeneous group but that each group or subgroup represented a unique set of individuals whose levels of drug use and delinquency were different.

Promising though these avenues might be, little research has been conducted on them and they remain largely unexplored. Parallels in the mental health field, where studies of co-morbidities (usually drug use and mental disorder) are much more developed, suggest this is promising area of research, but few drug researchers have taken up the challenge. As a result, the spurious model remains a minority interest.

Policy

McBride *et al.* (2002) argue that efforts to address the drugs–crime relationship must incorporate a realisation of how the development of policy and law has contributed to that relationship (p. 2). They go on to say that 'each time policy shifts the act of drug use takes on a slightly different character in relation to crime' (p. 3). They recognise that little research has been conducted in this matter but see it as a fruitful area of inquiry. They see American drug policy as having passed through the following three phrases:

1 *Libertarianism*. The individual should be allowed to do what he or she likes provided it does not harm others.

2 *Open markets*. A nineteenth-century policy orientation that limited government interference in the production and distribution of goods and services.

3 *Puritan moralism*. Individual behaviour with the potential to harm the community was seen as a community problem, with the legitimate purview of community action.

These three approaches have had, and retain, an impact on the relationship between drugs and crime. It is part of McBride *et al.*'s argument (2002) that we are in the Puritan moralist worldview, which led to the 'War on Drugs' and the subsequent demands for severe penalties for dealers and users. 'Puritan moralism' has a number of different forms, of which five subdivisions can be identified:

1 Prohibition – which emphasises severe penalties.
2 Risk reduction – which emphasises a public health approach.
3 Medicalisation – which calls for physicians to treat drug use.
4 Legalisation/regulation – which encourages increased access as permitted by the government.
5 Decriminalisation – which calls for an end to the use of criminal law and for a return to libertarianism.

These five subdivisions, although not mutually exclusive nor complete have been subject to considerable debate but not always within the framework defined by McBride *et al.* (2002). It is the wider, more general point about the way policy shifts and its subsequent impact on crime which is important; the research possibilities are considerable. What were, say, the effects of establishing treatment centres on crime, or restricting prescription to licensed doctors? And what are the effects on crime of allowing heroin to be prescribed under certain conditions? We simply do not know. And therein lies one of the many problems.

An overview

Few would dispute that there are links between drug taking and crime – irrespective of the mere fact that possession of selected substances is itself a crime. The problem is to determine the precise nature of that link.

As noted above, establishing causal connections (sufficient conditions) is additionally difficult; the best that can be done is to make a weak causal link (necessary condition) and begin from there. The main problem is that many drug users would have been offenders anyway, so that determining those offenders whose offences relate to drugs and those that do not is almost impossible.

None the less the research points to some important conclusions. First it shows that the links with crime are strongest amongst street heroin users than for almost any other group of users and for any other drug. And even within this group the rates of crime tend to be reduced when drug users are in treatment. This also supports the data on the link with crime amongst this group of users. However, as a general rule, research suggests less of a direct causal link and more of an association – a necessary rather than sufficient condition. At best many data sources establish a correlation. One of the main problems in establishing a causal link is that many drug users are not offenders, and the vast majority of drug-using incidents neither cause nor accompany criminality. None the less there is strong research evidence that drugs play a strong prob-abilistic role in some property offences and in some incidents of violence.

The Goldstein tripartite framework has been a boon to drug researchers, providing an invaluable organising scheme. Particularly interesting is the suggestion that the psychopharmacological properties of the drug should be identified as being linked to crime, although the evidence for this remains weak. Also interesting is to see the drug user as victim. These apart, Goldstein's concept of systemic crime (which grows out of the development of drugs markets) provides the most useful area of research and leads to a greater understanding of the drugs–crime nexus. Systemic crime, which involves the protection of drugs markets, can be extended to include those aspects which are related but at one remove. For example, systemic crime can include police corruption and those quasi-legitimate activities where local economies grow and develop as a result of drugs markets (i.e. where property owners let out their property to dealers, prostitutes, etc.).

Whilst the Goldstein framework is useful, it is time to go beyond this. Earlier theories are losing ground and are being replaced by modern theories, such as integrated theory, life-course transitions and eco-systems theory. Subgroups need to be examined especially those who are not lower class – i.e. the so-called celebrity users – and we need to look more closely at drug users' patterns of criminality, concentrating too on the extent to which drug use lessens crime.

The direct empirical evidence for the 'crime leads to drugs' model is less than for 'drugs-causes-crime'. None the less, some is available and sufficient to suggest that those who support this are on firm ground for they are able to draw on empirical data as well as on other theoretical models, including situational crime control, alongside an expanding area of research related to dual diagnosis. They may not have the popular appeal of the 'drugs-cause-crime' model, but so be it – there is support from basic empirical data, notably that about 50% of drug users were criminal before drug taking and about 50% were not. The situational crime model, which suggests that crime leads to drugs where offenders have surplus money from crime to start and continue their habit, is as plausible as the notion that drugs lead to crime.

Where the relationship is purely coincidental or based on a common origin, there are a number of submodels. Four have been identified: where drug taking and crime have the same antecedent history of behaviours; where the relationship is bi-directional; where the morbidities occur simultaneously; and where public policy shapes the crime link.

Numerous theories of drug use have provided useful and interesting areas of research but, for these purposes, a wider framework is required. Rather than looking for causal links or concentrating on one theoretical approach, the framework developed by Goldstein (1995) provides the basis of much that is to follow. The supply networks, particularly those within Britain, and the attempts to police them (and the corresponding drugs markets, whether local or otherwise), require attention. In using the Goldstein model, no assumptions were made that drugs use causes or leads to crime. The framework helps draw attention to the nature of crime in and around drugs markets.

Bruce Johnson et al. (1990) make the point that, whilst a few upper-level suppliers make 'crazy money' from cocaine and heroin sales, the vast majority of inner-city youths who enter this world rarely improve their economic positions. Instead the regular use of heroin, cocaine and crack frequently brings impoverishment (p. 43). The oft-heard lament from ex-dealers was 'dealing doesn't last' (Bean and Wilkinson 1988); they made their pile of 'crazy money'. Invariably, they lost it as quickly, whether from their own drug use or through burglary by other dealers, or simply by being 'busted' by the police, usually on a tip-off from an informer.

There is also the impact on the community – which is an under-researched area. Anecdotally, the impact could be devastating, especially amongst some ethnic minority groups where community structures are fragile. When a 15-year-old dealer taunts others with his new-found wealth, what does this do to a community where unemployment is high and job prospects limited? How do parents tell children that hard work and effort will lead to rewards, ten or 20 years hence, when the rewards are available now, with few entrepreneurial skills required and little by way of education? Or how do you cope with some of the more ill-considered comments from drug researchers who claim that drug use in Britain is 'normal'? Statistically this may be so, but how do parents tell their children not to take drugs when their response is that it is normal to do so? We do not have to live with high rates of drug abuse; there are things we can do, and one of these is to lay the appropriate foundations and then secure the political will to meet the task.

Notes

1 This literature review inevitably draws heavily on American sources. In an analysis of addiction abstracts from 1994 to 2000 taking over 5,000 abstracts from 30 specialist journals and 120 general journals, the National Treatment Agency in Britain found that the USA dominates. Over 50% of the abstracts were from American authors. Next was the UK with about 12% of all abstracts. About one third of those from Britain were on interventions (i.e. treatment and policy), one sixth on prevalence and one fifth on health behaviour, which includes co-morbidity and physical and psychological health matters. Furthermore, even in the UK it was found that a few research centres dominated, with little collaboration between them, and there was substantial variation and duplication. London provided the most (NTA pers. comm.). Clearly this leads to enormous gaps in the literature as well as in the planning and development of research programmes. In the UK for example, there is little research on drugs and ethnicity, and little with an international perspective (examining developing countries) or on drugs and older people (for these purposes those aged 35+). Nor is there much research on the links with policy.

2 Nothing has been said about contaminated drugs. In a study undertaken in Nottingham in 1993, we examined a small number of ecstasy tablets purchased in the street. The quality of the product was not related to price, to where they were purchased (club or street) or to the recommendation of the dealer. Most contained no ecstasy at all. Some were caffeine pills sold as ecstasy. Others contained small amounts of LSD or MDEA (a slightly different compound). For those who thought they purchased MDMA when it was caffeine, presumably they experienced a placebo effect.

Chapter 3

Sentencing drug offenders

In this chapter I want to look at the ways courts deal with drug offenders or, rather, with those charged with drug offences under the 1971 Act. There are two major types of offences: first possession – that is, illegally possessing one of the prohibited drugs; and, secondly, supply – that is, giving or selling one of those prohibited drugs. Of course, the 1971 Act is more extensive than this but these are the main types of offences. There will inevitably be numerous users charged with an index offence other than a drug offence. Unfortunately no official national data are available for this group, even though they may be in the majority. The research by Trevor Bennett (1998) is important in this respect.

Producing the data

The data on drug offenders appearing before the courts in the United Kingdom are described by John Corkery (1999) from the Home Office as 'very complicated, old fashioned and time consuming'. That means invariably that the data relate to a period some 12–18 months earlier, although a recent review is expected to lead to improvements, including the provision of more timely data (see http://www.homeoffice.gov.uk/rds/drugharmon1.html). There will always be some delay, but, even so, a greater sense of urgency would be welcomed (Corkery 1999). At present the courts supply their own data. In some areas the police also supply data taken from court records. The police also supply information on cautions – including reprimands and final warnings.

That the data are 'very complicated' is clear from the methods by which they are recorded. To show what this means consider the following. At present, the seizure data are compiled from a Crimsec 38 form which is used throughout England and Wales. This is apparently very simple to complete and can contain basic information – i.e. police force, date of seizure, drug involved, the type and quantity, and whether the drugs were sent for forensic analysis (Corkery 1999). Increasingly, more and more of the 43 police forces in England and Wales, plus the British Transport Police, submit data electronically on floppy disks, and steps are underway to encourage other forces to do so (*ibid*.). As of April 2003, 28 out of the 43 forces in England and Wales supply seizure data electronically (Corkery pers. comm.).

By contrast, the form used in Scotland and Northern Ireland is quite complicated. There the Crimsec 19 is a two-sheet partly carbonated form. The top sheet is completed when a drug seizure is made and sent to the Home Office once the substance has been forensically tested. In addition to the information outlined as being required by the Crimsec 38, other fields have to be completed (e.g. place of seizure and by whom). Details of the suspects are entered on to the form and these are copied through to the second sheet. This part of the form is supposed to be completed when the results of any police or court decision are known; it is then sent to the Home Office (*ibid*.).

The in-built delay concerning the time which cases take to come before the courts is further complicated in the case of Scotland because the courts there tend to 'roll up' offences. This means that, when an offender appears before the court, all offences of whatever nature are dealt with together. This makes it difficult for the police to decide on what action was taken for drug offences and hence what to enter on the Crimsec 19. These difficulties appear to have led to a significant shortfall in the number of forms being received by the Home Office, especially between 1994 and 1999. The second part of the Crimsec 19 form gives details of the date of offence, the date of the disposal (e.g. court appearance), the action taken (court sentence, amount of fine, etc.) and the drugs involved. This is in addition to basic sociodemographic data, such the offender's name, age, etc., as well as the court and police force area (*ibid*.).

To complicate matters even further, in 1995 and 1996, instead of supplying data on magnetic media in a format compatible with the Crimsec 19, HM Customs and Excise have provided data on floppy disk and computer printout for seizures and for offenders involved in unlawful import and export offences (almost exclusively the former). Since 1997 Customs data have been submitted as Excel spreadsheets.

Unfortunately, there is a fundamental difference between their data and that provided by the police and the courts in that the drugs seized by HM Customs and Excise are not attributable to individual suspects or offenders (*ibid.*). There were further problems with the supply of offender data in 2000 and 2001. Consequently, figures for import/export offences had to be estimated from court and police data. Information for drug seizures in Northern Ireland has been submitted in the form of Excel spreadsheets for the years 1997 and later. Information regarding cautions and court appearances in the province has been submitted for the years 1996 to the present in the form of summary tables (by the Police Service of Northern Ireland and the Northern Ireland Office, respectively), rather than raw data. However, this information is further limited because of the inability to provide breakdowns by drug type. One wonders, of course, why these variations persist and why it takes so long to introduce a coherent system.

Some of the information-gathering process is not as automated as it could be (*ibid.*). Some of the information on court disposals still comes from the police, who retrieve it from court records. This is true for the whole of Scotland as well as parts of England and Wales. The *Statistics Bulletin* 2001 and 2002 (not available at the time of writing) will include offender data which had to be updated as far back as to 1997. Forms were found lurking in the back of cupboards in some Scottish police forces (*ibid.*). Timeliness of data, both in terms of its submission to the Home Office and in regards to publication, is a major issue. Accordingly, the data presented below may well be the best available, but they should be seen as having obvious limitations.

There are two separate matters here. First there are the limitations imposed by the data themselves – that is, where data on drug offenders give but a partial picture. For example, many drug-using offenders may be charged with a non-drug offence. How best to interpret this? Or, how to interpret data on drug seizures? These limitations occur not as a result of defects in the data but because they are not sufficiently comprehensive.

To this end an independent review of drug seizure and offender statistics was undertaken in 2002–3 by the late Rodney Taylor. Doubtless this was prompted by the absence of centrally collected drug-related offender statistics since 1979 which, although important, is only part of the problem, albeit an important part. Data were collected originally by the Home Office Drugs Inspectorate and then by the Home Office Statistics Department. This information formed part of the data submitted by HM government in its annual report on drugs to the League of Nations and later the United Nations (see Bean 1974). The

Addicts Index has long since gone, and we have no satisfactory replacement. We have the National Drug Treatment Monitoring system in England and Wales and the Drug Misuse databases in Northern Ireland and Scotland, but these fall seriously short of what is required.

The second matter relates more to the validity and reliability of the data and directly to the collection of the data themselves. Take, for example, the accuracy of published data on drug trafficking and related crime in London, which come from the Metropolitan Police Database. Some Metropolitan Police Staff (MPS), especially in the Strategic Intelligence Unit (SIU), share these concerns, and with good reason. Since 1998, the SIU Drug Desk staff have been monitoring drug-trafficking crime in London. Analyses of the Crime Report Information Systems (CRIS) reports leave no doubt that MPS data are seriously flawed and present a distorted picture of drug trafficking. Geoff Monaghan (1999) analysed drug-trafficking offences involving Class A drugs. He found that nearly one third (31%) had been incorrectly classified. In a few cases 'possession of cannabis' had been incorrectly classified as 'production of cannabis' (a drug-trafficking offence). Important fields in CRIS (e.g. nationality, place of birth, drug type and amount) were all too often left blank. Obviously these missing data prohibit a meaningful analysis of offender profiles and seizure patterns. In our study of MPS records (Bean and Nemitz 2000), we also found numerous errors, such as where 'drug-trafficking offences' were listed without any supporting evidence. The results of our study supported fully those found by Geoff Monaghan.

Clearly, the situation is worrying. How can it be that the data are so poor, and why has so little attention been given to them? The recent review will hopefully improve matters but, as often happens, it is likely to be too little, too late.

Next are the sentences. Before looking at these, a brief overview is required of the legislation. The Misuse of Drugs Act divides the drugs it controls into three main categories, which determine the maximum penalties for possession, supply and other offences:

1 *Class A*. This is the highest class and includes heroin, methadone, cocaine, LSD, cannabinols (downgraded to Class C from 29 January 2004) and ecstasy. The maximum penalty for possession by the Crown Court is seven years' imprisonment and/or an unlimited fine, and in the magistrates court is six months' imprisonment and/or a £2,500 fine. For supply (i.e trafficking and dealing) the offence in the Crown Court carries a maximum life sentence and an unlimited fine.

2 *Class B*. The drugs included here are amphetamines (cannabis was a Class B drug but is now downgraded to Class C). In the Crown Court possession carries a maximum five years' imprisonment and/or an unlimited fine, and in the magistrates court thre months' imprisonment and/or a £2,500 fine. For supply in a Crown Court, the maximum is 14 years' imprisonment and/or an unlimited fine, and in the magistrates court it is six months' imprisonment and/or a £2,500 fine.

3 *Class C*. The drugs included here are the benzodiazepines, anabolic steroids, some synthetic opiates, gammahydroxybutric acid (GHB) (from July 2003) and cannabis. The maximum Crown Court penalty for possession is two years' imprisonment and/or an unlimited fine, and in the magistrates court three months' imprisonment and/or a £1,000 fine. Supply carries a maximum of five years' imprisonment in the Crown Court and an unlimited fine. (Note that the possession of cannabis is still an offence. Where small amounts are discovered and thought to be for personal use, it is likely the user will be given an informal warning or cautioned but the drug will be confiscated.)

In addition, the Customs and Excise Management Act 1979 prohibits the import and export of controlled drugs except for approved purposes (i.e. medicinal or research). The Drug Trafficking Act 1994 creates further offences in respect of money laundering and gives courts powers to order the confiscation of assets obtained through drug trafficking.

Now to the data themselves. First the data concerning drug seizures are a useful but not wholly reliable or valid indicator on the extent of illegal use, or of the extent of criminality associated with drug trafficking – except, of course, that the longest prison sentences are reserved for traffickers, especially large-scale international traffickers. John Corkery (2003) notes that the number of seizures within the UK involving Class A drugs increased by 10.3% in 2000, against the target set of 10%. Drugs with a street value of £789 million were seized by law enforcement agencies in 2000.

Data on seizures of controlled drugs in 1970–2001 are given in Table 3.1. The totals for each drug in the respective years do not tally with the subtotal nor do the subtotals tally with the main total as some seizures will be recorded more than once and the categories are not discrete. Some seizures include both possession and trafficking. However, from Table 3.1 it is clear that seizures have increased for almost all drugs in the last 20 years or so – few data were available before 1967.

Table 3.1 Seizures of controlled drugs (UK, 1970–2001)

	1970	1980	1990	2000	2001
Number of seizures					
Total	NA	17,617	60,859	125,079	130,894
Of which:					
Cannabis	NA	15,726	52,856	91,695	93,482
Amphetamines	NA	729	4,629	7,073	6,799
Heroin	NA	697	2,593	16,457	18,168
Cocaine	NA	445	1,536	6,005	6,984
LSD	NA	268	1,859	297	168
Ecstasy-type	NA	NA	399	9,784	10,411
Quantity seized					
Cannabis (exc. plants)					
(kg)	615	26,300	30,877	73,861	85,445
Amphetamines (kg)	NA	5	304	1,745	1,717
Heroin (kg)	1.667	38	603	3,386	3,929
Cocaine (kg)	0.203	40	610	3,948	2,842
LSD (doses)	460,23	400	143,000	25,400	9,400
Ecstasy-type (doses)	NA	NA	135,000	6,552,200	7,668,400

Source: Derived from Corkery (2002: Table 1.1); Corkery and Airs (2003); previous Home Office Statistical Bulletins, cited in Corkery 2003.

The pattern for 'quantity seized' is uneven: the quantity of seizures involving heroin, ecstasy and cannabis rose, but those of amphetamine and LSD fell – the latter by a very large amount. Clearly, the quantity seized has increased dramatically over the 30-year period, and that is for all drugs with the exception of LSD. Nowhere is this better illustrated than with amphetamines: 5 kg were seized in 1980 compared with 1,717 kg in 2001, and this was a small decrease over the previous year. The increase in the numbers and quantity of heroin seizures is disturbing. Cannabis still represented 73% of all seizures. Although cannabinols, cannabis resin, herbal cannabis and hash oil have been reclassified to a Class C drug, their status in terms of a Class A and Class B drug is still valid for the period under discussion.

Figure 3.1 puts the position of cannabis more clearly. This is a fascinating figure for a number of reasons. It shows how seizures of cannabis account for about 73% of all seizures. It shows, too, how cannabis seizures follow the same trends as for the combined seizures of all other drugs, and suggests there may be a link between cannabis

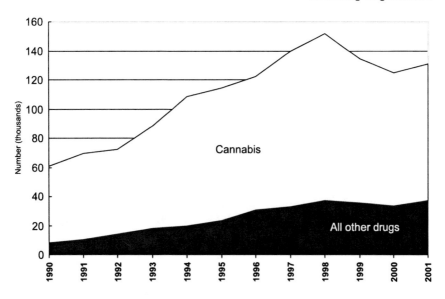

Figure 3.1 All seizures compared with seizures of cannabis (UK, 1990–2001)
Source: Derived from Corkery (2002: Figure 1); Corkery and Airs (2003), cited in Corkery 2003.

seizures and seizures generally. As we do not know details of the seizures (i.e. where they occurred), and the circumstances in which they occurred we are left to speculate. Of course some seizures were large scale but I suspect most were not. My guess is that many did not come about as a result of the police targeting small-scale cannabis users, whether in the street or their homes, but in the police station. The typical scenario would be something like this: an offender is brought into the police station and charged with a property offence, made to turn out his or her pockets and then cannabis is discovered. If I am right, the accusation that the police target otherwise non-criminal young people who happen to be cannabis users is false. I suspect the police are already 'on the back foot' when it comes to coping with drug offenders, and small-time cannabis users are not their priority. Small-scale cannabis seizures occur more due to serendipity than design. We know that many seizures of drugs, especially of amphetamines and cannabis, arise from stops and searches. Evidence indicates that, although only a minority of all stops and searches result in an arrest, they are relatively important in leading to arrests for drug use (see Brown 1997). Half all drug offences coming to the notice of the police do so as a result of stops and searches (see Phillips and Brown 1998).

At one level, seizure data can provide a useful indicator about the extent of use in that an increase in seizures may be reflected in use. This is clear from seizures of heroin: an increase in seizures occurred alongside an increase in use. Similarly with LSD, only here a decrease in seizures has accompanied a decrease in use. Or it might be that a new drug, say 'ice' (crystal methylamphetamine), is seized, and this might alert us to a new development or pattern of use. The problem, however, is by how much? As an indicator of use, seizures provide only a crude measure, if only because no one knows the extent to which the drugs seized relate to the total illegally imported.

A more interesting, and perhaps more useful feature, is to relate seizure data to price. Take, for example, heroin and cocaine. An aspect of current drugs markets is that, whilst the seizures of heroin and cocaine have risen, the cost of the drugs has actually fallen. The conventional wisdom is that users of illicit drugs, especially dependent users, are insensitive to price. However, as MacCoun and Reuter (1998) point out, this is not so. If the price increases demand falls and vice versa. Accordingly, how then to interpret seizures? It seems that where seizures have increased, whether in quantity or numbers, as shown in Table 3.1, and the price has not risen, we can assume that the seizures are but a small part of a larger market or in Peter Reuter's terms, 'seizures constitute little more than a random tax collection' (Reuter 2001: 22). On the other hand, where seizures have had an impact on price, as with the famous 'Operation Julie' for LSD (i.e. where the seizure led to a massive price increase), it was correct to assume the seizure was part of a smaller market. As it turned out this seizure was of a monopoly supplier. If law enforcement is about reducing availability then it must aim to increase the price to the point where the use of drugs is almost impossible or essentially unobtainable (MacCoun and Reuter 1998: 214). Unfortunately, with the exception of that LSD seizure, the quantities seized for other drugs remain a long way from realising those aims.

Secondly, the drug offenders. As noted above, a limitation of the official data is that they relate only to those convicted of offences against the principal Act which, in Britain, is the Misuse of Drugs Act 1971. They do not include those convicted for a different index offence who are none the less drug users. For those where the index offence is a drug offence, the numbers appearing before the courts or dealt with by the police in the UK from 1970 to 2000 are given in Table 3.2. Figures 3.2–3. 4 show the actions taken against drug offenders over the period 1990 to 2000 – that is, how the offenders were dealt with by the courts and the police (by way of cautioning, etc.) for the principal drug offences. The term 'offender' will be used in this and subsequent chapters although, legally, an offender must have been convicted of an offence but the term is used here when the person may have been found not guilty or may not yet be convicted.

Table 3.2 is in two parts: first, it gives data on the total number of offenders (i.e. not offences) and on the sentences passed for those offenders. Incidentally, the subgroups in Table 3.2 will not tally with the subtotal as more than one offender is in the subgroups. The second part lists the drugs. The table shows the relentless rise in the number of possession offenders over the 30 -year period from 1970 to 2000 (i.e. from 8,412 in 1970 to 104,390 in 2000). From 1990 it has gone up from 44,942 to 104, 390 (i.e. more than double in ten years). Secondly, it shows a massive increase in the number of heroin offenders, especially in the ten years

Table 3.2 Drug offenders (UK, 1970–2000)[1]

	1970	1980	1990	2000
Total offenders	8,412	17,158	44,922	104,390
Of which:				
Unlawful possession	7,107	14,030	39,350	92,877
Trafficking[2]	594	2,496	6,680	14,928
Of which:				
Immediate custody	1,068	1,676	3,402	9,386
Fine	4,389	11,720	16,437	26,515
Caution	–	239	17,025	42,021
Compounding[3]	–	–	1,184	NA
Fiscal fine (Scotland only)	–	–	–	681
Of which:				
Cannabis	7,480	14,912	40,194	75,985
Amphetamines	NA	827	2,330	6,637
Heroin	281	751	1,605	12,297
Cocaine	162	476	860	5,451
LSD	757	246	915	260
Ecstasy-type	NA	NA	286	6,630

Notes:

1 Data not yet available for 2001 at the time of writing.

2 Unlawful production of drugs (exc. cannabis), unlawful supply and possession with intent to supply unlawfully, unlawful import and export. Production of cannabis included from 1995.

3 Financial penalty imposed by HM Customs and Excise in lieu of prosecution. Typically used for unlawful importation of small amounts of drugs for personal use.

Source: Derived from Corkery (2002: Table 3.2); previous Home Office Statistical Bulletins, cited in Corkery 2003.

1990 to 2000, and an equally large increase in cocaine offenders in the same period. However, possession offenders constitute the bulk of the drug offenders (92,847 out of 104,390 in 2000), in spite of a mammoth rise in trafficking offenders.

Any hope (such as there may be) comes from the Home Office *Bulletin* (2000). Comparing 1999 with 2000, the number of 'drug offenders' fell by 14% to 104,400 in 2000. There was no clear pattern in the number of persons dealt with for Class A drugs. Whilst the number of ecstasy-type drugs and 'crack' offenders rose by 49% and 7%, respectively, to record levels, cocaine offenders increased by only 2% and the number of heroin offenders fell by 5%. The number of persons dealt with for offences involving Class B drugs fell: for cannabis by 15% and for amphetamines by 46% (Corkery 2003). The number of persons dealt with in Great Britain for supply offences involving Class A drugs rose by 24.7%, well above the target set of 10%.

Sentencing and the treatment of drug offenders

Next come the sentences. The way these offenders were sentenced over the last ten years is shown in percentage terms in Figure 3.2. This figure gives a different slant for, *inter alia*, it shows how the numbers of those sent to immediate imprisonment may have risen, yet the percentage has remained roughly the same – or if anything has fallen. It also shows how the fine has lost ground, almost certainly to the caution. The caution is not a court disposal but a police one in England, Wales and Northern Ireland. Reprimands and final warnings are counted as cautions in the published statistics – this would include the use of informal warnings for cannabis possession, as in the Lambeth pilot project. There has been an increase, too, in those sentenced to 'other found guilty'; probably this means being sentenced to probation, community service or to a combination order. Figure 3.3 shows that the proportion found 'not guilty' remained fairly stable.

This broad overview of the number of offenders and of the manner in which they were sentenced sets the scene for a wider discussion on the sentencing practices of the courts where, as shown above, only about 10% of drug offenders are sentenced to immediate custody and about the same number are placed on probation, with rather more (but falling numbers) being fined. What this shows is that most drug offenders never appear at court but are cautioned by the police, having admitted their offence. Here I want to look at the four major sentences of the court. as shown in Figure 3.2, they are probation, the fine, a caution and imprisonment, to determine their contribution to drugs crime reduction.

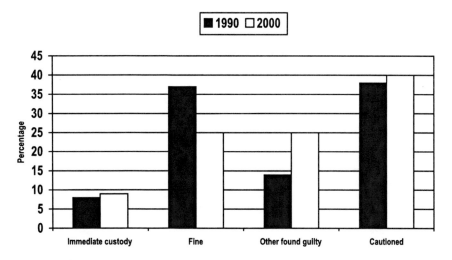

Figure 3.2 Action taken against drug offenders (for principal drugs offences, UK, 1990 and 2000)
Source: Corkery (2002: Table 1.1)

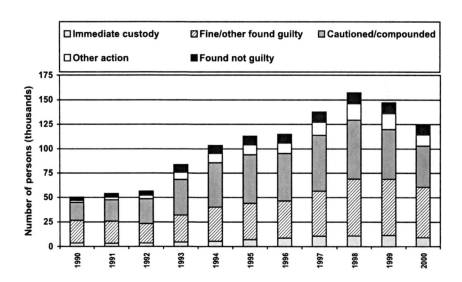

Figure 3.3 Persons dealt with by action taken (UK, 1990–2000)
Source: Corkery (2002: Figure 10)

First, probation which accounted for about 8% of drug offenders in 1997, falling to 5% in 2000, and was the least used of the four major sentences (for our purposes cautions are called sentences). On the face of it the probation order would seem an obvious method of dealing with drug offenders. It is primarily rehabilitative in approach, concerned to assist with the welfare of the offender, with facilities to assist in treatment, and with officers who have knowledge of local facilities. In practice the probation order appears not to work well with drug users: supervision can be patchy and the type of treatment offered does not always appear to have much impact. For example, in a study of the Inner London Probation Service, the results were anything but clear cut or favourable to the Probation Service. When asked what had been the greatest help overall in tackling drug use, most of the offenders in the population who were on probation mentioned factors other than probation. However, in doing so most of those interviewed felt their probation officer had played a part in securing this help (Hearnden and Harocopos 2000). Or, again, over two thirds of respondents felt that the Probation Service's relationship with drug users could be improved. Many judged their officer to have little understanding of drug issues and terminology, so that probationers who were not prepared fully to discuss or divulge their drug use said it was easy to mislead their officer – a matter which is of deep significance when we come later to discuss the Drug Treatment and Testing Order. On the other hand, these interviewed offenders said that they did not necessarily think their officer's knowledge needed improving, regarding it as sufficient that their officer could refer them on to a drugs specialist, either within the Probation Service or elsewhere (*ibid.*: 3). There was some success in reducing drug use whilst on probation, but it seemed too often that the demands of the drug were more powerful than the demands of the probation officer.

There is little doubt that the Probation Service is in the front line when it comes to dealing with drug offenders. The study quoted above shows that a significant minority of the Inner London Probation Service (ILPS) caseload has consistently been identified as problem drug users. Data from the ILPS Drug and Alcohol Demonstration unit suggested that, in 1989, around 1,800 (20% of the caseload) fell into this category (*ibid.*). In a study by Claire Nee and Rae Sibbitt for the Home Office (1993), the conclusions were depressingly similar – that is, there was substantial variation amongst probation services in terms of the kind of response made, the effectiveness of the responses, the number and range of drug agencies available, and the relationships with these agencies. Nee and Sibbitt state that 'in many ways the responses appeared inadequate; probation officers had not been trained to recognise drug misuse and drug programmes did not always have the support of management' (*ibid.*). Of significance are matters relating to the conditions of treatment that can be attached to a probation order. Nee and Sibbitt say that 'once they had made a referral probation officers were usually unable to get feedback from drug agencies as a result of the agencies' policies on confidentiality' (*ibid.*). As will be shown in the next chapter the Probation Service has learnt its lesson from that one; under the Drug Testing and Treatment Order, those undertaking the treatment are required to report directly to the probation officer and to be responsible to the Probation Service.

Within the Probation Service there remains ambivalence about the need to control drug users – a casework mingled with a harm reduction approach is sometimes seen as more appropriate than one based on abstinence and control. This ambivalence produces all sorts of problems and uncertainties when it comes to securing and enforcing treatment. The criticisms made of the probation officers in this respect are sometimes unfairly directed at them when they should be directed at those doing the treatment, as the treatment providers often fail to co-operate with the Probation Service for reasons which are sometimes difficult to determine. It is strongly suspected that the treatment providers co-operate unwillingly because they do not want to be involved in court proceedings or, worse, that, as is often said, the treatment provider does not want to inform the probation officer of the patient's failings as this 'might damage the relationship with the treatment provider'. To which the obvious retort would be that the relationship could not be very strong if it could not stand that measure of honesty.

The facilities which offer the best opportunities are those of a probation order with a condition of treatment attached. Briefly, the Powers of the Criminal Courts Act 1973 permits the court to attach a condition of treatment to a probation order (which may be as an inpatient or outpatient) if the court is satisfied on the evidence of a duly qualified medical practitioner that the offender's condition is such as requires and may be susceptible to treatment, but is not such as to warrant detention in hospital under the Mental Health Act 1983.[1] The main advantages of this type of probation order are that it can be employed in cases not warranting detention in a hospital, perhaps under the Mental Health Act 1983, and it is able to provide treatment in conditions falling outside the Mental Health Act definitions of mental disorder (e.g. because they can include alcohol and drug misuse).

There seems to be general agreement that what is commonly called the 'psychiatric probation order' – or, more accurately, a probation order with a condition of psychiatric treatment as essentially determined by

s. 3 of the Powers of Criminal Courts Act 1973 – is underused, under-valued and under-researched. As far as can be seen, the high point of the order was in the mid-1970s when approximately 1,000 outpatient and 500 inpatient orders were made – 'approximately' because, surprisingly, there were few accurate national statistics on the orders made. By 1987 it appears that the figures had dipped to 870 and 150, respectively, and by the late 1990s had dropped even further. Of course, these figures are not just for drug offenders but for all offenders on the probation order with a condition of treatment, some of whom may not use drugs.

It is difficult to explain this lack of interest. It may have something to do with a general reluctance on behalf of psychiatrists to accept patients on an order, and a similar reluctance by the Probation Service to negotiate with psychiatrists about resolving existing tensions. The courts, too, seem to have lost interest, or perhaps have simply gone along with the prevailing climate. No one seems to know. Only one detailed research study has been undertaken, and that as far back as 1980 (Lewis 1980). This study looked at the use and effectiveness of such orders. The conclusions were generally favourable, with Lewis arguing for greater use, especially amongst the less severe mentally disordered. Sadly, the study produced little general interest and has hardly been referred to again.

The Criminal Justice Act 1991 attempted to revive things by placing community treatments at the centre of the criminal justice system. For example, s. 9 allowed the court to require the offender to comply, during the whole or part of the period on probation, with such requirements as the court considered desirable. The 1991 Act seems not to have improved things, with the decline continuing. It is difficult to know how that decline can be reversed.

In addition there are bail and arrest referral schemes which, strictly speaking, are not part of probation but are often run by the Probation Service. These constitute a catch-all group and are available where an offender requires assessment or treatment and an early investigation of the options. These can be provided through the bail scheme. Bail schemes may also involve the services of a consultant psychiatrist. The accommodation is usually in local bail hostels – the West Midlands Probation Service in Birmingham has one such hostel. If the offender is on police bail the police may choose not to prosecute if the offender is being successfully diverted. Sometimes the police will refer to the CPS for advice (NACRO 1993: 15).

There are various types of arrest referral schemes, some of which may involve nothing more than supplying the offender with an address to seek assistance or accommodation; others involve treatment agencies attending the police station and offering advice on treatment. Others offer incentives contingent on receiving treatment. Much is made of these schemes with the potential for diverting drug offenders out of the criminal justice system (although the caution does that successfully), but there is little information on the number of such schemes or on their effectiveness, and without this it is difficult to evaluate them.

One study by Sondhi *et al.* (2002) showed that in the period from October 2000 to September 2001, those who made a treatment demand were broadly similar to problematic users presenting for treatment elsewhere. Males accounted for 81% of those screened. The average age was 27 years (range 10–66), and 90% were 'white'. The percentage reporting use in the last month were, in descending order: heroin 56; cannabis 34; alcohol 27; crack 22; benzodiazepines 14; methadone 11; and cocaine, amphetamines and ecstasy each 6. Nearly half (47%) had injected in the last month. What appears to be happening is that about 30% of offenders offered treatment accept it, but whether they are a representative sample of drug users is difficult to say.

What is more important, however, is to see what happens to them afterwards. Are they accepted for treatment and, if so, do they stay? No one seems to know, although anecdotal evidence suggests only a small number make contact with the treatment services, and an equally small number stay. Sometimes this is due to a lack of treatment services, in which case it is all very well offering treatment, or rather suggesting offenders go into treatment, but if the services are not available or there is no requirement to remain in treatment, we should not be surprised if the long-term results turn out to be poor. The other possibility is that offenders may lack the motivation to succeed in treatment.

The following point will be developed in the final chapter but the opportunity arises here to flag it up, as it were. A major problem with all arrest referral schemes is they can only offer treatment to offenders; the Bail Act does not permit treatment to be a condition of bail – and arrest referral schemes operate at the point where the offender is arrested and then bailed. Everything we know about treatment tells us that drug users are at their most vulnerable, and therefore most susceptible to treatment, when arrested. Yet offering treatment is never enough; at best most will accept one or two appointments and then relapse. Treatment for offender populations works best when there is a compulsion to remain in treatment, supported by mandatory drug testing, and a period of treatment lasting at least 60 days. Anything less than that and one should expect failure. Arrest referral schemes may pick up one or two offenders who are ready for treatment and sufficiently motivated to succeed, but these are a small minority. To catch the majority we need something much more.

Secondly is the fine. The use of the fine fell from 37% in 1990 to 21% in 1996, before ending the decade at 26%. The interesting feature of this is not the decrease in use but that the fine is used at all. It clearly has no place for street junkies whose lifestyle makes them unsuitable for that type of sentence, or for the serious trafficker. It may have more of a place for a possession offence where the drug involved is not a Class A and the charge involves a small amount (e.g. cannabis or perhaps even a similar amount of ecstasy).

How, then, to account for its use? The key is found in Table 3.2 (and Figure 3.3), which gives the principal offences and the sentence. This table shows that the drug most likely to lead to a prosecution was cannabis (75,985 in 2000), followed by heroin (12,297), amphetamines (6,637) and then by ecstasy-type drugs (6,630). The number of prosecutions for drugs such as cocaine has also risen considerably. It is reasonable also to assume that most of these offences were for possession, given the data in Table 3.2. What this table shows, then, is that most drug offences are for possession of a drug which does not normally carry a severe penalty (e.g. cannabis), and this is why the fine has been used.

The implications go beyond the use of the fine or sentencing policy generally. They extend to matters surrounding policing, which are discussed in Chapter 7, as they raise questions about the effectiveness of policing. How is it that most drug offences are for the possession of a small amount of cannabis? How are the police spending their time? They also raise questions about introducing drug courts into Britain. Could drug courts be introduced for this group of offenders who would otherwise expect only the minimal punishments? And they also raise questions about the type of drug policy that is pursued. Is it correct to use up the court's time for these relatively minor offenders or should sentencing policy be more severe to produce a more deterrent effect?

There is no information available as to the effectiveness of the fine for drug offenders, neither in terms of reconviction rates nor as to whether the fine was paid. Compounding, which is a fine in every respect except it does not involve a court appearance and can be imposed by HM Customs and Excise remained steady over the ten years from 1987 before falling at the end of the 1990s. There is no information on its effectiveness, but payment is made direct to the Customs service at the time the drugs were discovered. The numbers of offenders given the fiscal fine, for Scotland, were comparatively small. The fine carries no treatment requirements.

Now follow cautions. Table 3.2 shows that, as the use of the fine has declined in relation to the caution, so it is reasonable to suppose the caution has replaced the fine at this lower end of the sentencing tariff. Briefly, there are two types of cautions, the informal and the formal. The first is given in the form of a warning, no record is made of the incident and no further action is taken. (Presumably this will be given to selected cannabis users after 29 January 2004.) The formal caution is different. It arose in the late 1940s with juveniles in Liverpool where it was found that children who were made subject to the juvenile court proceedings did rather worse in terms of reconviction than those who did not go to court. It is a pragmatic device aimed at cutting down court appearances and avoiding reconvictions. It is a peculiarly British device, being hardly used outside Britain, but it is cheap, effective and thought to be especially useful for juveniles, although it is increasingly used for adults. Formal cautions (like informal cautions) carry no treatment provisions, although there is nothing to stop the police from advising those cautioned where they can receive treatment should they so wish.

The use of the caution for drug users increased from 38% in 1990 to 52% in 1993, remaining at around that level before falling back to 40% in 2000. The Advisory Council on the Misuse of Drugs (ACMD: 1994) saw cautioning as a 'particularly appropriate way of dealing with minor drug offences' (para. 7.6), adding that 'the effect of cautioning in reducing re-offending remains in question', although for most first offenders the likelihood of reoffending appears no greater than after conviction by the court. It defined cautioning thus:

> In England and Wales the police may formally caution an arrested offender instead of initiating prosecution by the Crown Prosecution Service. The procedure is not used in Scotland. Although the practice of formal caution has statutory recognition it is nowhere defined in legislation, and is essentially an administrative act based on the discretion the police have in whether or not to prosecute offenders (*ibid.*: para. 7.2).

A major problem is the variation in the rates of cautioning throughout Britain: some police forces caution only on a first offence; others would not caution if the offender had a previous drug offence, and some would not caution for supply. At one level, of course, this offends the principles of natural justice – equals should be treated equally. At another level a national policy might be quite inappropriate, and recognised as such by many police forces who said they wanted to operate a policy related to the conditions in their area. So, for example, they would not want to give a caution to a drug user in an area where drug use is rare as it would send the wrong message to other users and potential users, but where drug use is common a caution might be more appropriate. Home Office Circular 18/1994 encourages greater consistency between the police forces and tries to meet other criticisms that cautions are a soft option. The circular, for example, discourages the use of cautions for the most serious offences (*ibid.*: para. 7.36). To what extent that advice is heeded is difficult to say, but the ACMD were correct to say that they were convinced of the value of cautions in dealing with drug offenders (*ibid.*: para. 7.1) and, accordingly, we can expect their use to continue.

Finally comes imprisonment. The use of imprisonment has remained relatively steady over the last decade, and currently (2000) runs at about 9% of total drug offenders. The proportion of drug offenders sentenced to immediate custody matches the rise in drug offenders generally. Imprisonment is used less for possession, more often for trafficking offences (defined in Table 3.2 as the production of drugs, the unlawful supply and possession with intent to supply unlawfully, and unlawful import and export). The longest sentences are awarded to the most serious traffickers.

Generally, the main aims of imprisonment are to punish according to individual and general deterrence, retribution and rehabilitation. Treatment is part of a rehabilitative framework and is provided in prisons alongside mandatory drug testing. The latter was introduced into all penal establishments in England and Wales in March 1996 and is primarily a deterrent against using whilst in prison but, if provided alongside a treatment programme, it can be beneficial.

I want to look at some of the features of treatment in prison. It seems there are three main reasons why treatment programmes should be run in prisons. The first is to provide treatment for those who say they want it – prison provides an opportunity to give treatment, and that opportunity should not be missed. Secondly, treatment programmes help reduce the extent of drug use in prisons generally (the extent of which is large).[2] Thirdly, treatment in prison also provides a means by which drug users can plan for their release (most relapses occur soon after release). Determining the effect of these programmes is impossible with current data sets; there are no measures of the numbers of drug users in prison generally, so it is not possible to estimate the impact of the programmes let alone compare one programme with another. Nor is it clear what the criteria should be to measure the impact of programmes or to determine to what extent incarceration itself was of greater importance than the treatment. Reconviction, and perhaps continuing drug use, are the only measures generally available, but these are not always valid measures and are rarely reliable.

The range of programmes for prisoners must of necessity be limited, whether due to the available facilities or the length of stay of prisoners. (Treatment programmes in whatever setting should last at least three months.) In an American study of over 100 jails providing treatment, it was found that few had comprehensive services, most had poor screening facilities and few were linked in any systematic way to community agencies on release. The services provided, which varied greatly in content (and one suspects also in quality), were available only to a small proportion of inmates who should have been receiving them (Peters 1993: 47–9; Weinman and Lockwood 1993). Most of the treatment consisted of a mixture of group therapy and psycho-educational approaches within therapeutic community settings, often determined by the interests and qualifications of the staff and the amount of time the prisons allocated to this rather than to other requirements. Similar results were found in prisons in Britain, where John Burrows *et al.* (2000: 3) reported that the provision of drug services throughout prison establishments was uneven, and where prisoners reported that treatment often depended on what was available rather than what was appropriate to their needs.

There is little doubt that treatment services are required. Burrows *et al.* (*ibid.*) report that drug taking amongst prison populations prior to incarceration is high, with use in the 12 months before entering prison ranging from 40% to about 70%, and findings from self-report studies show that many continue to use drugs whilst in custody. Many (66%) cited heroin as their main drug and had used it every day in the 30 days before being sentenced. In addition, a third said they took crack and a half took cannabis. Overall most were polyusers (*ibid.*: 2). The researchers also note that the primary means of identifying prisoners with drug problems is when they themselves seek help. However, many are reluctant to do this as it means the authorities know they are drug users, and the prisoners fear they will be targeted during their sentence – for additional searches, etc. These are some of the impediments to receiving prison treatment. Add to these the increasing numbers of substance-abuse prisoners with a coexisting mental disorder and dual diagnosis (about 11% in US jails according to the US Department of Health and Human Services 1998), and the problem is huge.

The Office of National Statistics (ONS) carried out a survey of inmates in English and Welsh prisons during 1997 (Singleton *et al.* 1998). It revealed that nearly half of sentenced males and a third of females reported using drugs during their current prison term. Cannabis use was reported by 46% of male and 31% of female sentenced prisoners. However, women were just as likely as men to report use of heroin. Around two fifths of both male (43%) and female (41%) inmates reported dependence on drugs, somewhat lower than the rates for remand prisoners – 51% and 54% of males and females, respectively. Females reported higher levels of dependence on heroin and non-prescribed methadone. By the end of March 1996, John Corkery (2003) reports that mandatory drug testing (MDT) had been introduced into all penal establishments in England and Wales. Results for these countries, show that whilst there was an overall decrease in the proportion of inmates testing positive for cannabis (from 10.2% in 1999–2000 to 6.8% in 2001–2), there were rises in the use of opiates and benzodiazepines (Home Office 2001, 2003). The proportion for opiates rose from 4.3% to 4.7%, and that for benzodiazepines from 1.1% to 1.3% in 2000–1, but it fell slightly in 2001–2. Of note is that 1.5% of inmates in some establishments in the north east of England tested positive in 2000–1 (and 1.2% in 2001/2) for buprenorphine, which is becoming more widely used in the treatment of opiate dependence (Corkery 2003).[3]

What is particularly disturbing is that some prisoners reported that their detection and punishment had not affected their use. In a sample of 148 prisoners from five establishments, Edgar and O'Donnell (1998) found that 37 claimed they did not use drugs whilst in prison. However, of the remainder (111), almost half (53) said they had not changed their drug taking whilst in prison, four said they had tried heroin for the first time and cut down on cannabis use, seven reported altering their pattern of consumption (taking less cannabis but continuing to use heroin) and 17 out of the 111 said they had reduced their consumption, i.e. not stopped. An outcome of MDT is that many prisoners will spend longer in custody at a significant cost to the Prison Service. Edgar and O'Donnell report that, in 1997, about 159,000 days were added to prisoners' sentences as a direct result of MDT (roughly equivalent to 360 prisoner years or about £7 million in additional running costs) (*ibid*.: 4). A criticism of MDT, at least from the prisoners' point of view, was that not enough attention was given to identifying serious drug use and directing prisoners to treatment, and rather too much attention was given to deterrence.

The US Department of Health and Human Services (1998) talk of what they call 'obstacles to effective post release transitions' – in other words problems about providing adequate throughcare facilities. The obstacles they say are the most substantial (with most coming from the structure of public sector systems) are the fragmentation of the criminal justice system, the community providers' lack of attention to offender issues and funding barriers (*ibid.*: 4). Burrows *et al.* (2000) paint an equally dismal picture for Britain when they say: 'Drugs throughcare provision is characterised by structural impediments where delivery is restricted by disputes over professional boundaries, areas of responsibility and fragile funding. Successful schemes are typically the product of one or two charismatic individuals and unusually strong interagency partnerships.' Yet without adequate throughcare the inevitable will happen: prisoners will return to drugs, as most appear to do, and speedily upon release. This may result in fatal overdoses (Seaman *et al.* 1998; Singleton *et al.* 2003).

The Prison Service is clearly alive to the problem, and its 1998 strategy was aimed at providing an equitable provision of basic and enhanced specialist services to meet low-level, moderate and severe drug problems. In practice this means developing what is called a Counselling, Assessment, Referral, Advice and Throughcare Service (CARATS) within and across the Prison Service with greater emphasis on the inputs of the treatment services. At the same time security is strengthened and drug testing continues; the usual mixture of carrot and stick is in evidence.

The problems posed by drug users in prison are immense. Some (e.g. those convicted for trafficking) are unlikely to be drug users and are more likely to come from the organised crime syndicates described in Chapter 6. They pose particular control problems as their sentences are wholly for retributive or for deterrence reasons and are likely to be lengthy. Rehabilitation, whatever that might mean to drug offenders generally, is not likely to be available for this group, nor will there be treatment whilst in prison for these traffickers. Yet there are many other drug offenders where the principles of rehabilitation do apply; treatment is needed and supervision is required.[4]

No one wants to underestimate the difficulties. Some drug offenders are reluctant to disclose their drug use when first taken to police stations or when first subject to a report from a probation officer, believing such a disclosure might result in a longer sentence, especially if a woman and certainly if pregnant. Nor are they the most rewarding offenders to deal with; for some, the concept of rehabilitation does not apply, not because they are not worthy candidates for a rehabilitative approach but because rehabilitation assumes that they were once habilitated, and that assumption may be unwarranted. They may have never received the basic skills (social, technical or otherwise) in the first place. Many are unemployable, having reached their mid-twenties without ever having had a proper job. Their life experiences have largely been shaped by periods in prison and the drug scene, where interpersonal violence and the demands for instant rewards are commonplace. Supervising these offenders is always going to be difficult, whether inside the prison or on discharge – monumental even. Yet all too often these are the offenders who cause enormous expense to the criminal justice system and take up a disproportionate amount of resources.

Some concluding comments

Looking at the numbers of drug offenders and the number and length of sentences passed tells us little about sentencing policy, about changes in policy or about the practices of the courts. Drug offenders (as defined in Table 3.2) are only a small proportion of the offenders who appear before the criminal justice system with a drug habit. Countless others (where the Index offence is not a drug offence) will appear regularly. In some cases the court will not know there is a problem and, if it does, it is not clear whether or not the court considers the drug problem when passing sentence.

Secondly, even if we knew of all the drug offenders, the numbers of offenders sentenced to each specific sentence are insufficient to identify a sentencing policy; at the very least we would need to know the ratio of sentences to offences – that is to say, we need to know the years of prison time, the amount of the fine, the period of probation, etc. Even so, the answer we would obtain would give only a crude figure because it would ignore other key factors such as previous convictions, the amount of the drug involved and so on. We are left, therefore, able to do little more than describe the sentences themselves, examine the changes over time and infer likely trends.

The principal rationales for sentencing apply equally to drug offenders as to others; there are no special defences for drug offenders and no particular reasons to deal with drug offenders outside the usual justifications for imposing sentences on any other offender. Sentencing involves a mixture of legal principles, moral assertions, theoretical justifications and legal precedents, which can occasionally be reduced to the notion of a tariff – that is, a rough-and-ready guide based on a common law tradition about what a particular crime is worth as far as a sentence goes. To say that one crime is worth a more severe sentence than another is to invoke a multitude of arguments about proportionality, deterrence and rehabilitation, plus a mixture of mitigating circumstances which can include the nature of the offence, the way it was committed and the character of the defendant. In this respect sentencing drug offenders is no different from sentencing others. The sentence will contain the following components: a need to deter others from committing the offence; a need to deter the individual from committing the offence again; sentencing the offender because he or she has committed an offence and therefore deserves to be punished; and the offer of a form of rehabilitation whilst being punished. The final decision will also take account of the mitigating circumstances, which may include the offender's dependence on drugs, but this may not always work to the offender's advantage as the court may think this is a self-inflicted condition and justifies a heavier sentence than otherwise.

However, in one respect drug offenders *are* different. It is increasingly being recognised that they need to be sentenced according to principles of rehabilitation rather than deterrence or retribution. This has occurred because of the links with treatment – 'Treatment Works' – a recurring theme that is to be found in later chapters. Rehabilitation was the dominant philosophy of the 1960s and 1970s but has since been discredited, to be replaced by a just-deserts model which draws on retribution as its intellectual inspiration. The basis of a rehabilitation philosophy is that offenders require help, not punishment. Help is usually provided through some therapeutic intervention or by medical services. Rehabilitation has been criticised for being too soft on offenders and too concerned with their welfare, at the expense of the victim, whilst at the same time too harsh because it permits detention until the offender is cured – which may be longer than would have been the case had a retributive sentence been passed.

The paradox of the present position is evident: the treatment of drug offenders resurrects the theory of rehabilitation and, with it, all those arguments which were left behind when the just-deserts philosophy became dominant. Rehabilitation has within it a set of apparent contradictions: it is regarded as too soft when drug offenders are given treatment in the community rather than being sent to prison, and too harsh when they are detained in prison for treatment longer than they would have otherwise. For those conducting the treatment, rehabilitation promotes them into an increasingly powerful position, for they will be asked to decide when the drug offender is ready to be discharged. They will also be asked who will be given treatment, what will be given, the cost, the length of time it is likely to take and, above all, who is suitable. They will have their say about who is to be let into treatment and who is to be excluded.

At the moment rehabilitation as a dominant theory of sentencing is being held back by a shortage of treatment services, which are scarce and poorly developed; there are about 500 drug treatment agencies in England and Wales (Royal College of Psychiatrists 2000), but these have a relatively minor part to play within the criminal justice system. Rehabilitation could change that and, indeed, in later chapters I argue that there should be a greater level of co-ordination between the criminal justice system and treatment services. In saying this I recognise that I am advocating a return to a rehabilitative philosophy (with all its attendant problems) but, in doing so, I am suggesting that it be resurrected in a form which avoids the failings of the past. It will still have an impact on the sentencing practices of the courts and will exert an influence but in ways less destructive than those of earlier years. The extent of this re-habilitative influence will become increasingly apparent as the demands for treatment increase.

At present most energy in Britain seems to be taken up with less important pursuits, such as whether drugs, mostly cannabis, should change from one class to another, typically from Class B to Class C, or whether ecstasy should change to Class B from Class A. The argument for doing so is that a more accurate 'hierarchy of harm' will help to target prevention and treatment resources more effectively. Whether that will be so remains to be seen for, as will be shown later, the policing of drug offenders is more haphazard than this, as most prosecutions (especially for cannabis) occur when the offender is arrested for a non-drugs offence and is found to be in possession of cannabis. Few offenders are targeted for possessing cannabis, although more may be for possession of ecstasy, but reclassifying this to a Class B drug is not likely to make much difference as far as policing is concerned. Moreover, as shown in this chapter, most of those offenders charged with a possession offence are given a caution or a fine, and this is so irrespective of the class of the drug. It is more likely that the reclassification argument is part of a wider demand for decriminalisation or legalisation and has little to do with sentencing, policing or public policy.

Of the many aspects of sentencing which are important, there are two which need to be emphasised as likely to be of significance for the future. First, drug offenders in Britain are not likely to go to prison for a possession offence but are very likely to do so for illicit supply. Secondly, the links with treatment align sentencing closely with a rehabilitative philosophy. Consequently, the development of treatment facilities is becoming increasingly important. The nature and extent of drug misuse in the UK – as established from official statistics, surveys and studies of sentencing – will need to be considered if only to avoid the defects of rehabilitation, which were glaringly obvious when rehabilitation last assumed its measure of dominance. I shall return to these points again in later chapters.

Notes

1 There is an apparent confusion here which turns out to be resolved thus: a person on a probation order with a condition of treatment can be detained in a hospital but, unlike those patients detained under the Mental Health Act, his or her condition will not be as severe and, whilst on probation, he or she has the same rights whilst in hospital as an outpatient to refuse treatment and discharge him or herself. That of course may lead to a breach of probation, but if a refusal to undergo treatment is reasonable, having regard to all the circumstances (s. 6(7) Powers of Civil Courts Act 1973), no breach would be implied.

2 A survey of Scottish prisoners conducted in 1998 found that 44% of prisoners had used drugs whilst in prison during the previous six months (Wozniak *et al.* 1998). Nearly two fifths (39%) had used cannabis; the rates for other drugs were heroin 31%, diazepam 16%, dihydrocodeine 14%, ecstasy 9%, amphetamines 8%, methadone 4% and other opiate-based drugs (e.g. Temgesic – buprenorphine) 23%. There was a significant increase in the use of heroin between 1994 and 1998, from 9 to 31%. Levels of drug use reported by inmates varied from 11% in Peterhead to 59% in Glenochil. Drug use was more likely amongst young offenders, especially males. On average, 5% reported injecting drugs in prison; again this varied from prison to prison, reaching 19% in Aberdeen. About four-fifths (82%) of injectors reported sharing injecting equipment. Remand prisoners and long-term prisoners nearing the end of their sentences are less likely to have these practices. The 2001 sweep of this survey found that 38% reported having used drugs in prison in the previous month (SPS 2001). Of these, opiates were reported by 76%, and cannabis by 70% . Four per cent of this drug-using group reported injecting, and of these 77% had shared their 'works'. Drug use ever in prison was reported by 58%, of whom 43% had received help, such as counselling or prescriptions, whilst in prison. Three quarters said that their drug use had changed during their current period inside: for 80% use had decreased, but 12% reported more use, and 8% had used different drugs. The latest sweep (SPS 2002) indicates that, whilst the use of opiates and Temgesic has fallen since 2001, there have been increases in a range of other drugs. These changes have been accompanied by a doubling (to 8%) in the proportion reporting injecting drugs, and a higher proportion of these sharing (92%). However, the percentage of those receiving help for their drug problems had risen to 50%. Other patterns remained similar to 2001.

3 MDT results for Scotland show that the proportion of positive tests for any drug fell from 36% in 1996–7 to 21% in 2000–1 before rising to 22% in 2001–2 (ISD 2002: 152; 2003: 165). The rates for cannabis and opiates fell most from 29

to 9% and from 16 to 11%, respectively. The rate for benzodiazepines fell from 9 to 4%. The rate of detection for Temgesic has ranged between 1 and 3%. The levels of drug use amongst prisoners at reception increased in Scotland from 73% in 1998–9 to 77% in 2001 but fell to 75% in 2001–2 (ISD 2003: 164). The use of cannabis rose from 49 to 63% in 2001 but fell to 45% in 2001–2 as well as for benzodiazepines (from 43 to 52%). Methadone use increased from 8 to 12% before falling to 10% in 2001–2, probably reflecting its wider use in the treatment of dependence. Opiate use varied between 34 and 44%, and amphetamines between 2 and 4%. Cocaine use rose from 4 to 9%. These results relate mainly to the prison establishments in Aberdeen and Perth. A study in October 2000 found that there were substantial geographical differences in the use of all types of drug (ISD 2002: 151). For example, cannabis use ranged from 29% in Inverness to 93% in Perth; opiates from 11% in Polmont to 61% in Cornton Vale (a female establishment); and benzodiazepines from 12% in Dumfries to 84% in Aberdeen.

4 The National Offender Management System (NOMS) now brings the Probation and Prison Services together. The aim here is to link prison and probation programmes making them more effective.

Chapter 4

Coercive treatment and mandatory drug testing

In the previous chapter an overview was given of the facilities available within the criminal justice system for dealing with drug offenders. In this chapter the aim is to look more closely at treatment within the criminal justice system which, for these purposes, means coercive or enforced treatment. This examination will take place alongside a look at mandatory drug testing (for a more detailed discussion on treatment generally, see Bean and Nemitz 2004).

From the mid-1990s onwards, British governments have shown an increasing willingness to fund and thereby increase the range of treatment facilities for substance abusers and, correspondingly, have shown a willingness to increase drug testing. They have done so because they recognise that treatment provides one of the few options for containing the drug problem, coupled with a belief that it breaks the link with crime. Drug testing is included because it is thought that, without that backup, treatment will fail. Drug testing is the building block of treatment within the criminal justice system.

Briefly, the background to the various government initiatives is as follows. In 1995, *Tackling Drugs Together: A Strategy for England 1995–8* was produced for England; that for Wales and Scotland followed soon afterwards (Ministerial Drugs Task Force 1994; HM Government 1995; Welsh Office 1998). *Tackling Drugs Together* (HM Government 1995: para. 1.3) committed the government 'to take effective action by vigorous law enforcement, accessible treatment and a new emphasis in education and prevention'. There were no details of the treatment programmes in these strategies but promises were made that these would be provided in a later task force report. The emphasis in *Tackling Drugs Together* was on reorganising local services, including replacing them with Drug Action Teams.

The later *Task Force Report* (Department of Health 1996) assessed the range of treatment services and commissioned some research; its terms of reference included 'a comprehensive survey of clinical, operational and cost effectiveness of existing services for drug misusers'. In 1998 a second drug strategy was introduced by the newly appointed Anti-drugs Co-ordinator, entitled *Tackling Drugs Together to Build a Better Britain: The Government's Ten Year Strategy for Tackling Drug Misuse* (HM Government 1998). This largely reiterated the themes of the 1995 document whilst adding performance targets for drug reduction for the next decade. Finally, in 1999, guidelines on the clinical management of drug users gave advice to the medical profession about how best to implement the drug strategy.

The National Treatment Outcome Research Study (NTORS) – the biggest study of drug treatment ever conducted in Britain – showed that there were considerable benefits in bringing drug users into treatment. However, the rates of improvement were less than in the USA (Gossop *et al.* 1997, 1998). NTORS followed the progress of 1,100 drug misusers through treatment and concluded that there were no 'magic bullets' to cure drug problems. In a review of treatment using NTORS data, the conclusion was that drug abuse was a chronic relapsing condition which required treatment to fit the client's needs. Drug treatment, which embraces social care and support as well as clinical intervention, can be effective in reducing drug-related harm, but most substance misusers require several attempts at treatment before noticeable success occurs (Gossop *et al.* 1997).

In June 2001 the post of Anti-drugs Co-ordinator was abolished, and the Drugs Czar was initially given a part-time job as an international adviser, but that ended soon after. The centre of the government's strategy moved from the Cabinet Office to the Home Office, presumably on the grounds that policy had traditionally come from the Home Office and that two centres of policy-making produced unnecessary duplication.

In April 2001 the National Treatment Agency (NTA) – a Special Health Authority within the National Health Service – was launched (see Bean and Nemitz 2004: chap. 7). The NTA covers England; other arrangements are in place for Scotland, Wales and Northern Ireland. The aim of the NTA is 'to co-ordinate the drive for better and more consistent treatment for people with drug problems'. This includes 'the commissioning and delivery of high quality effective treatment for drug misusers (which) is fundamental to the success of the Government's drug strategy' (NTA undated). This statement of purpose is in line with the government's strategy 'To increase participation of problem drug misusers including prisoners in drug treatment programmes which have a positive impact on health and crime by 66% by 2005 and by 100% by 2008' (*ibid.*). In February 2002, the NTA produced *Models of Care for Substance Misuse Treatment* aimed at providing a framework 'intended to achieve equity, parity and consistency in the commissioning and provision of substance misuse treatment and care in the UK' (p. 2).

All these government initiatives emphasised the need for treatment. Treatment was to operate alongside law enforcement, prevention and control – the latter mainly through the criminal justice system. Treatment was endorsed as a desirable platform in the government's strategy, which inevitably concentrated on Class A drugs controlled by the Misuse of Drugs Act 1971 (i.e. mostly heroin and cocaine). In its strategy the government called on substantial evidence from America (now transformed into British thinking), which shows that 'Treatment Works' – a slogan particularly favourable to Britain which, nationally, has well developed, widespread treatment services.

Legislation has been introduced that requires some drug offenders to submit themselves to treatment – these in addition to facilities already in existence. The DTTO provided for under ss. 61–64 of the Crime and Disorder Act 1998 (and drug testing in prison carried out under s. 16A of the Prison Act 1952) links the treatment services with the criminal justice system in ways that require them to work according to criminal justice requirements. The Criminal Justice and Court Services Bill, which was then before the House of Lords, illustrated government thinking: 'Identifying drug misusing offenders at every stage in the criminal justice system is now a prime objective of the crime reduction strategy and will make an important contribution to the overall drug strategy' (House of Commons, Explanatory Notes 2001: para. 28). Additional powers require offenders and alleged offenders to be drug tested at various points in their contact with the criminal justice system. These are at a national implementation cost of £45.5 million, of which £20 million will be police costs (*ibid.*: paras 133 and 134). Clearly this is where the government is putting the funding. There are also drug abstinence orders which require the offender to refrain from misusing Class A drugs and to undertake a drug test on instruction, as well as pre-sentence drug testing.

Why are these additional facilities required? There have long been facilities to treat offenders under a probation order, perhaps with a condition of treatment as an inpatient or outpatient. There have been also opportunities to require some offenders to be inpatients as a condition of their probation order. However, these appear not to have been taken up, for reasons which have not always been understood. Briefly, the Criminal Justice Act 1991 tried to boost the use of treatment under a probation order and gave the courts powers to impose treatment as part of a sentence of probation – as it was then called. It was rarely used. The Home Office Probation Inspectorate said this was because:

- The Home Office and Probation Services adopted a neutral stance, declining to issue guidance.

- Probation officers did not believe coerced treatment would work so were reluctant to recommend it in their pre-sentence reports.

- Sentencers lacked information on the treatments available.

- Within the criminal justice system treatment providers were un-enthusiastic about operating coercive systems.

The result is new legislation where the overall effect is to shift towards more forms of treatment (some of which are coercive) and away from the earlier approach, which is still beloved by many of the treatment services – that treatment should at all times be voluntary. This is not the place to discuss the philosophy of treatment (see Bean and Nemitz 2004 for a discussion on treatment generally), but the government has clearly been influenced by the American research which proclaims in unequivocal terms that treatment is successful (Anglin and Hser 1990).

Yet behind the slogan 'Treatment Works' lies a range of difficult questions. First there is a group of empirical questions, such as with whom does treatment work? Can successful treatments be given over a single period, or do they require subsequent treatments even after the success of the first? Is a single type of treatment appropriate to all patients? Then there are questions about the principles of treatment. What are the aims of treatment? What should be the remit and to whom should treatment be given (it clearly cannot be given to everyone who takes drugs)? Finally, there is a group of questions specifically sur-rounding treatment within the criminal justice system, such as: what are the aims of treatment in criminal justice? Do they or should they differ in a qualitative sense from that provided outside the criminal justice system – that is, can treatment be effective if the offender is coerced, or does it always need to be voluntarily? The questions to be dealt with here centre on the links with the criminal justice system and the corresponding matter of coercion. Others of a more general nature are considered in another volume more directly concerned with treatment generally (see Bean and Nemitz 2004).

The aims and nature of treatment

The treatment of substance abuse, whether in or out of criminal justice, uses a mixture of traditional medical interventions, including treatment talk, which is likely to dominate treatment programmes. In the early stages when the offender enters the programme, the focus tends to be narrow, perhaps centring on detoxification or other forms of withdrawal. As treatment progresses it becomes more inclusive (i.e. more therapeutic), taking in wider aspects of the drug takers' lives. The Royal College of Psychiatrists (2000: 155) sets out the aims of treatment: to prevent and reduce the harm resulting from the use of drugs. The Royal College says this definition includes social, psychological or physical harm, and may involve medical, social or educational interventions. It also includes prevention and harm reduction – prevention presumably means for everyone, but harm reduction is for those who are chronic substance misusers (*ibid.*).

The straightforward definition provided by the Royal College differs in content hardly at all from that found in most standard texts on the rehabilitation of offenders, although it differs in form in that rarely are definitions as succinct as this. This is to its advantage as it spells out the treatment aims in a clear, unequivocal manner – a quality rarely found in textbooks on treatment. More likely there will be a discussion, or rather a description, of the nature of drugs and addiction; there will then be a discussion of assessment, followed by an examination of measures of intervention – usually including a discussion on the range of treatments and the special types of problems encountered – with a final section on follow-up and outcome. The central questions will be neatly bypassed, such as what should treatments aim to achieve, and for what reason?

Within the drugs field the language of treatment is predominant medical. There is little to suggest, however, that treatment is aimed at curing an 'illness', although the patient's condition during the withdrawal period may be akin to this, requiring expert medical intervention. The model of addiction most favoured in Britain, including that by the Royal College of Psychiatrists, is a socio-behavoural one; an alternative, the disease model, has little support outside the rather narrow confines of AA/NA (Alcoholics Anonymous/Narcotics Anonymous), who provide programmes such as the '12 Steps' and other self-help groups.

Treatment has, and will continue to be, thrust into prominence for two main reasons. First, there has developed a wider understanding of the links between drug taking and crime, initially promoted during the late 1980s when drug cases began to escalate dramatically alongside an ever-increasing crime rate, particularly property crime. Within this research, studies confirmed what many had suspected – that large numbers of offenders on arrest were testing positive for a range of drugs and were claiming they committed crimes while under the influence of drugs (Bennett 1998). Overwhelmed by this increase in drug use and the apparent criminality it produced ('apparent' because, as shown in Chapter 1, the links with crime are more tenuous than at first appears), the government's response has been to increase the range and numbers of treatment programmes. This, it expects, will provide relief from the so-called revolving door of crime, where drug users endlessly move between the courts, the criminal justice system and the world of criminality. The NTORS is a clear example of government interest (Gossop *et al.* 1997). Of course not all drug users are part of the revolving-door syndrome, but those who are create the biggest problems.

Secondly, treatment has been revitalised by the growing belief that it works. The veracity of this is more alive in America than in Britain as Britain does not have the complement of research data to verify it, but it has been picked up in Britain, none the less, and the NTORS study goes some way to redress the balance. Research has not always made clear how treatment works with whom it works, or whether some treatment modalities work better than others, but there has arisen the popular belief that it does work. Perhaps this slogan has been accepted because it provides the only way of dealing with a problem that is almost out of control – treatment provides a life-raft and gives hope against an otherwise relentless increase in drug use. Whether this is the case or not, treatment (and the expected success it will bring) is imbedded in the popular image, and governments are prepared to invest heavily in treatment programmes.

However, does treatment work only when the offender seeks it, or does it work when the offender is coerced? This is one of the key questions, not simply because of the empirical questions about outcomes and success rates but because treatment within the criminal justice system must operate according to different parameters than those involved in the traditional freedom of the doctor–patient relationship. Criminal justice is about control; the classical model of treatment, however, involves freedom on behalf of the doctor and patient to break the relationship. Small wonder that those treatment agencies wedded to the traditional model find it difficult to work within a criminal justice framework. Too often they insist that treatment must be voluntary but find themselves involved with a system that does not permit their patient – the offender – to make his or her own decisions; this is essentially a coercive system. The problem is compounded by the demands made for treatment by the criminal justice agencies. The group most in need of treatment almost certainly comes from the criminal justice system and, indeed, about 60% of all those seeking treatment come from this source. What, then, of coercion?

Coercive or enforced treatment of substance abuse

It seems axiomatic that any increase in the treatment services will be directed towards the criminal justice system, for this is where the government sees the problem at its worst and, consequently, is most likely to spend its money. Governments no longer live in that world where they hope the drug problem will magically go away; they recognise its enormity and the cost it brings, socially and otherwise. This would suggest (whether the treatment services like it or not) that there must be a closer working relationship between the treatment services and the criminal justice system. This has already happened in the USA. In the 1980s there occurred a so-called 'paradigm shift' where the treatment services and the criminal justice system agreed on a development programme and a strategy about how best to implement it. This included decisions about who should and who should not be treated, about the best way to move forward and about how to remove existing barriers to co-operation. It meant sharing beliefs and accepting a new set of aims and objectives. In practice, the changes were almost all one way: the criminal justice system shifted its position hardly at all. That 'paradigm shift' has not yet occurred in Britain but it cannot be long before it does.

A likely implication of a closer working partnership is that the treatment services will lose some of their independence and, with it, their more theoretical approach to treatment. A possible outcome is that treatment agencies will be subcontracted to the criminal justice system, providing treatment to offenders on court orders, whether at the pre- or post-sentence stage. This is already happening under the DTTO, but the change is likely to be accelerated in the short and long term as governments seek new ways to control drug offenders. Treatment agencies will also have to face demands to evaluate their work (most of which have been able to avoid this type of scrutiny hitherto). The effect will be to bring about an erosion of some cherished beliefs and a corresponding change in some of the assumptions underpinning the agencies' work.

One established cherished belief likely to come under threat is that which asserts that treatment ought only be provided if the patient seeks it voluntarily. (This was one of the first casualties of the 'paradigm shift' in the USA.) This view, which, like so many others, has been promoted and sustained with little or no research evidence to support it, has become one of the shibboleths of the treatment world. It is based on a set of assumptions that suggests the patient must give of him or herself fully and freely to a treatment programme or it will not be successful. A coerced patient will be a failed patient.

Much confusion centres on the term 'coercion', as if there was something sinister about the fact that offenders are coerced. Yet coercion or enforcement is a *sine qua non* of the criminal justice system. Treatment agencies working within the criminal justice system must expect to work within a coercive apparatus; that some appear to try to operate otherwise shows they misunderstand the nature of their task. It is not therefore whether coercion is acceptable for, by definition, coercion is part of criminal justice. The questions are, or should be: what is an acceptable level of coercion and what should be the powers of those able to coerce? What should the boundaries be of a coercive regime?

As far as coercive treatment is concerned, two major legal forms of coercion can be identified, each with its own subtypes:

1 Those involving *civil* commitment. The agencies undertaking civil commitment usually include the courts sitting as a civil court, created government agencies (including the police) and a medical agency.

2 Those involving *judicial* commitment. This occurs where commitment is a condition of a sentence, as in a probation order or compulsory after care. Imprisonment for the Index offence is not included in this category.

First comes civil commitment. There are no provisions in Britain for the civil commitment of substance misusers. The Mental Health Act 1983 expressly forbids including drug addiction as a category of mental disorder, although a mental disorder resulting from drug abuse could warrant compulsion. The first Brain Committee report (Department of Health 1960) considered introducing civil commitment provisions for substance abusers but rejected it, and the Review of the Mental Health Act 1959 (which led to the Mental Health Act 1983) noted that government advisory bodies said it was incompatible with current thinking to regard drug dependence and drinking problems as a form of mental disorder:

These conditions are increasingly seen as social and behavioural problems manifested in varying degrees of habit and dependency. However, it is recognised that alcohol and drug dependency can be associated with certain forms of mental disorder (Department of Health 1978: para. 1.29).

However, the distinctions have increasingly become blurred. Substance abuse is frequently found in mentally disordered patients and mentally disordered patients are frequently found to be substance abusers – the so-called dual diagnosis patients. Moreover, substance abuse can mask or mimic disorders, making diagnosis difficult and treatment equally so. None the less, as a general proposition, the Brain Committee were correct to make and establish the distinction, and the recent review of mental health legislation was also correct to leave things as they are.

Civil commitment has been used extensively elsewhere; in a United Nations' survey of 43 countries, 27 had civil commitment provisions for substance abuse (Porter *et al.* 1986). In America, civil commitment was introduced early in the twentieth century when users were referred to so-called narcotic farms and, later, to hospitals (as in Lexington, Kentucky). It was used again in the 1960s in California and New York, again through the civil law, based on assumptions that, whilst some drug abusers are motivated to treatment, others are not. Accordingly, a mechanism had to be established to deal with the less motivated users (what was called 'rational authority') but which Inciardi *et al.* (1996: 28) say was a euphemism for appearing not to be punitive, yet able to exercise mandatory control. The California programme permitted commitment for up to seven years – without, of course, having convicted the drug user of any offence. In New York it was similar.

Few civil commitment programmes have been properly evaluated, including those in America. Inciardi (1988) says of the New York programme (that is, where such evaluation as there was existed) that it was an abject failure. This, he says, was not because the idea was wrong but because it was poorly funded, had poor treatment facilities, appointed untrained staff, had a poorly developed aftercare programme and lost public support, leading to a wave of bad publicity. Anglin and Hser (1991) evaluated the California programme and concluded that civil commitment was an effective way of reducing narcotic addiction, yet added that this conclusion should not necessarily lead to immediate implementation. It was useful for bringing users into treatment, but it could not take the place of treatment (Leukefeld and Tims 1988; Anglin and Hser 1991). Anglin and Hser (1991) believe that drug abusers should be given greater encouragement to enter treatment voluntarily and, unless funding is provided to create new programmes or extend existing ones, the coercion of an individual into drug treatment may make the situation worse.

There are, of course, civil rights questions to be asked about civil commitment. People in Britain rightly object to the notion that a person can be detained without having been convicted of a criminal offence because he or she abuses substances. (In Britain there are, incidentally, fewer qualms about compulsory detention of the mentally ill without due process of trial.) It may be true that the extent of abuse makes a user a danger to him or herself as death rates are high. So, too, are they amongst motorcyclists or young car drivers – are these to be detained also? The justification for civil commitment in the USA is also based on health/economics (that is, detention is justified because of the expected cost to the public health services if left untreated). Of course the same could be said for anyone engaged in dangerous pursuits, from skiing to working as a steeple-jack. The more serious point, however, can be made with those who directly care for children, including pregnant women, where substance abuse can damage the physical and mental health of those in their care.

The second type of commitment (judicial commitment) is, however, used extensively in Britain, as shown by the data in Chapter 3. This involves committal to treatment by a court order and, whilst the offender is given a choice about accepting the order (as in the DTTO), in practice this choice is illusory – resembling more of a Hobson's choice than a real choice. Judicial commitment has existed for some time through the probation order and it has been extended through the DTTO (through parole and for offenders in prison).

Critics of judicial commitment, many of whom are from the treatment services, see judicial commitment as coercive and, by implication, wrong. They see it as standing in stark contrast to voluntary treatment which, they say, by definition, is their approved form of treatment. This assertion is at best misleading and at worst simply wrong. It produces a *coercion* v. *voluntary* dichotomy which fails to take account of the possible shades of meaning within each of the terms. For example, judicial commitment does not mean the drug abusers always feel coerced into treatment; some may enter willingly and be glad of the opportunity to be offered the options. Nor does it mean that coercion from the courts is the only source of coercion; greater coercive pressure might have come from elsewhere, family, friends, employers, etc., which may be more powerful and influential.

It makes more sense to talk of different levels of coercion operating at different points on a continuum, and coming from different sources. Take the court and the legal system as an example. De Leon (1998) suggests that the court offers different levels of coercion, able to invoke a range of options based on different degrees of severity (Farabee *et al*. 1998). First, de Leon (1998) says there is *legal referral* which operates according to an explicit procedure where the offender is referred to treatment according to a sentence of the court or by some other formal practice as in probation or parole. Secondly, there is *legal status* where the offender is referred according to an administrative device, as with bail or arrest referral schemes. Finally, there is *legal pressure,* which refers to the extent to which the offender experiences discomfort over the potential consequences of non-compliance, such as where the court makes clear that failure in treatment is likely to lead to a long prison sentence. *Legal pressure* is the form most likely to be regarded as coercive, but even then coercion might not be excessive – for example, some offenders might regard a prison sentence as a less fearful option than a spell in a treatment programme. Moreover, levels of coercion may vary within programmes: some probation orders with a condition of treatment may appear coercive but, in practice, the treatment agencies rarely report shortcomings and failures, including the failure to attend for treatment and that, to all intents and purposes, means the offender does what he or she likes.

Or consider social and family coercion. Family coercion could be seen as qualitatively different from the coercion of friends and employees, as it is more likely to be sustained and to have longer-term consequences. It might also be more effective in driving offenders into treatment. It is more useful, then, to see coercion as existing where the offenders enter at a certain point and stay or leave at the same or different points. The source of referral does not determine the level of coercion, although it might (O'Hare 1996).

To concentrate for a moment on *legal pressure* as this is likely to be the mainstay of the opposition to court-based programmes, the assumption has been that the level of coercion will always be high. Assume, however, that it is. Does this warrant opposition to providing treatment under those circumstances? Not in terms of ethical or jurisprudential matters. Courts have traditionally been permitted to require treatment as part of punishment (for various conditions including mental disorder or alcoholism) and have been allowed to impose conditions attached to sentences. What are the research results? The case for coercion would be weakened if it were shown coercion does not work. In fact the research evidence, albeit American, shows that the circumstances under which an individual is exposed to treatment, voluntarily or under coercion, are irrelevant. The important point is that the drug user should be brought into an environment where intervention occurs; the more routes into this environment the better, even if they include coercive routes. Treatment outcomes are not based on the reasons for entering treatment but the length of time remaining in treatment. That is to say, the longer the period in treatment the better the outcome. This makes sense: the longer a person spends in treatment, the greater the number of options and the greater the possibility that the choice will be abstinence (Anglin and Hser 1991).

The initial motivation to enter treatment may not be high for many of those brought before the courts, but motivation to enter the programme is not that important. Motivation is less important than retention: 'Considerable research demonstrates a direct relationship between retention and post treatment outcomes' (Lipton 1995: 46). 'How an individual is exposed to treatment seems irrelevant. What is important is that the narcotics addict must be brought into an environment where intervention can occur over time' (Anglin 1988). Or, this time, from Sally Satel: 'It is the length of exposure to treatment that powerfully predicts patients' success', which, she says, occurs 'no matter what the treatment setting' (2000). In a review of a number of studies, Satel says two major findings emerge: first the length of time in treatment is the most reliable indicator of post-treatment performance so that, beyond a 90-day threshold, treatment outcomes improved in direct relationship to the length of time spent in treatment. Secondly, coerced patients stayed longer and therefore were the most successful. Weaknesses occur where the offenders do not experience consistency or uniformity about the treatment demands; outcomes are higher when they know the rules, when the rules are enforced fairly and consistently, and when there is appropriate pressure to meet treatment demands. Coercion then might turn out to be irrelevant, except in a moral sense; success seems to be more about how the regime is operated and the length of stay.

In practice the enforced (coerced) treatment of drug users appears to sit uneasily on the shoulders of many treatment agencies. They seemingly prefer to treat only those patients who are apparently sufficiently motivated to enter the treatment programme voluntarily. Given the otherwise consistent research findings, might it not be time to rethink that ideology, doing so in a way which permits a more receptive approach to new ideas and allows a more flexible approach to the problem? To remain within the existing boundaries might produce a measure of certainty, albeit misplaced, but it does not provide much of an opportunity to move forward. As things stand at present, the courts and the treatment services talk past each other, yet the point made by Anglin and Hser (1991) is a sound one: 'that members of both systems need to move away from adversarial stances and towards collaboration to produce the desired behaviour change in drug users'. The suspicion is that, if the treatment services do not make the appropriate move, they might well be the ones who are coerced, this time to accept the enforced patient. Already their hand is being forced; the DTTO is on the statute books and, were the American-style drug courts to be introduced into Britain, they would eclipse existing provisions.

Mandatory drug testing

Jay Carver (2004) is scathing about the way criminal justice systems fail to make use of drug-testing facilities. He says that some offenders with drug-taking histories are not tested at all. He reminds us that some supervision programmes test only infrequently, and then on regular, scheduled reporting days, and that some drug-testing programmes have so few internal controls that offenders find it easy to avoid detection through any number of techniques:

> Even if a probationer tests positive, the most likely response will be nothing but a warning from the probation officer at the next reporting date, which could be a month after the test was taken. If the violation does come before the judge, the hearing is likely to be months after the fact (*ibid.*).

He gives an example from data taken from the District of Columbia, collected as of November 1997 and concerning probation violations. This example shows that only 29% of the infractions reported to the court were handled within 60 days, whilst 71% either were never reviewed by the sentencing judge or were handled more than 60 days after the violation. He says:

> Judges are likely to do one of two things. They may revoke probation and impose the remainder of the sentence in prison. Or they may admonish the person not to use drugs again. In summary, we have a system where there is a low rate of detection for drugs. There is a low rate of enforcement for violations. There may be high punishment severity *if punishment is actually applied* (*ibid.*) Emphasis original.

His conclusion is salutary: if one sets out to design a system to produce failure, it is hard to imagine a better one.

Mandatory drug testing is not confined to the criminal justice system; certain occupational groups are routinely tested (for example, airline pilots and athletes), whilst some employers insist on testing their employees. It becomes a moot point about which occupational groups should be tested: train drivers perhaps, or bus drivers even? Or anyone working in a highly skilled occupation, or anyone where public safety is concerned? In fact, Corkery (2003) reports there has been a surge of interest in drug use in the workplace, with some firms operating a drug-testing policy.

The data are interesting. For example, in 1998 the Institute of Personnel and Development (IPD) surveyed 1,899 firms, of which 18% reported illegal drug taking by staff – an increase of 3% on the corresponding figure two years previously. Although 81% of firms encouraged individuals to seek counselling and help, time off for treatment was only allowed by 38% of companies. Dismissals were used by firms in 31% of cases. It was noted that the level of work performance deteriorated as a result of drug taking, at least according to 64% of respondents. There was seen to be a worsening in working relationships with co-workers as a result of drug abuse by 57% of companies, and in 27% relationships with clients deteriorated. Yet surprisingly only about half (53%) of companies surveyed had a drugs policy, and only 15% had an illegal drugs awareness policy. The two main ways in which personnel or management departments became aware of drug misuse were deterioration in work performance (75%) and notification by other members of staff (72%). Accidents in the workplace accounted for 14% of notifications, but random drug testing only 4% (IPD 1998b; Corkery 2003).

That apart, the theory behind mandatory drug testing is based on the proposition that, with the development of cost-effective technology, we can now intervene more appropriately in drug users' lives (Wish and Gropper 1990: 322). Without mandatory drug testing it is suggested there is no possibility the courts (which, in Britain, also means probation officers) will be able to know the extent of the problem. Self-report studies are valuable as they provide useful information and give some data on the extent of drug use, but they are not always valid in that they do not give the whole picture. There is evidence that, when drug users are questioned about their drug use, especially at the time of arrest, they understate it, although they will often correctly admit the extent of lifetime use or use in the distant past (*ibid*.: 325). Drug testing is used to detect and provide that information which would be otherwise absent. Carver (pers. comm. 1999) goes further and says that, without this information, the justice system is unable to obtain quick, accurate information on the offender's drug use so that the court environment is one in which the offender can remain in denial with no immediate consequence for continued use: 'In a very real sense the criminal justice system becomes an enabler for the addict. The judge is in the dark, the defendant knows the judge is in the dark, and the con game continues' (*ibid.*: 1). He goes on (*ibid.*) to ask: 'Is it any wonder then that the justice system is viewed as ineffective in dealing with the underlying addiction that fuels the problem? Is it surprising that there is widespread scepticism on efficacy of treatment and rehabilitation?'

Drug testing can also be used as a deterrent to future use or, equally, to verify compliance with conditions of release – which will in turn deter future use. Deterrence in drug testing operates as in all other forms of deterrence; it deters the individual and it deters others, although the evidence suggests it works best when it is tied into a treatment programme. The aim, as far as drug treatment is concerned, is to monitor treatment and provide accurate up-to-date information on the extent of use.

A short note on drugs and driving

The Road Traffic Acts prohibit driving under the influence of drugs and alcohol. Whilst there has been considerable research on driving under the influence of alcohol, there has been much less for drugs. Testing for driving under the influence of drugs is a much more difficult matter than for alcohol. A self-report study involving 1,008 drivers aged 17–39 shows that 9% said they had driven under the influence of any drugs, and 5% had done so in the previous year (Ingram *et al.* 2001). These figures represent 26% and 36%, respectively, of those who had used drugs ever or in the last 12 months. Not surprisingly, males were 2.6 times more likely than females to have ever driven under the influence of drugs, and 2.7 times more likely in the last year.

Research by the Transport Research Laboratory covering the period October 1996 to June 2000 shows that there has been a significant increase in the number of road traffic accident fatalities involving the consumption of drugs (Tunbridge *et al.* 2001). In 1985, 7.4% of a sample population in a similar study were found to have used medicinal or illicit drugs, and 35% alcohol (Everest *et al.* 1989). A decade later, the proportion taking drugs had risen to 24.1% but that for alcohol had fallen slightly to 31.5%. In a study involving a total of 1,184 fatalities 17.7% tested positive for a single drug and 6.3% for multiple drugs (i.e. in a quarter of cases where drugs were detected multiple drugs were implicated). This contrasts with only 5.3% in the earlier study. Where two or more drugs were found cannabis (11.9%), opiates (5.6%), benzodiazepines (4.8%) and amphetamines (4.5%) were the drugs most commonly detected. Most of all illicit drug consumption (75.3%) was in those aged under 40, whilst the majority (78.3%) of medicinal use was in those aged 40 and over.

99

The number of studies concerning driving whilst under the influence of drugs remains small. It goes without saying that this is an important area of research which must include those who use licit drugs (i.e. prescribed drugs and not necessarily those covered by the Misuse of Drugs Act). One wonders how many drivers in the morning rush hour are driving under the influence of medication (sleeping pills, etc.) taken the night before, or whether reclassifying cannabis to a Class C drug will increase the extent of drug driving. More research is to be welcomed on all these matters.

An overview of the types of tests available

Basically there are six types of drug tests: sweat, saliva, blood, hair, eye and urine. Urine tests remain the most widely used and, for all their limitations, are still regarded as the most suitable. Others are used to complement urine tests or to act as a screener, or are used when a urine test is inappropriate.

The sweat patch

This testing system identifies drugs through perspiration. It involves a small patch being placed on the offender's arm for between 10 and 14 days. It measures the presence of selected drugs but not the amounts. It is not intrusive, although, sometimes, the arm has to be shaved before the patch can be applied.' It is easy to apply and has the advantage of being what is called 'tamper evident' – although claims have been made that the patch can be successfully adulterated through the use of certain types of bleach. The disadvantages of the sweat patch are, first, that there are large variations in the amount of sweat produced from one offender to the next, and this has, it has been claimed, produces distortions in the results, although whether this is true or not is far from clear. There is, secondly, the risk of accidental removal, especially in areas of high humidity. More importantly, however, the offender is given a 'licence' to continue drug use if the baseline proves positive. This means that, if the offender tests positive for certain drugs at the time the patch was put on, he or she might as well continue to use those drugs for the duration of the patch. The cost is about £3 per patch, with a further cost of between £8 and £10 for analysis. The general conclusion is that the patch has its uses (e.g. when other tests could not be given over a specific period of time) but it is not as successful as urine analysis, in that the patch system only gives results when the patch is taken off and sent for analysis.

The saliva test

The saliva test, which tests for oral fluids, has been available for alcohol since the 1950s and is now used for a variety of drugs, including the amphetamines, cocaine and the opiates. Typically, two swabs are taken, the first for screening and the second for confirmation. Test results tend to support the use of saliva tests in that there is a good correlation between drug and saliva concentrations. The saliva test is therefore seen as a useful additional test, having a number of advantages over the urine test in that it is neither demeaning nor invasive (it avoids the so-called 'ugh' factor which is present when handling urine specimens). It has, however, a number of disadvantages. First, there is no agreement as to the cut-off points, and the courts in the USA have produced no precedents about these. Accordingly, the FDA has not approved the saliva test. Secondly, there is strong cross-reactivity to certain over-the-counter medicines, especially amphetamines and ecstasy, where, typically, adulterants are placed under the tongue at the time the test is taken. Moreover, the so-called 'window of opportunity' is limited. This is the period between the ingestion of the substance and the time during which it can be measured. This varies between drugs; for cocaine it is about 12 hours, for cannabis it is 3–5 hours and for methadone it is 12–16 hours (incidentally, there is little agreement about these times; they vary depending on whom one talks to. The strongest supporters of saliva tests give the longest times). The unit costs are about £4 per test, before analysis (i.e. quite low) but without the FDA's or the Supreme Court's approval, its use is limited in the USA.

The blood test

Blood tests are rarely used, being more appropriate for tests for infectious diseases. There are a number of problems with blood tests. First, they are invasive. Secondly, blood tests have to be taken in a hospital so as to remove all possibilities of contamination at on-site testing facilities – and they have to be done by a trained paramedic such as a nurse, thereby excluding most (if not all) court staff. They are also expensive at about £30 per test. Moreover, clinicians must turn up at court to present the findings – this is, incidentally, true for other off-site hospital tests, including hair analysis. Finally there is the problem of the disposal of the sample but, again, a problem not exclusive to blood tests. Largely for these reasons blood tests are not regarded as a viable option. They have an advantage in that agreement exists about the cut-off point at which the test is accepted as positive unlike, say, that for saliva. There is little future for blood tests despite the obvious validity and reliability of the results. What courts are looking for is a form of testing that is quick, reliable, valid, not intrusive and that does not require a laboratory to produce the results. There is no test yet devised that fits all the criteria, but blood tests are thought to fail most.

Hair tests

The history of hair testing goes back to the 1970s. However, the reasons why there are drug samples in hair are still not fully understood, but all types of body hair can be tested (the tests need not be confined to head hair). Many of the problems of blood testing apply to hair testing – that is, there can be no on-site testing facilities, tests have to be undertaken at the laboratory and the unit costs are high – about £75 per test. The main advantage of hair testing is that it can provide details of the history of substance abuse going back about six months and, for that reason, it is used more frequently at the workplace or in post-mortems than in the courts. It takes about one week for a substance to show up in a hair analysis test so it is of little value if results are required about recent drug-taking incidents, as they invariably are. An advantage is that, like blood tests, hair analysis is tamper resistant. The advantage of blood and hair tests is that they can give information on the amounts used. This, however, is not regarded as important; it is more important to know if the offender has taken (say) cocaine than if he or she is a heavy user.

Eye testing

Eye testing operates on the basis that certain substances will produce significant changes in the eye's reaction to light. Eye tests measure dilation, the saccadic velocity of the eye (i.e. the speed the eye moves from side to side), the constructive latency (i.e. the speed the eye constricts down) and the constructive aptitude (i.e. the way the eye returns to normal). Drugs affect the eye in different ways so that eye tests can pick out specific drug use in the same way as other tests. However, each person must have their own baseline established before assessments can be made and interpreted, and this baseline must be established at a time when the offender is drug free. The technology is still in its early stages, although eye testing is not new. It is currently being marketed as a screening test able to bring to the attention of the court possible drug misuse. Its value is that it is not invasive, it is easy to administer, accurate (or reasonably so), gives immediate results and detects most abused substances. It has a low unit cost; the equipment can be hired at about £3,000 per month and, as some courts test about 1,000 offenders per week, this is a relatively cheap screening test. The general consensus of opinion is that eye testing will, if the technology is improved, be the flagship of the future. It has many advantages.

Urine testing

Little needs to be added to what is already known about urine testing. In spite of certain disadvantages it remains the most favoured test. The technology is effective (it has been available for over 30 years), it has been given High Court approval, has been cleared by the FDA and has an agreed and accepted cut off-point. Recent developments have been directed less at justifying the use of urine tests and more towards reducing unit costs (it costs about £4 per test). Urine testing remains preeminent, with the only likely rival being the eye test or the patch, but the latter only when other forms cannot be used. There are two likely developments to urine testing. First, attempts are being made to measure the amounts of drugs taken – but this then raises again the question: to what end? Secondly the aim is to facilitate presentation which, for these purposes, means being able to download the data directly from the testing device to the printout in a way that removes any human contact, including the interpretation of results. The aim is to restrict further human error, as well as further reducing unit costs.

The procedures are fairly standard. Usually, the offender is given a screening test and, if positive, then he or she is given a confirmatory test. Screening tests provide rapid results, are inexpensive and have an accuracy level of about 97% or 98%; confirmatory tests are more expensive but give a greater level of accuracy. The most common screening test is urine testing and the most common confirmatory test also uses urinalysis. Operating these tests requires considerable skill, and there are numerous pitfalls to avoid, both legal and technical. The procedures must be sufficiently foolproof to minimise arbitrary or erroneous decisions, at least to the extent that it is feasible to do so. Insuring a completely error-free process is the aim, albeit a distant one, but a positive drug test can lead to deleterious results, including incarceration or other restrictions on liberty. Accordingly, drug-testing procedures must be as reliable and valid as possible. Moreover since drug testing (urine testing, that is) is relatively new, the possibilities of legal challenges are considerable. Ideally tests should be undertaken in laboratory conditions, and never by poorly trained assistants.

Likely errors and ways of tampering with the tests

Two types of errors are likely. The first creates false positives. These occur when a test result proves positive for a given drug when that drug is actually absent in a urine sample or present in concentrations below the designated cut-off level. The second creates false negatives. These occur when the test result indicates a negative result for a given drug yet that drug is present in the sample. What constitutes a false positive or false negative can be largely determined by the cut-off level for the test. This is defined as the concentration of a specific drug in the urine, usually in nanograms per millilitre (ng/ml), and this is used to determine whether a specimen is positive (at or above the cut-off level) or negative (below the cut-off level). The point at which the cut-off level is set is critical to the results; a cut-off level set too low will produce false positives – one set too high will produce false negatives. Tampering by users (where the aim is to neutralise the results) can lead to false negatives.

Some errors can be produced by defects in the equipment, others by a failure to use the correct procedures and yet others by tampering. Equipment errors occur when, for example, licit drugs cross-react with the urine sample to produce a set of positive results which are wrong. For example, codeine, pholcodine (found in some cough syrups) and even poppy-seeded bagels will produce positive results on some tests. This is especially so for saliva tests. Ephedrine (found in some cold medications) can cross-react with amphetamine, and urine samples containing enzymes can mimic certain drugs to produce false positives (Meyers 1991: 298).

Other errors are more concerned with the way the system is used. One commentator (Wish 1988: 151) says, from his experience of using urine tests in offender populations, that the problem of false negatives is much larger than for false positives – laboratories simply fail to pick up the drugs. He says his studies show that, even when a person admits to taking a drug one or two days before the test, it is discovered in only 70%–80% of cases. Moreover, most tests fail to identify the quantity of the drug taken, its purity and the time since ingestion.

Then there are administrative errors. These can produce false positives and false negatives. These are much more common and much more difficult to control – at least those described above are well known and expected. Robert Blanke puts it this way: 'The most difficult errors to control are administrative ones. Labelling errors, spelling errors, transposition of numbers, all can lead to a correct test result being assigned to the wrong subject. In fact most laboratories have learned that these occur more frequently than errors in testing procedures'(cited in Meyers 1991). Contaminated systems and temperature variations cause other administrative errors which can also produce false positives. Meyers (1991) says the very ease of performing these tests belies the care with which they must be undertaken, and the consequent reliance on people not trained to laboratory standards may lead to an underappreciation of the dangers of cross-reactivity and of the importance of other potential threats to their accuracy. He cites the case of *US* v. *Roy* (1986) where the defence introduced log sheets that reflected sloppy and careless operations in the Superior Court's system. Claims of an accuracy of 97% can only be achieved in ideal laboratory conditions, and these are rarely met outside. Errors in prisons produce false positives ranging from 46% to 13% (*ibid.*).

The use of a confirmatory test is one way of reducing errors. Generally speaking, confirmatory tests are used after the initial screening test is recorded as positive, although some confirmatory tests have been used when the results are negative. Not all courts are able to obtain confirmatory tests, especially when the testee is in the criminal justice system and will be tested regularly, perhaps weekly, in which case a second screening test is likely to be used alongside a diagnostic interview (Wish 1988: 151). When tests are intended to trigger further investigation or to determine whether a person is involved in drugs, a confirmatory test is not usually seen as necessary; they will be deemed more necessary if the offender is in a treatment programme (*ibid.*). Things are different outside the criminal justice system as a confirmatory test is more likely and the consequences more immediate. For example, in one reported case in the USA a private sector employee was fired because he tested positive (i.e. as a false positive) and he consequently received $4.1 million damages against the laboratory (Meyers 1991: 288). Offenders in the criminal justice system have a better chance to set the record straight than employees, but, nevertheless, errors in whatever form and for whatever reason are damaging.

Then there are problems surrounding the officials who supervise and man the tests. These officials will quickly find that clean urine is a valuable commodity: it is worth a great deal of money to those able to market and sell it. Within the drug-testing world there is a trade in clean urine. As early as 1986 a case was reported of an American defendant who allegedly bribed an employee to have his urine result reported as negative when it was actually positive (*Washington Post* 12 July 1988). This is but one of a number of examples where officials have been open to bribery. In Britain, the Prison Service insists that two prison officers are present when urine samples are taken in prison (this, incidentally, would be regarded as wholly unsatisfactory in some circles for there still remains the possibility of bribery at a later stage, such as at pre- and post-analysis). What is needed is a system that virtually eliminates human interventions so that the opportunities for bribery are eradicated; that is, a system that is fully automated, that excludes transcription errors and is not open to falsification by corrupt officials. The American system works under the slogan: 'If the system is not foolproof, don't bother testing.'

Drug testing in general (and urine testing in particular) has to meet and cope with constant attempts to undermine the validity of the tests. It has been reported that, in the USA, the number of attempts at tampering have increased, alongside a proliferation of tampering products. The public perception is that the safeguards are weak and ineffective. Hence the view that tampering is the 'number one issue'. Moreover, a clearly expressed view is that if you are not directly involved in the test (i.e. you cannot observe it directly), 'don't bother doing it'. Or again: 'There are some very clever drug users out there.' Specimen validity tests (SVTs) are a group of procedures which determine whether the urine has been tampered with in some way or the test compromised after the specimen has been given.

One way of beating the test is to dilute the sample. A diluted sample is defined as being less than 20 mg/dl, which is not consistent with normal urine. Dilution can occur as a result of drinking large quantities of water prior to being tested – 4–8 pints of water will sufficiently dilute the sample to make the test invalid. Creatinine, a nitrogenous-based compound, measures the strength of the sample to determine its concentration.

Another way of determining the concentration is through its specific gravity. This is a measurement of dissolved solids in a liquid. It can also be used to measure the strength or concentration of a urine sample. So, if the levels are between 1.003 and 1.001, the sample is said to have been diluted and is therefore invalid. In some American states a diluted sample is regarded as a positive drug test; in others the test would have to be retaken. Dilution can occur at the pre-test stage (taking salt to affect the specific gravity is one way to dilute the sample) or it can occur at the post-collection stage when drug-free liquids are added to the sample.

A pH measurement determines the acidity or alkalinity of a specimen. The purpose of a pH test is to detect the presence of certain adulterants (acids, etc.) which have been added to distort the test results. These adulterants can cause the pH level to change in ways which disrupt the chemistry of the drug-testing procedures, thereby distorting the results. (A favoured, but ineffective, way of altering the pH level is to drink vinegar before the test.) The generally accepted rule is that if the pH is equal to or less than 3 or greater than 11 (i.e. it is very acidic or very alkaline), adulterants have been added.

Finally there are the nitrates. There are tests to measure the concentration of nitrates in urine which are intended to act as adulterants. The most common adulterants are sodium or potassium-based compounds which come in the form of proprietary brands of some soda drinks. If the results show a level greater than 500 mg/ml the urine is considered to be adulterated. As with other compounds, the aim of nitrates is to distort the test results.

The main impact of SVTs is to restore confidence in the procedures. They provide safeguards against tampering, especially as there is a proliferation of tampering products and devices. The aim must always be to be one step ahead of the field or, if not, then never too far behind so as to allow too many tests results to be successfully distorted. SVTs also help reduce the costs of tests by ridding the system of those which are invalid, and they help to reassure the public that tests are carried out according to appropriate guidelines. In America, the formation of a national Drug Testing Advisory Board has assisted in this. This comprises a selected group of toxicologists who meet quarterly to set standards, advise on testing policies, draft guidelines, determine cut-off points and examine and approve certain laboratories to establish whether their testing procedures are adequate. Tampering is taken very seriously.

The debate in America is not whether drug offenders should be tested – this has long been accepted. The debate is about how to improve procedures, whether at the unit-cost level, through the development of new technology (as with eye tests), or in reducing tampering. The appointment of a national advisory board shows how seriously the USA takes the latter. Unfortunately Britain has not taken the matter on board or treated it with the same sense of urgency. That is a serious failing.

Some legal and social issues concerning testing

A central jurisprudential question is the extent to which governments might order random drug testing in the absence of reasons to suspect a person of using drugs. As a general rule, courts have held that mandatory drug testing is permissible when it serves a special need of government. So, for example, in America in *Skinner v Railway Labor Executives Association* (489 US 609 (1989)), government testing was justified because there was a special need to maintain the safety of the railway system. In another case, this time involving customs officers (*National Treasury Employers Union* v. *von Raab* 816 F2nd 170 5th Circuit 1970), the court held the government has a special need to maintain the integrity of its border to ensure public safety. In both cases the demands of the government were said to outweigh individual privacy. The argument was that certain employees in the public sector have a reduced expectation of privacy because they are required to produce high levels of public safety, and their health and fitness are important aspects of their jobs. Similarly, such officials as customs officers should reasonably expect scrutiny into their probity and fitness. Similar arguments have been used in Britain where it has been suggested there should be mandatory testing of airline pilots, police officers and members of the armed forces (*The Times* 14 June 1997, *Sunday Times* 15 June 1997).

As in the world of sport, those who test positive will always seek to discredit the system, and offender populations are no exception, and rightly so if they believe an injustice has been done. Clearly, training programmes are required and should be set at a high level if the system is to be free of bias and error. The fear is that too little training is provided and, where it is, then not always at the appropriate level (i.e. not undertaken up to that required for laboratory conditions).

A special problem for offender populations is that, once in the criminal justice system, they may lose many of their rights. British customs officers have unrivalled powers to search someone on the basis of reasonable suspicion of an offence being committed. Police surgeons under the 1984 Police and Criminal Evidence Act (PACE) can use 'reasonable force if necessary to take non-intimate samples' – which include urine (PACE 1984, Code of Practice, para. 5.5, as amended by s. 58 of the Criminal Justice and Public Order Act 1994). The balance is already tipped towards those doing the testing, so the least the offender should expect is that tests will be as free from error as possible. I am not always certain this is so.

An offender in prison (alongside those on probation or parole) can be subject to searches, and some of an intimate nature. Those who test positive therefore run the risk of additional sanctions. Exceptionally, these could involve incarceration but, more likely, a restraint on liberty, such as requiring the offender to report more frequently or to provide additional samples. An unintended consequence of a vigorous testing system is that it may lead to an increase in the prison population as more offenders test 'dirty' and violate their probation or release conditions. An increase in the prison population under these circumstances may be neither cost effective nor part of the overall strategy. However, it is a possibility, at least initially, or until treatment services are properly organised and offenders dealt with under treatment programmes, a point to be developed in the last chapter.

There is still the tricky problem of interpreting the results. Put simply, what does a positive test mean? Assume an offender on a treatment programme is required to be tested weekly. In the first week he tests positive for heroin, cocaine, cannabis, amphetamines and ecstasy. He does so again in the second week but says that he has reduced the amount. In the third week he no longer tests positive for heroin and cocaine, but does so for cannabis, amphetamines and ecstasy. This pattern is maintained for three more weeks, except that he no longer tests positive for amphetamines. What then? Presumably the best that can be hoped for in the next few weeks is that things do not get worse. But is the offender to be reported to the court, taken off the programme or what?

The fashionable answers would be that progress has been made and we should be satisfied with that, or that the drugs being currently taken are not dangerous and, anyway, should be legalised. The unfashionable answer is that officials making these decisions ought not to be required to decide what is and what is not lawful. Parliament, in its wisdom, has decreed that certain substances are illegal, and the job of officials is to enforce that. It is the Benthamite distinction that insists 'is' should be distinguished from 'ought'; it is not about the law as it ought to be but what the law is that is the deciding matter. Moreover, failure to deal with substance abuse, whatever the form or type, is as presented in these tests a de facto way of legalising the drug, and thereby undermining Parliament's wishes.

Part of the muddle we get ourselves into is that we are unclear about what we are trying to achieve. Are we trying to achieve abstinence or harm reduction? If the latter, then it is difficult to see how this can be achieved within the criminal justice system. Harm reduction might be an appropriate response for non-offender populations, or may be used as a strategy to progress towards abstinence at a later date – drug users are rarely able to become abstinent overnight – but it cannot be an end for offender populations. Harm reduction allows the use of less harmful drugs in preference to those that are more harmful, which means that the criminal justice system is required to turn a blind eye to continued use and use which is unlawful. The alternative (abstinence) is more logical and straightforward; abstinence means the offender stops all drug taking and so, by definition, stops breaking the law. That after all is what a court order should involve. Abstinence, however, is not a fashionable proposition nowadays, but it has the obvious virtue of making treatment goals compatible with the goals of criminal justice, and it avoids the confusions involved in clinging to a harm reduction philosophy. It might be an advance that an offender stops injecting heroin but smokes cannabis. Yet that cannot be the aim of a drug treatment system working within a criminal justice setting. That must be compliance with the law.

Questions about who should see the test results are no less easy to resolve. A positive test can produce the stigmatising effect of being labelled a drug user on the court record. Clearly, sets of regulations are required to determine who should or should not have access to test results if only because most people would equate a positive drug test with being a drug user – perhaps even a persistent one, although the proportion of offenders who are found positive and are seriously involved in drugs is unknown (Wish 1988: 152). Protecting the rights of the offender in this respect is never going to be easy. The history of pre-sentence reports (PSRs) in Britain is testimony to that. PSRs find themselves in all sorts of establishments with all sorts of people having access to them, even though they were prepared for the court. It raises the point about the dangers of making test results available to employers or potential employers and, even more difficult, whether there should be a duty to do so if employment involves matters of public safety, such as being in the transport industry – a train driver perhaps.

Finally there are questions about what lawyers refer to as 'search and seizure'. In 1989 the US Supreme Court held that urine tests that were compelled by the government constitute a search under the Fourth Amendment. Traditionally only those tests which necessitated an actual physical intrusion (such as a blood test) were afforded Fourth Amendment protection. In a famous case *Skinner* v. *Railway Labor Executives Association* (489 US 609 (1989)), Justice Kennedy said:

> There are few activities in our society more personal or private than the passing of urine. Most people describe it by euphemisms if they talk about it at all. It is a function traditionally performed without public observation: indeed its performance in public is generally prohibited by law as well as social custom.

The court held that urinalysis is a search because it implicates expectations of privacy. It does so in the act of urination and in the subsequent analysis of the urine specimen. Urine analysis could reveal highly personal information about the testee (e.g. such as pregnancy, epilepsy or diabetes). As far as the English legal position is concerned, urine analysis also constitutes search and seizure and for similar reasons to the USA. That is, urine is 'of possessory interest', and its analysis can reveal features about a person's life. An aggravating factor is that it is necessary to ask additional personal medical information before the sample is given, otherwise the test results could be interpreted wrongly (e.g. such as whether or not the testee is taking other medication). And because these personal questions need to be asked, urinalysis becomes increasingly intrusive. What appears, then, on the face of it to be a relatively straightforward exercise – that is, testing for illegal substances – turns out to be highly complex with issues far beyond that of the tests themselves.

Conclusion

I have tried to untangle some of the knots we have tied for ourselves, especially in the fields of coercion and drug testing. There are many examples of sloppy thinking surrounding these topics which have led to numerous problems and, hopefully, in this chapter some have been eased. In the next chapter an examination is made of some instances where coercive treatments and drug testing have been introduced. The questions asked here are: what effect are these new provisions likely to have on the solution to the drugs problem? Where are these proposals likely to lead us in the future?

Chapter 5

The drug treatment and testing order and drug courts

It was noted in Chapter 2 that relatively little use had been made of the arrangements under Schedule 1A (6) of the Powers of Criminal Courts Act 1973 (as inserted by the Criminal Justice Act 1991) to impose treatment as part of a sentence. The findings of the Home Office Probation Inspectorate as to why there had been a failure to make use of these services have been given earlier, but two of those findings need emphasis:

1 Reluctance on the part of probation officers to make such proposals in their pre-sentence reports, based on the view that coerced treatment is unlikely to be effective.

2 A perception of a lack of enthusiasm on the part of treatment providers to operate mandatory programmes.

The implied criticisms by the Home Office were that the Probation Service retained an outdated view that coercive treatment was unacceptable in moral terms, or not likely to be effective, illustrating again the alliance of probation with traditional social work values – an alliance not to the government's liking. One result of this was an order, the Drug Treatment and Testing Order (DTTO), introduced in the Crime and Disorder Act 1998 (see ss. 61–64). It remains the government's flagship and, according to the official government publication, will solve many of the earlier problems by strengthening the courts' powers. Its aim is to toughen up the probation response to drug abuse and requires the offender to undergo treatment, either as part of or in association with an existing community sentence. It will be targeted at serious drug misusers and aimed at reducing or removing the amount of crime committed to fund their drug habit (Home Office 1998a). The government identifies two crucial differences between this and earlier provisions: the DTTO will review the offender's progress through a court review hearing, and drug testing will be mandatory. It adds somewhat darkly and prophetically that 'The success of any new legislation will depend on the availability of treatment and the resolution of cultural differences between the criminal justice system and treatment providers, under-pinned by strong interagency arrangements' (ibid.: para. 4). What the government calls 'cultural differences' I have called 'ideological differences ' – it is the same point with different terminology.

Briefly, the legal provisions are that, under s. 61 of the Crime and Disorder Act 1998, the court by or before which the offender is convicted may make a drug DTTO. This will require offenders to undergo treatment for their drug problems, either alone or in tandem with another community order. The DTTO lasts for not less than six months and not more than three years, and includes the following requirements and provisions.

A Drug Treatment and Testing Order shall include a requirement (the treatment requirement) that the offender shall submit, during the whole of the treatment and testing period, to treatment by or under the direction of a specified person having the necessary qualifications or experience (the treatment provider) with a view to the reduction or elimination of the offender's dependency or propensity to misuse drugs (s. 61).

The section also gives the courts powers to test and states:

A drug treatment and testing order shall include a requirement (the testing requirement) that, for the purpose of ascertaining whether he has any drugs in his body during the treatment and testing period, the offender shall provide during that period, at such times or in such circumstances as may (subject to the provisions of the order) be determined by the treatment provider, samples of such description as may be so determined.

The order is for offenders over the age of 16 years (ibid.). They will be supervised by the Probation Service, and supervision includes provisions for the order to be reviewed at intervals of not less than one month. Under s. 63 the offender is required to attend a review hearing although, if progress is maintained, the order can be amended so that the offender need not attend. Where treatment is not satisfactory, or the offender commits another offence, the court may consider the order within the meaning of s. 6 of the Criminal Justice Act 1991, that is, it may sentence the offender again for the offence for which he or she was made subject to the original order.

Section 62 requires a DTTO to include a treatment requirement stating whether the treatment will be residential or non-residential. It must identify the treatment provider and include a testing requirement with a specified frequency of drug testing. Treatment providers are required to give each offender the minimum number of tests required by the court and to submit the results to the supervising probation officer who will report them to the court. The offender must report to a probation officer as required, and notify the probation officer of any change of address – this is in line with probation orders generally.

The model for the DTTO is that of the American drug court although nowhere is there any public recognition that this is so. The DTTO uses the three central platforms of the drug court: first, treatment is provided by outside agencies (called treatment providers in the legislation, itself an American term); secondly, treatment is backed by drug testing; and, finally, treatment is reinforced by supervision, which in this case includes that of the Probation Service mixed with frequent court appearances where progress is reviewed. However, differences between this and the drug court are immense, not the least because in the DTTO these features are poorly integrated. In practice, the DTTO turns out to be a weak carbon copy of drug courts, lacking certain essential features necessary to make the system work.

Take two examples: drug testing and the review hearing. In the first there are questions to be asked about the link between drug testing and the treatment programmes. Some American commentators say that positive urine tests should always be backed by other information (progress in the treatment programmes, etc.). Experiments in Texas, where drug-testing programmes were introduced without the necessary treatment backup, showed how it failed. The conclusion was that drug testing was a poor deterrent on its own; it works best as part of a wider strategy where it is incorporated into a programme.

It is doubtful if that measure of integration exists within the DTTO. This is due to a number of reasons, one of which is a lack of clarity in the guidelines (Home Office 1998a) on the drugs to be tested. For example, the *Guidance for Practitioners Involved in Drug Treatment and Testing Order Pilots* (Home Office 2000) says that, 'The index drug or drugs (i.e. the drug most closely implicated in the offender's criminal behaviour) should *always* be tested for. Treatment providers and supervising probation officers should consider in addition if it would also be valuable to test for the presence of other illicit drugs.' If the supervisor does not know which drugs are being taken, it is difficult to see how treatment can be properly assessed. The lack of clarity or, rather, a lack of urgency pervades the system.

Another is the manner in which results are obtained. The *Guidance for Practitioners* (*ibid.*: para. 5) says that 'Test results should be returned to the treatment provider within 5 working days of dispatch'. Most judges in the American drug courts have the results sent to them immediately or within 20 minutes. They say delays allow the offender to manipulate the system, whilst decisions based on past events are of little significance to current treatment requirements. The aim in American courts is to integrate test results into the programme immediately; the judge and the supervisor need up-to-date information if supervision is to be meaningful. Delays up to five days would be regarded as unacceptable.

Then there is the rather vague manner in which the review is to be conducted. Under review hearings (s. 63 (1) of the Crime and Disorder Act 1998), we are told in the *Guidelines* (Home Office 1998a: para. 8) that the aim is to examine progress under the treatment programme. Here it is said these are not breach proceedings but a unique opportunity to assess the effectiveness of the sentence (*ibid.*: para. 7). The order can be amended at the hearings, depending on progress or lack of it, and the court will have reports from the probation office. One obvious problem is that there is no guarantee that the offender will appear before the same bench of magistrates; indeed, it is highly likely that he or she will not and, again, continuity is lost. The *Guidelines* (*ibid.*: para. 8) say that where this occurs 'it is vital that magistrates are made aware of the history of the order, particularly what was expected in the time immediately prior to the present review'. Damage limitation, perhaps, but hardly satisfactory given the nature of the exercise.

A second problem concerns the style of the review hearings. On the one hand, whilst in very broad principle they follow the style of drug courts, they lack the sense of firmness of purpose that drug courts possess. Drug courts may have an informal style but this is deceptive if informality is seen as being lax or lacking strength. In Britain, for example, the bench is encouraged to acknowledge success and to be firm in seeking explanations for missed appointments. It is also encouraged to permit active participation by all concerned, and there is to be no format for the hearing (*ibid.*: para. 9) – presumably individual benches may vary in their approach. But there the matter ends. In contrast, the drug court has all the informality, allows encouragement and blame to be accorded, and there are enormous variations in practice. The difference is that they act quickly and forcefully against any shortcomings and, they *require* all involved to be present. For the DTTO, the *Guidelines* (*ibid.*: para. 6) say: 'It is also expected that in the vast majority of cases either the probation officer or a drugs worker would attend the hearings to assist the court.' In the drug court, sanctions are imposed immediately; DTTOs have breach proceedings at some later date.

In addition there are the ethical and jurisprudential questions of testing, which seem to be ignored in the DTTO. As said earlier, erroneous results place the offender in jeopardy, as indeed do all positive tests. Everyone who tests positive for drugs within the criminal justice system runs the risk of incarceration or some other punitive decision. In the USA, drug-testing laboratories that report erroneous positive test results to the court are civilly liable to defendants injured by the erroneous information. One wonders what would happen if the same threat existed in Britain under the DTTO.

As discussed in detail in Chapter 4, errors also occur when the samples are contaminated:

> False positive results are also caused by contamination of samples or equipment, improper calibration, inadequate maintenance of the equipment, temperature variations, or failures in the chain of custody system. The very ease of performing these tests belies the care with which they must be done, and the consequent reliance on persons who are not trained to laboratory standards may lead to an under-estimation of the danger of cross reactivity and the importance of other potential threats to the accuracy of the tests (Meyers 1991: 299–300).

As for testing 'up to laboratory standards' there is little hope that this will be achieved in Britain. The *Guidelines* say that:

> The sample should be divided into two containers in front of the offender, who should be asked to sign two labels for the sample containers. These should be affixed to the two containers in his/her presence. One portion of the sample should be offered to the offender ... [who] ... should be advised to refrigerate the sample immediately if they wish to undertake independent testing. The remaining portion should be split again and one portion refrigerated to be dispatched for confirmatory testing. The remainder should be frozen and retained for one year in case of judicial review or challenge (Home Office 1998a: para. 10).

The American system aims to produce a drug-testing system free of all possible errors, and that means reducing the possibility of any human contact, whether with the offender or the drug-testing equipment. In Britain, as reported in the evaluation of the DTTOs, there was a certain laxness when it came to supervising urine tests. Sometimes offenders were handed the container and allowed to give a sample in the privacy of a lavatory; in one probation area there were no facilities for supervised testing (Turnbull et al. 2000: 36). The possibilities of error, of providing false samples, of corrupt officials (as said earlier, there is a trade in clean urine) are endless. It is difficult not to conclude that, in Britain, the rules and regulations for this part of the DTTO fail to provide the necessary protection, whether for the offender or the person doing the testing. They could well produce trouble for all concerned, whether from the Court of Appeal or elsewhere.

The pilot studies

Before they were introduced nationally, the DTTOs were piloted in three areas, Gloucestershire, Croydon and Liverpool. Inexplicably, the government decided to introduce DTTOs before the evaluation was completed, suggesting that a political decision had been reached rather than a criminological one. Had they waited they might have been able to iron out some of the problems thrown up by the evaluation. The results of the pilot were not wholly convincing. It is difficult to summarise them all, but the main ones were as follows: the use of drugs of the offender population, urine testing, interagency working and supervision of the offenders whilst on the order.

First comes drug abuse. This appeared to be the most successful feature, at least on the face of it. Offenders substantially reduced their drug abuse, at least at the beginning of the order, and the six-months' follow-up confirmed this. Of those who completed or nearly completed the order, a similar pattern emerged: a number said they were drug free and crime free, except for cannabis use. However, without a comparison group, it is difficult to state to what extent the DTTO was responsible for the change and, with the small numbers interviewed, it is difficult to draw firm conclusions. None the less, on the basis of these results (and many were based on self-report data which are not the best from which to draw conclusions) the DTTO made some impact on the use of some drugs.

Secondly is urine testing. The frequency of urine testing varied markedly between the pilot areas. The evaluators thought that testing needed to be integrated fully with treatment programmes, with testing regimes tailored to the objectives set for individual offenders. They suggested a minimum standard – twice per week for the first three months of the order with discretion to reduce this to a minimum of once per week after that period (Turnbull *et al.* 2000: 85–6). Croydon administered the test three times a week throughout the order; Gloucestershire averaged two tests a week; and Liverpool about one a week.

There seemed little to suggest a standardised approach was being operated for the testing procedure, and observation was not always undertaken with care. The evaluation reported as follows:

> Before administering the test DTTO staff asked drug using offenders if they had used drugs. It was not uncommon for drug using offenders to admit to drug use, in which case staff recorded a positive result without testing, in order to save money. Croydon was the only site where urine sample giving was observed routinely. Observation was frequently undertaken in Gloucestershire although there was emphasis on an offender being observed if falsification of a sample was suspected. Of the comparison sites only the STEP programme routinely observed the provision of urine samples. The Hastings programme had no facilities for supervised testing: PASCO and Fast Track occasionally observed the provision of urine samples (*ibid.*: 36).

Thirdly, there is interagency working. All three teams struggled to develop an effective model of interagency working, in spite of training for team members at all pilot sites. The evaluation said that: 'although inter-agency relationships improved at all three pilot sites only the Croydon team resolved conflicts and disputes sufficiently thoroughly to be operating as an effective team whose whole was greater than the sum of its parts' (*ibid.*: 53). One wonders how it was possible to run an effective programme in these circumstances. Interagency co-operation, always difficult in any circumstances, is likely to be additionally important in a project such as this where responsibilities for tasks need to be made clear, and where processes are outlined to review supervision goals.

Finally comes supervision. Supervision, which is another critical component, suffered in similar ways to that of interagency working. The guidelines, such as there were, appeared not to be clear or, if they were, they were not appropriately implemented. The evaluation says the teams had different expectations: 'The three sites had widely differing approaches to warnings, breaches and revocations. In all three sites offenders quite often failed to meet the conditions of the order. The main form of non-compliance was failure to attend but ... many continued to use illicit drugs especially near the start of their order' (*ibid*.: 80). Again it is difficult to see how such a situation arose. From the offender's point of view, these variations violated basic principles of natural justice in that one team, the Gloucestershire team, applied much stricter requirements about drug abuse and attendance and produced the highest revocation rate at 60%. This compared with Croydon at 40% and Liverpool at 28%. For the probation officer, it highlighted levels of uncertainty about the object of the exercise as, apparently, teams found it quite difficult to give precise definitions of breach criteria (*ibid*.: 42).

The general conclusion, as reported in the evaluation, is not one which leads to a measure of confidence in DTTOs. At best, the failings can be explained by reference to the uniqueness of the programme, the expected teething troubles which were bound to arise and the lack of preparation – which was clearly not adequate. The alternative explanation is less charitable and points to a failure in training, preparation and planning, which should have been resolved earlier, and where the obvious question is: if this was the outcome for the pilot stages, what are we to expect now that DTTOs are made nationwide?

Given these failings, how are we to interpret the results? Considerable time has been given to an examination of the DTTO if only to show how, without training and built-in safeguards, failure is inevitable and immediate. The testing procedures were not adequate to produce valid results, and the data on drug use were based largely on self-report information, especially at the end of the order. It is difficult to see how credence can be given to these results given the shortcomings of the data and the processes involved in their production. At best it seems that the data should be treated with caution. Can we assume, then, that the failings in the procedures will be ironed out in the national implementation? Probably not, as many are not failings or shortcomings due to a lack of preparation but structural failings created by the isolation of organisations from one another, and from their reluctance to change traditional ways of working.

The *Guardian* (22 May 2002) described the way the DTTO was introduced: 'the early pilot results were so bad that Home Office ministers, anxious that they might lose the money promised by the Treasury, simply rolled them out nationally before the final results came through and lied about the pilots.' These are severe criticisms of a key measure of criminal justice policy. The journalist in question, Nick Davies, quoted a Whitehall source saying 'Breach is the norm with DTTOs' (*ibid.*), adding that 'last year [2001] only 6,186 orders were made but there were 5,419 proceedings against users for breaching them'. Apparently offenders do not accept the treatment available and are willing to take their chances if the court decides to punish them. Davies (*ibid.*) says: 'The Government has come up with a remedy; regardless of the failure. Downing Street last year asked the Treasury to fund yet more DTTOs; the Treasury agreed to put up an extra £20m. but only if the Probation Service agreed to increase their targets by 50%.' Davies reports that the Probation Service had no chance of hitting these targets, but the Home Office accepted and rewrote the rules to produce a new DTTO which imposes only minimal requirements on offenders. This, according to Davies, is dubbed the 'DTTO-lite' by drug workers.

The manner in which DTTOs were introduced highlights the methods used by the government to deal with the drug problem: seek quick solutions and then throw some money at them. Above all, do not disturb existing structures or operate on the basis of a research-led programme.

Drug courts

In 1987, Chief Judge Wetherington, alarmed at the ever-growing numbers of convicted drug users appearing at the Miami courts, sent Judge Klein on a sabbatical year to come up with a solution. The result in 1989 was the first American drug court or, rather, the first drug court to use the approach known as the 'Miami drug court model'. Other drug courts existed, but their aim was to process drug users more speedily through the system – these are called fast-track administrative courts. The Miami model is different; it is a slow-track treatment court where the aim is to provide court-based treatment programmes to treat the offender's addiction. From a relatively modest beginning in 1989 there has in the space of a decade been a burgeoning growth to well over 400 Miami drug courts in the USA (or simply drug courts henceforth) in every state, as well as in Australia, Canada, Ireland, Scotland and Puerto Rica.

Drug courts arose for three main reasons. First, the existing system was not working. Early efforts to speed up the process for the large numbers of drug offenders appearing before the courts (the so-called 'expedited case management courts' merely produced a faster, more efficient system by reducing the waiting time between arrest and conviction. Paradoxically, this had the reverse effect: these courts hastened the offender's progress through the revolving door from court to prison and back to court. Other attempts to deal with the problem fared no better. The so-called 'build out' approach, which meant building more prisons to deal with more and more offenders, produced no relief. All that happened was the prison population grew exponentially with an alarming increase in costs. As one Miami drug court judge said: 'Before the Miami drug court began the strongest prisoners slept on mattresses, the weaker on the floor and the weakest standing up' (pers. comm.).

A second reason was the link between drug taking and crime. As in Britain, the research evidence shows that large numbers of American offenders tested positive for drugs at the time of arrest, and many claimed that their criminality was a direct response to their habit. In the circumstances it was reasonable to infer a direct link – with more certainty where the users were street addicts. The crack/cocaine epidemic of the late 1980s and beyond produced large numbers of offenders charged with possession offences, especially from the inner-city areas. Efforts to reduce crack/cocaine use became a high priority.

Thirdly, there are the courts themselves, especially the judges, who were critical of legislation which redefined the criminal codes and escalated penalties for drug possession and sales. The 'three strikes' policy restricted judicial action, as did other sentencing guidelines, so that judges increasingly saw themselves tied into a sentencing straitjacket. They believed these guidelines produced no tangible results, except perhaps longer sentences and, where they did not, offenders were moved through the system in ways which did nothing to reduce their drug taking on discharge. The 'three strikes' policy invariably produced sentences of 30 years plus, sometimes for a relatively small amount of cocaine, and many judges saw this as neither sensible nor productive. The drug court became a judge-led movement where judges wanted a more humane, effective programme which dealt directly with the problem of drug abuse.

These features alone did not account for the popularity of the drug court, the shape of its programmes and the ethos surrounding it. For that there needs to be an assessment of drug courts as a social movement, which is beyond the scope of this book. There are, however, a number of aspects worth highlighting. First, drug courts operate according to an abstinence model which sits easily within the compass of the earlier prohibition movement. Also, there is within the drug court system a strong evangelical approach that is part of an American cultural worldview which is not used elsewhere. Thirdly, drug courts operate under a free-market model where the offender is expected to pay towards the treatment, and where the aim is to return the offender to being 'a productive member of society' – terminology rarely used outside the USA. The European perspective is suspicious of abstinence, preferring harm reduction, is suspicious of evangelism and is unused to talking in terms of a 'market model of treatment'.

Yet for all these criticisms drug courts have produced the largest number of clean addicts to be found anywhere; the drug court movement is burgeoning and, at present, unstoppable; and it has already attracted international interest and acclaim. Evaluations of drug courts are promising but not as hopeful as were earlier thought. As less tractable offenders enter the programmes, rates of compliance and graduation will decline and recidivism rise; this is an inevitable feature, especially as the earliest drug courts dealt with less serious offender groups. None the less, drug courts still achieve their aim of reducing levels of addiction and are more successful than any other programme.

Drug courts have also been introduced into the juvenile justice system, and there are similar courts for drunken drivers, domestic violence offences, mentally disordered offenders and for 'dead beat dads'. More recently, drug courts have moved into the prison system where pre-parole prisoners are placed on a drug court programme and, if successful, are granted parole. It has been said that we should expect only one good idea in criminal justice per decade; that being so, the drug court makes up for two.

Drug courts are not a homogeneous group and, within the Miami model, there are differences. Some place offenders on a diversionary or quasi-diversionary programme, others are post-adjudicatory – that is, the offender is sentenced to a drug court programme after conviction. Some drug courts deal only with minor offenders; others will not take offenders with convictions for violence; and yet others will take only those charged with a possession offence. As the movement develops, so the population of offenders has become more varied, but one of the main criticisms is that, too often, they have concentrated on low-level offenders (Gebelein 2000). It is interesting that the Australian approach has been to target the persistent drug user and high-level offender.

The National Association of Drug Court Professionals (NADCP) lists the following as ten key components of drug courts. These are taken from its document, *Defining Drug Courts: The Key Components* (NADCP 1997), where each component is explained, followed by performance benchmarks (some of which will be given here). These key components provide the most useful means of examining and explaining drug courts.

1. *Drug courts integrate alcohol and other drug treatment services with justice system processing.* This is one of the most important of the components as

it sets out the mission of drug courts, which is to stop the abuse of alcohol and other drugs and related criminal activity through a co-ordinated team approach that includes all the court personnel and the police, alongside community organisations such as education services, housing, etc. Drug courts operate on the basis that the criminal justice system has the unique ability to influence a person shortly after a significant triggering event, such as an arrest, and thus persuade or compel that person to enter and remain in treatment. This mission statement repeats the point made in Chapter 4, which is that research indicates that a person coerced to enter treatment by the criminal justice system is likely to do as well, if not better, than one who volunteers.

One of the many innovative features of the drug court is that the court supervises the offender. Elsewhere, the offender is handed over to another criminal justice agency (such as the Probation Service), who decides on the nature of control and treatment. Often that agency will itself subcontract some or all of that control and treatment to another agency – perhaps psychiatry, where the subcontractor is required to report to the Probation Service on the offender's progress. That they rarely do is another criticism of the traditional approach to treatment, irrespective of the type of treatment or the type of offender. In the drug court, the court retains supervision and control, and directly employs the treatment providers. This means hiring and firing according to the demands of the programme. The treatment providers work for the court, as do those involved in drug testing, and probation officers. In the drug court, judicial control is pervasive, with the judge at the centre of the programme – this being a way of using the status and power of the judge to impose the programme on the offenders.

2. *Using a non-adversarial approach, prosecution and defence counsel promote public safety whilst protecting participants and due process rights.* Drug courts make much of the importance of the team approach where, it is claimed, in order to facilitate an offender's progress in treatment, the prosecutor and defence counsel must shed their traditional adversarial courtroom relationship and work together. This, of course, is easier said than done or, rather, when it is done it may work to the detriment of the offender's rights. The drug court has provoked intense criticisms in some quarters by shedding the non-adversarial methods and opting for a team approach (Boldt 1998; Bean 2001b). As it turns out, the prosecuting attorneys seem to experience fewer problems than the defence, for the former has a duty to protect public safety by ensuring that each candidate is appropriate for the programme. That is relatively straightforward. The defence counsel, on the other hand, is required to

seek a not-guilty verdict or, if not, then the most lenient sentence, as well as to protect the offender's due process rights. According to the NADCP, the defence counsel does this by advising the offender on the nature of the drug court (one of the benchmarks for this component), whilst encouraging the offender's full participation in the programme. But what happens if the defence believes that a successful rebuttal of the charges can be achieved, or that it would be possible to receive a more lenient sentence than in the drug court? Should he or she go for that and forgo the possibility of his or her client receiving treatment for his or her addiction? The drug court movement has never answered these questions satisfactorily – nor can they be, for they centre on a subsidiary question about priority. That is, should priority be given to the offender's rights or to his or her welfare?

3. *Eligible participants are identified early and promptly placed in the drug court programme.* The period after arrest is seen as a critical time for an offender, who conveniently gives the drug court a window of opportunity for intervening and introducing the value of treatment. Judicial action, taken promptly after arrest, capitalises on the nature of the arrest. Entering the drug court typically takes place as soon as possible after being convicted, and the programme itself will usually begin within 24 hours of coming before the drug court judge – this is one of the benchmarks to be achieved. The offender enters the drug court after being found guilty of one of the accepted offences: 'accepted' in the sense that it must be one of the types of offences and offender the drug court will take. Instructions will be given immediately about reporting to the court (usually three or four times a week at this stage), followed by the first of many regular drug tests when the offender will be promptly allocated to a treatment programme.

Generally speaking the programme will last for two years, and if the offender successfully completes it, he or she will have the original charge dropped and, possibly, have it taken off the file. This is important especially for those subject to the 'three strikes' policy. In exceptional cases, as in the Superior Court at Washington DC, successful completion will lead to a two-year probation order.

4. *Drug courts provide access to a continuum of alcohol, drug and other related treatment and rehabilitation services.* The drug court claims that the treatment experience begins in the courtroom and continues throughout, making it a comprehensive therapeutic experience. On entering the drug court, there will be an initial screening and evaluation period, lasting about 24 hours, after which the offender enters the programme.

Successful completion, however, requires more than abstinence. The Delaware drug court, for example, not only requires four months of abstinence but also requires that the offender meets the other demands of full employment, etc., in order to graduate. Different criteria operate throughout, but abstinence plus full employment are likely to be the most common. However, treatment also includes dealing with co-occurring problems (such as mental illness, primary medical problems, HIV and sexually transmitted diseases, homelessness and domestic troubles), some of which may include domestic violence. It will certainly expect to be long term for, unless these other factors are addressed, success in treatment will be impaired.

5. *Abstinence and use of alcohol and other drugs are monitored by frequent drug testing.* Drug testing is an essential feature of the programme as accurate testing is seen as the most objective and efficient way to establish a framework of accountability to determine the offender's progress. Those who do well – that is, do not test positive – and advance in treatment and, if they fulfil other requirements such as hold down a job and become a productive tax-paying citizen (the drug court is more than about being drug free; it is about being fully rehabilitated), they will be allowed to report less frequently. Drug testing is almost always through urinalysis and the results are made available immediately. One of the benchmarks is that failure to comply (i.e. testing positive) and missing treatment appointments and court appearances will produce immediate sanctions. In some courts the local police give a high priority to those who fail to attend and are in breach of the programme. Another benchmark is that drug testing must be certain – the samples must not be contaminated. Alcohol is invariably included as one of the drugs to be tested, as the NADCP argues that alcohol use frequently contributes to relapse among individuals whose primary drug of choice is not alcohol. Contracted laboratories are held accountable to established standards.

6. *A co-ordinated strategy governs drug court responses to participant compliance.* An assumption behind the drug court is that addiction is a chronic relapsing condition, so that becoming drug free is a learning experience in which failures, especially in the early stages, are to be expected. None the less, sanctions are imposed for continued drug use, and responses increase in severity for failure to abstain. In contrast, if the offenders complete the programme successfully they are rewarded. This may be praise from the judge, encouragement from the treatment staff or ceremonies in which accomplishments are recognised and applauded; or

they may be an award of a diploma or some other means of official recognition at the graduation.

Drug courts have what is called a co-ordinated strategy to deal with non-compliance, which will often involve short periods in prison. State legislation permits these multiple sanctions, which are almost unique in common law jurisdictions. Normally, there will be no more than one sanction imposed for each offence and, when that punishment is served, the offence is expiated. The exception is on a probation order where it is possible for the offender to be dealt with on more than one occasion for breaking the conditions of the order, but it would be very rare for that to occur more than once.

7. *Ongoing judicial interaction with each drug court participant is essential.* The judge heads the team, which includes the prosecuting and defence counsel, the police and all other officers of the court. This team approach is another of the innovations of the drug court, which was traditionally absent in the adversarial system where collaboration and co-operation are at a minimum. Competition is more common. In the drug court, all work together for the common good – stopping the offender from taking drugs. The origins of the team approach can be found in the TASC programme (Treatment Alternatives to Street Crime), which itself emerged from research showing that treatment was more effective in settings in which legal sanctions and close supervision provide incentives for offenders to conform with treatment protocols and objectives (Lipton 1995). To operate successfully, there had to be a team offering co-operation rather than a number of agencies pulling in different directions. However, TASC (unlike drug courts) did not seek to fuse the criminal justice system with the treatment services but to provide a bridge by supplementing traditional adjudication with treatment services, usually through diversion. (The TASC programme is discussed in more detail later in this chapter.)

8. *Monitoring and evaluation measure the achievement of programme goals and gauge effectiveness.* From the outset, drug courts have been evaluated. Evaluation is often a condition of funding, where process and outcome evaluations are built into the programme. Process evaluations are concerned with the way the system operates; outcome evaluations are about the success, achievements or failures of the programme. In spite of this, only a small number of evaluations have been sufficiently rigorous to meet acceptable standards; most have varied in quality, comprehensiveness, types of measures used and the appropriateness of comparison groups (Balenko 1999: 7). Initially, the drug court movement claimed

results which have not been validated, and some of the earlier claims have had to be scaled down. More realistically, later evaluation results are consistent with some, but not all, of the earlier findings – that is, drug courts continue to engage drug offenders in long-term treatment, providing more regular and closer supervision than that received by those in other forms of criminal justice supervision in the community. Drug-use rates and criminal activity, as measured by urine test results and recidivism, are reduced whilst participants are on the programme. In the evaluations of outcomes that use a control group, post-programme rearrest rates and drug use, the rates are lower than for those who drop out or who are terminated from the programme (*ibid.*: 4). The overall conclusion is that drug courts are more successful than any other drug-involved prevention activity, and cost evaluations suggest that for every US$1 spent on drug courts there is a saving of US$7 in the criminal justice system.

9. *Effective drug court operations require continuing interdisciplinary education.* Those working in drug courts, at whatever level, are expected to participate fully in the training programmes. One reason is to bridge that gap (noted in Chapter 4) which exists between criminal justice and treatment personnel. Criminal justice personnel need to be familiar with treatment goals and the many barriers to successful treatment, whereas treatment personnel need to be familiar with criminal justice account-ability and courtroom operations. All need to understand and comply with drug-testing procedures. Drug courts operate best when a spirit of commitment and collaboration is promoted, and this can be achieved through education and training programmes – which should always take place before the drug court is up and running and where, as a bench-mark, attendance is regarded as essential, whether at the outset or later.

10. *Forging partnerships among drug courts, public agencies and community-based organisations enhances drug court effectiveness and generates support.* Most communities are proud of their drug courts, believing that they offer a serious attempt at dealing with an otherwise intractable problem. One of the lessons learnt by the earlier drug courts was to seek and obtain support from the media, especially in the formation stage, as opposition from the media was a severe disadvantage to their success. Accordingly, drug courts have learnt to promote themselves and present themselves favourably to the local community. Federal funding has rarely been sufficient so that drug court judges have had to raise monies themselves – selling lottery tickets was not unheard of, alongside other popular activities. Promoting and producing public support have been

an important way of securing funding and help restore faith locally in the criminal justice system.

Some additional comments

The ten points listed above cover much of what constitutes a drug court. They do not, however, convey the flavour of the court, the dramatic intensity which is often present and the interactions between judge and offender (for a full description of the drug court and its personnel, see Nolan 1998). Drug court, in Nolan's terms, produces personalised justice and, with it, a set of attendant dangers. There is little doubt that it has raised again the spectre of rehabilitation which was widely discredited in the late 1970s but which has appeared again under a new guise and a different banner. The emphasis on treatment, the belief that treatment breaks the link with crime and the transformation of the judge into a type of judicial social worker have helped push rehabilitation into the forefront (for a critique of this, see Bean 2001b). But anyone who has experienced a drug court in full swing will know how easy it is to be pulled along on that tide of enthusiasm. Drug court workers believe in their crusade, for a crusade it certainly is.

It would not be impossible to introduce drug courts into Britain on a larger scale than at present (see the discussion of the Scottish drug courts below), but it would need a political commitment and require the courts and their appropriate government departments to be persuaded of the need to be innovative. Opposition would be expected from the Probation Service, who would find itself marginalised with a less dominant part to play than under the DTTO. In the drug court, the judge is doing what the Probation Service does, and much more. As one drug court judge said: 'There is nothing the Probation Service can do that I cannot do, and I can do a lot more than the Probation Service' (pers. comm.). The voluntary sector might also find it difficult to work in the drug court, although initial reservations in the USA diminished when voluntary agencies saw that the work was worth while and profitable. There is little doubt that drug courts would produce stresses and strains on the existing system, but there will always be such stresses with radical change, and the drug court is nothing if not radical. Its supporters talk of reinventing justice and, to some extent, this is so.

The judge is an integral part of the court structure – it is the unique power of the court and the status of the judge that drive the system along. Attempts to weaken the system by handing over responsibility for treatment to, say, psychiatrists or probation officers emasculate it to the point where it ceases to be a drug court. There is no one else able to command the same respect as the judge or to have powers to enforce the order in that way. Judges promote a type of regime which mixes sympathy with control; no excuses are accepted for not reporting or for returning to drugs, whether it be a family bereavement, doing overtime or the car breaking down. (One drug court judge urges new offenders on the programme to call all their families together as, from the judge's experience, most will die during the treatment programme – some more than once!) It is not unusual for a drug court judge to have a caseload of over 80 each day. Burnout rates are high and, when a drug court judge steps down, it is not always possible to find another sufficiently motivated to continue and, without a highly motivated judge the drug court does not work well (Gebelein 2000).

Drug courts and the DTTO: a comparison

Too often claims are made that a drug court has been introduced in Britain where the 'drug court' in question turns out to be nothing of the sort. Or demands are made to introduce 'drug courts' where there seems little understanding of what this means. Sometimes the so-called 'drug court' places the offender on probation, and the offender returns occasionally to the court to report on progress. Or the 'drug court' involves a few probation officers who have found a group of treatment agencies willing to take an interest in treating drug offenders. These are not drug courts in the sense in which the terms are used here: they are traditional courts using probation orders with bells and whistles attached.

Table 5.1 compares selected features of the two systems, although it needs to be emphasised that, within the Miami model, there are differences between drug courts, and sometimes between states as well as with a state. Differences are usually about the type of offenders, the length of the programme and the manner in which the original conviction is retained on file. They do not differ in their basic methodology.

The table compares the two systems and, incidentally, shows the types of changes necessary were drug courts to be introduced more generally into Britain or, for that matter, into any common law jurisdiction. It is not simply about bolting drug courts on to the existing system but of making structural changes to the way the courts operate.

The differences between the DTTO and drug courts are considerable and show, first, in the ideologies and aims of treatment. In drug court it is abstinence; in the DTTO it is harm reduction.

Table 5.1 Drug courts and the Drug Testing and Treatment Order (DTTO): a comparison

Drug court	DTTO
Aim is abstinence. That may include alcohol	Aim is harm reduction, especially heroin or cocaine
Treatment providers are employed by the court	Treatment providers work for the Probation Service
Judge conducts the supervision	Probation Service conducts the supervision
Adversarial system replaced by team approach	Adversarial system remains intact
Judge can impose multiple sanctions	Court restricted to breach proceedings defined in legislation
Drug test results sent to the judge immediately	Drug test results take up to 5 days before arriving at court
Courtroom procedure is less formal	Formal procedures remain
Offender may be required to pay for treatment	Treatment is part of NHS provisions
Drug court judge concentrates on drug offenders	Judges retain full range of offenders
Probation Service has only a minor part to play	Probation Service is central to the order

The second major difference is that the court employs the treatment providers. This is a radical departure from existing practice and has profound implications, whether at the criminological, jurisprudential or political level. Treatment providers in Britain have traditionally been employed by voluntary agencies or the major national agencies, such as the NHS. Working for the court, as opposed to working with the court, would be a new experience, where some professionals, including those in medical and allied practices, might find it difficult being an employee of a judge or panel of magistrates. Some psychiatrists, for example, have said they could not accept such forms of employment; on the other hand, some directors of voluntary agencies say they would welcome the opportunity, seeing the introduction of drug courts more generally in Britain as a new, challenging, profitable experience.

The third major difference is that the judge conducts the supervision. Judges in drug court have invariably made themselves knowledgeable about addiction and its associated effects, and have become experts in their way. They may not be entirely suited for the social work role they are required to undertake, but there is little doubt most conduct themselves with confidence. They have been prepared to break the mould and engage in activities not always to the liking of some of their colleagues. Their position is not without justifiable criticism and, were drug courts to be transferred on a larger scale to Britain, the British counterparts may not be expected to engage in the more extreme activities, nor may they want to. On the other hand, a few changes by the magistrates might be welcome.

The fourth difference produces the most controversy, for this changes the complexion of a common law adversarial system of justice that is deeply ingrained in the ways things are done. To a large extent claims by drug court to 'reinventing justice' are hyperbolic, although there is no doubt that they have made things different. Operating as a team changes judicial roles and produces a loss of procedural rights, as well as the protection those rights provide. The question for the offender is how much is he or she prepared to trade off or forgo rights when there is the prospect of being drug free. For the judicial system, the key question is: how far is it prepared to go in the direction of that 'team' approach? Legal restrictions can be imposed on drug courts and the powers of the judge could be limited, or it could be allowed an unbridled development. The latter would not seem a sensible option.

Fifthly, there is the question of multiple sanctions. Were drug courts to be developed more widely in Britain, legislation would be required should they operate on the Miami model. Multiple sanctions, the key to drug court success, are not permitted under current legislation, yet without them the drug court becomes not much more than an extended type of probation order.

Tests results are given to drug court judges immediately. Under the DTTO, delays of up to five days are to be expected. The difference is critical if decisions are to be made about the offender's current position and, if they are not, one wonders how they can ever be effective.

The courtroom procedure in drug court is less formal than is likely in the hearing for the DTTO. Offenders in the drug court believe that the informal contact with the judge is an important ingredient for their success. Some drug courts operate more like a legal circus; others are more muted in their response. There is no evidence to suggest one is more successful than the other, but offenders are clear that personalised justice, in some form, is important to them.

Some drug courts require the offender to pay for his or her own treatment, on the basis that he or she produced his or her problem and should pay for it to be removed. Their view is that it is not the business of the state to pay through the taxes of its citizens for a self-inflicted disease. The European perspective is more corporate and unused to this rampant individualism. Given the manner in which many American ideas have arrived in Britain, usually first being considered outrageous and unacceptable, how long, one wonders, will it be before this one is accepted? Drug court is what it says – a separate court with a specially appointed judge who hears drug court cases only when drug court is sitting. There is no court set aside for offenders on a DTTO.

Finally, in the drug court the Probation Service has a minor part to play; under the DTTO, the Probation Service is central. Opposition to drug courts is likely to continue to come from the Probation Service, who would be a major loser. On the other hand, treatment services would be the major victor, albeit employed by the court, for they would have increased funding and would assume a dominant position in the new drug court structure.

Clearly, the DTTO is the government's flagship to deal with the problem of drug abuse and crime. It has within it certain flaws and, as such, it will, in my judgement, be a failure. I say this more from sorrow than anger, yet the omens were not good at the start: the pilot results were hardly satisfactory, but the government pressed ahead none the less. Everything that one hears about the way it operates confirms that pessimistic view. It will be another example of doing too little too late and, in part, of not grasping the nettle about coercive treatment. It is also another example of a fudge and of having an eye on the professionals so as not to make too many changes, not to spend money and to tinker with existing institutions rather than reform them.

There are, of course, other models of treatment, but the drug court remains a persuasive one which other countries are using, but Britain, with the exception of Scotland, is left with a system already outdated and creaking at the seams. It is not only that the DTTO will not work. It is that time and energy have been given to it which should have been directed elsewhere. The DTTO leaves too many pertinent questions unanswered, including: what types of actions are likely to produce the best results when tests are found to be positive? Will testing work more effectively on certain types of offenders than others? Can strategies be developed for estimating a person's risks on the basis of drug-test results? These are what we should be asking, but they must remain for the future, at least until we have sorted out the current predicament. No one suggests that drug courts are free of blemish, but they have produced a more coherent and considered approach than the DTTO, and should have at least been considered.

Drug courts in Scotland and Ireland

Scotland is ahead of the rest of the UK in that the first pilot drug court began in Glasgow in the autumn of 2001, and another opened in Fife a year later. Their history is interesting. A working group entitled 'Piloting a Drug Court in Glasgow' was established in February 2001 on the initiative of the Scottish Justice Department. The remit was 'to make proposals to the Scottish Deputy Minister for Justice and report by Easter on a model within existing legislation of a Drug Court and on the arrangements for its operation in Glasgow Sheriff Court by the Autumn of 2001'. The timetable was commendably tight, allowing two to three months to prepare a report and a further six months to complete preparations.

The working group proposed that the objectives for the Glasgow drug court should be to:

1 reduce the level of offending behaviour;
2 reduce or eliminate offenders' dependence on or propensity to misuse drugs; and
3 examine the viability and usefulness of a drug court in Scotland using existing legislation and to demonstrate where legislative and practical improvements might be appropriate.

Point 3 is interesting because the aim in Scotland was to produce a drug court within the existing legislative framework and then see which new features were needed. The working party concluded that, in comparison with other courts generally, drug courts are successful in engaging and retaining offenders in treatment services; that drug courts provide closer and more intensive supervision; criminal behaviour was lower; and drug courts save money.

The court operates in the same way and with the same authority as other courts. Initially, there was the same range of powers and sentences available, but as will be shown later, sentencing options have been expanded. In the early stages the sentencing options were a probation order with a condition of treatment, a DTTO, a concurrent DTTO and a conditional probation order, and a deferred sentence. What the drug court did was to impose on these sentences the principles and practices of the Miami model and, in so doing, adapt the Miami drug court model to the Scottish system. In addition to the usual conditions of probation, etc., the Scottish drug court requires the offender to:

1 submit to treatment with a view to the reduction or elimination of dependency on or propensity to misuse drugs;
2 conform to the directions of the treatment provider;
3 agree to be tested for drugs;
4 attend review hearings; and
5 abide by any such additional conditions as may be inserted.

It could be argued that the court could act in this way already under the DTTO, so that the drug court is doing little more than operate as a DTTO with another name. But that is wrong; it is doing much more. It is taking the Miami system and recasting it to fit the Scottish experience and, in so doing, maintaining many distinguishing features:

1 It has a specialist bench consisting of a Sheriff who develops a considerable measure of expertise.
2 A multi-agency team who oversee the operation of the drug court.
3 Regular and random testing of all orders, including offenders on probation.
4 Regular review of the offender's progress.
5 A multi-disciplinary screening group and interagency working.
6 Fast-track court procedures to get the offender into treatment quickly.
7 Initiation of breach proceedings by the bench.
8 Use of summary sanctions at reviews.

Point 1 is new; point 2 is also new but does not go so far as giving the team the powers and responsibility of the American system. Point 3 constitutes a departure from existing practices, as does point 4, and point 5 moves close to the American team approach. Point 6 is not new except that the existing system is slow, but point 7 certainly is new. Point 8 is interesting: the aim here was to seek legislative change to allow multiple sanctions to be introduced so that the offender can be dealt with on breach of the order and the order be allowed to continue.

These have now been introduced under the Criminal Justice (Scotland) Act 2003. This Act, *inter alia*, designates a court or class of court as a drug court: 'that is to say, as a court especially appropriate to deal with cases involving persons dependent on, or with a propensity to misuse, drugs.' The 2003 Act gives the drug court additional power to impose a limited period or periods of imprisonment or a community service order for failing to comply with the requirements of a DTTO or probation order, without affecting the continuation of the order. Community-based supervision and treatment options include DTTOs, probation with a condition of drug treatment, combined DTTO and probation, and deferred sentence.

The court in Glasgow (as in Dublin) is closely aligned to an American model of designated drug courts. As such, both courts are characterised by:

- dedicated judges (Sheriff and District Court judge);
- dedicated supervision and treatment teams; and
- powers to impose multiple sanctions, including periods of custody before final disposition.

Currently, a Sheriff with the same range of sentencing powers available to a Sheriff court as under summary proceedings constitutes the Glasgow court. The Sheriff operates a 'fast track' procedure so that breaches of an order are dealt with by the next scheduled review. Depending on the circumstances, if a breach is proved, the court may allow the order to continue and impose a fine, or community service order in the case of a probation order. Alternatively, the order could be terminated and the offender sentenced for the original offence. Irrespective of the new power to impose interim custodial sanctions, the court would have the opportunity (in dealing with multiple sentences for a number of offences) to impose a custodial sentence for one offence whilst allowing other orders to continue.

By agreement with the legal profession, lawyers do not appear after the first review hearing (if they do, legal aid fees are limited). The 2003 Act does, however, require that written details of alleged breaches of the DTTO or probation order are given to the defendant, who must be informed that there is an entitlement to be legally represented and that he or she need not answer the allegation before an opportunity has been given to take legal advice.

Referrals to the drug court are considered at a steering group convened by an assigned procurator fiscal with a range of professionals in attendance. The supervision and treatment team consists of social work (probation) staff and staff from the Glasgow Drug Problem Service (health and addiction workers). A multi-agency drug court group representing the Sheriffs, Sheriff's clerk, drug court procurator fiscal and project leader of the supervision and treatment team oversees their work. The status and authority of the drug court procurator fiscal contribute in no small measure to the efficiency and effectiveness of the overall operation of the scheme.

The Glasgow drug court takes some of the so-called 'hard to treat' users. It is thought about 8,000 drug users in Glasgow could benefit from the drug court but it will be able only to take about 150 per annum. The criteria for entry to the drug court are as follows:

1 The age group is over 21, but those over 16 will be considered in exceptional circumstances – there is a steep upward failure rate in American drug courts for those under 28 years of age.
2 Male or female.
3 Prosecuted summarily at the Sheriff court.
4 Known pattern of substance misuse susceptible to treatment.
5 Known record of drug-related crime.
6 No dual diagnosis of drug misuse and mental illness.
7 Past record of community supervision does not preclude referral.
8 Must reside in a defined geographical area.
9 Must plead or be found guilty.
10 No outstanding petition matters.

Drug testing is central to the programme, although treatment could include substitute prescribing (including methadone maintenance) (Glasgow Drug Court undated). The results are encouraging. For the first 18 months of the Glasgow drug court (up to the end of April 2003), the court received 144 referrals and placed 86 people on drug court orders. The majority were DTTOs (60 out of the 86). The majority of these orders were for 18 months. The offending history shows that there were no serious traffickers in the drug court, the majority of offenders having convictions (past and present) for dishonesty and minor drug offences. Most offences were acquisitive. In the 18-month period, there were seven completions and ten breaches of the order. This suggests a fairly low failure rate and, whilst there are grounds for optimism, not too much should be read into these figures as the numbers are too small to make a more confident interpretation (Price pers. comm.). And, of course, the success rate should be high; after all, a condition for entry into the drug court is that the offender has been assessed as 'motivated to change'. There are no data available for the second Scottish drug court in Fife, which began in September 2002.

Ireland has a drug court which began in January 2001 in Dublin and, in the first four months from January to May 2001, there have been 22 referrals. The Dublin drug court team consists of two probation officers, a liaison nurse, two community workers and an educational assessor. Cases are referred from other courts and then assessed. If the offender is suitable – and the Irish court takes those who have failed under voluntary programmes as well as serious offenders – he or she is sent to the drug court. The programme lasts for two years.

The Dublin court is a bail bond court (it operates with the offender on bail). Being on bail, the offender can opt out at any time. He or she has not been sentenced but, whilst on bail, must abide by the conditions of bail. The Irish Bail Act says it is a breach of conditions of bail if the offender is no longer of good behaviour, and this is what gives the court its powers. This is another example of the way in which drug courts can be adapted to local conditions yet retain the spirit of the drug court (Haughton 2003 pers. comm.).

The district judge in the Irish drug court exercises no sentencing powers as such. By agreement with the legal profession, once referred to the drug court, the legal representative will not appear. The court enforces conditions of bail, which include drug treatment and testing.

A feature of the bail bond entered into by an offender is that the terms and condition of bail may be varied from time to time by the judge, and that bail may be suspended for a period of not more than eight days for failure to comply with the conditions of bail or any drug treatment programme. The drug court judge has suggested that an offender's record of convictions could be expunged on completion of the treatment programme, though we know of no authority for this. Suspension of bail for a period (or periods) is clearly less satisfactory than primary legislation for interim sanctions with the safeguard of legal advice and representation. However, the court functions without challenge.

To be eligible, an offender must:

1 be 17 years or over;
2 have lived within the catchment area for a minimum of one year, but the area covered is to be expanded;
3 have pleaded or been found guilty of a current non-violent criminal offence related to dependency and/or abuse of drugs;
4 be likely to be sentenced to custody;
5 be abusing or dependent on drugs;
6 understand the implications of participation in the drug court; or
7 be willing to co-operate with supervision.

Table 5.2 sets out the position of the Irish drug court as of March 2003 in terms of allocation and the numbers of offenders.

The treatment programme is tightly structured and has the benefit of an education programme too. In many respects the treatment pro-gramme in Ireland is more extensive and demanding than that in Scotland. There are three phases of treatment. Phase 1, the stabilisation

Table 5.2 Irish drug court: allocations and numbers (March 2003)

Allocation	Number
Graduated	4
Ineligible	38
Terminated	16
Assessment	8
Phase 1	11
Phase 2	12
Phase 3	10
Total	99

Source: Haughton G. (2003 pers. comm.).

and orientation phase lasts about three months. In this phase the offender is expected to reduce illicit drug use and demonstrate an ability to remain free for a significant period, to cease criminal activity and begin treatment. In phase 2 (expected to last between six and eight months), the offender has to demonstrate the ability to remain permanently free of illicit drugs, to address life issues through counselling and to commence study, vocational training or employment. Phase 3 requires the offender to remain consistently free of illicit drugs and crime and to be well established in study, a vocation or employment. Phase 3 is expected to last about 12 months. The supervision and treatment team is much the same as that in Scotland, though accountability is directly to the workers' respective agencies. This is a disadvantage as it could divide loyalties.

The intention in Ireland (as in Scotland) has been to take the hard-to-treat and serious offenders. This is based on the assumption that, if drug courts have anything to offer, they should be able to deal with those offenders who cannot easily be dealt with elsewhere. In this respect the first 35 participants had a total of 872 prior convictions (with a range of 1–85 prior convictions), 60% of which had over 11 convictions. All had been to prison and all had been on probation (Haughton 2003 pers. comm.). The effect of the drug court has been measured in terms of recidivism and response to drug testing. However, there is no control group with which to make comparisons. First comes recidivism. Table 5.3 shows that the number and percentage of arrests decreased as the offenders went through the programme, as did the frequency of bail revocation. In terms of responses to drug testing, the data are presented in Table 5.4.

Table 5.3 Outcomes of the Irish drug court treatment programme

Period	No. of participants	% arrested in programme	% with new charges	% with bail revoked
First quarter	9	86	86	56
Second quarter	15	47	33	47
Third quarter	28	36	36	21
Fourth quarter	35	31	28	19

Source: Haughton, G. (2003 pers. comm.).

Table 5.4 Responses to drug testing, Irish drug court

Period	No. of participants	No. of tests	No. of clean tests
First quarter	9	100	42 = 42%
Second quarter	15	144	81 = 56%
Third quarter	28	324	203 = 63%
Fourth quarter	35	509	417 = 82%

Source: Houghton, G. (2003 pers. comm.).

Clearly, the frequency of clean tests improved throughout the programme: in the fourth quarter they were up to 82%. Notice the difference between the results here and those surrounding the DTTOs.

An overview and summary

What is most apparent and common to both the Scottish and Irish systems is the justifiable enthusiasm of the participants, including, surprisingly enough, those on the receiving end of the criminal justice system. The speed with which recognisable and distinct drug courts were able to be established without primary legislation is also a tribute to those who planned and operate them. Recognition also has to be given to the co-operation of all the agencies and professionals involved and to the ability of the systems to deal with offenders with long-established drug use and a considerable history of offending.

The systems offer a 'carrot and stick' approach by providing an opportunity to expunge convictions on completion of treatment but by imposing penalties for backsliding. What is also impressive is the manner in which the dignity and authority of the courts have been maintained and, indeed, for many offenders even enhanced, by the drug court judge, notwithstanding the more informal processes of periodic review.

Both the Glasgow and Dublin courts show what can be achieved under existing legislation to create a more focused and knowledgeable approach to drug misuse. The designated judges play a major role, commanding respect and retaining authority. The example of Scotland perhaps offers a more securely based model, even without the more recent powers provided by the 2003 Act. Multidisciplinary teams can present problems however structured. The attitude of the legal profession appears not to be an issue, nor has the cost of the programme.

As the English courts have the same sentencing options (with the exception of powers under the 2003 Act), given the will and the co-operation of the professions, including the police, there are no legal procedural restrictions on what could be achieved in England with district court judges or stipendiary magistrates. The time is ripe to benefit from the experience gained in Glasgow, Fife and Dublin.

Improving treatment services

The clear and obvious aim of the DTTO is to provide treatment under a court order. The assumption that 'Treatment Works' is there for all to see; what is missing is a deeper understanding of what is required to implement such a programme. The DTTO was simply added on to an existing framework, plus a few modifications, as if that is all that matters. It is not (nor can ever be) as simple as that. Taxman (cited in McBride *et al.* 2002: 27) sets out what are called 'threats which impede the implementation of treatment services':

1 Lack of clear crime control goals for treatment services.
2 Lack of clear assessment and eligibility requirements.
3 Insufficient treatment duration to effect behavioural change.
4 Lack of supervision and sanctions/rewards to reinforce treatment goals.
5 Lack of objective drug testing to monitor treatment services.
6 Insufficient case management services.

Taxman (*ibid.*) argues for a system in which 'correctional and treatment agencies build a delivery system that cuts across and integrates the systems, reduces duplication in efforts to create and recreate processes for unique programmes and emphasises empirically driven programmatic components'. The DTTO does little of that; in fact the six 'threats' identified above all apply to the DTTO. It is almost the perfect example of all that Taxman says should be avoided. For example, there was a 'lack of clear crime control goals for treatment services' as in threat 1, and an equally 'lack of clear assessment and eligibility requirements'. So, too, for the others. However, I want to examine more closely the sixth threat – what Taxman refers to as the 'insufficient case management services'. I regard this a key 'threat': it needs to be implemented before the others.

By 'case management services' I mean the manner in which offenders are identified as being suitable for treatment, as being transferred into treatment and being supervised therein. A tried-and-tested model is that developed by TASC in the USA – originally standing for Treatment Alternatives to Street Crime but now changed to Treatment Account-ability for Safer Communities. It aims to span the boundaries of the treatment and justice system by identifying appropriate treatment referrals through clinical screening processes, assessing the treatment and other needs of clients from the justice system, referring clients to treatment and other services, and providing client-centred case management. TASC case management can be distinguished from more traditional types of case management by its level of assertiveness; its ongoing nature; its focus on long-term positive outcomes resulting from multiple interventions; and its continual interagency and inter-system communication (Goodman 2004).

TASC began operations in Wilmington, Delaware, in 1972. There are now over 150 TASC programmes in 40 states. It has continued under state and local auspices, and has been described by many commentators as the largest and most widely respected organisation of its kind. Its purpose was (and still is) to serve as a link between the traditional functions of criminal justice and the treatment community. The objective is to provide an effective bridge between two groups with differing philosophies: the justice system and community treatment providers. Whereas the justice system sanctions reflect community concerns for public safety and punishment, the treatment community recommends therapeutic intervention to change behaviour and reduce the suffering associated with substance abuse and related problems. The basic goal of TASC is to identify offenders in need of drug treatment from within the criminal justice system and, under close supervision, provide community-based treatment as an alternative or supplement to more traditional criminal justice sanctions. TASC is in part a diversion pro-gramme yet also a supervisory programme, for it not only refers drug users from the courts to the appropriate treatment programmes but it also undertakes the supervision, monitors progress whilst in treatment and links the programmes to the courts. Some TASC programmes undertake the treatment themselves, but that is not a critical element of the standard TASC model. TASC takes offenders sentenced to deferred prosecutions, community sentences, probation and pre-trial services as well as taking those on parole.

TASC programmes make the links, place the offenders, undertake the supervision and monitor progress, whilst acting as a bridge between the courts and treatment. The bridge is required because of the philosophical differences between the two systems. Presumably in Britain the Probation Service already acts as a sort of TASC, able to operate in the same manner; but could it, or would it, behave like TASC if required? Probably not. TASC operates under what it calls 'vigorous or aggressive supervision'. This is what it means by case management. It is doubtful if the Probation Service in Britain would work in that way.

TASC began as a federal initiative to foster and improve the delivery of treatment and other services to drug offenders and others in the justice system who disrupt the community, endanger their families and threaten public safety because of their substance abuse. It has developed approaches which, it claims, are applicable to those involved in criminal and civil matters, and in all stages of the justice continuum. A number of states now have 're-entry courts' for prisoners on parole or licence, and TASC also provides services to these courts. The TASC model is now used with mental health, family and juvenile court cases.

TASC aims to reach people wherever they are in the justice system and place them in the appropriate treatment programme. The methodology and practice are designed to deal with the multiple co-occurring problems of substance abuse, mental and physical health, social disorder, etc. – so often a feature of those going through the criminal justice system. TASC provides links between treatment agencies, the support services and the criminal justice system to ensure the systems work together. The programmes are designed to secure the delivery and monitoring of services and effective operational standards. Protocols and service agreements are designed to illustrate its approach to case management. (For a full discussion on TASC and how it operates, see Goodman 2004.)

One of TASC's strengths is that it assists in providing treatment services by negotiating with the treatment system and providing advocacy for those in the criminal justice system who might otherwise fall through the cracks. TASC programmes also provide information and training to treatment and justice on effective strategies for managing substance abuse. It serves as a central point for managing policy and information, as well as managing those referred for treatment and other services. The direct services provided include screening, assessment, continuous case management, alcohol and drug testing, and treatment network development. Formal communication protocols have been established to assist the integration of justice and other systems.

The benefits claimed from TASC programming include the following:

- Providing the organisational structure to manage substance abusers referred from the justice system in a logical, organised and cost-effective fashion.

- Developing and improving treatment delivery networks.

- Using resources efficiently by screening, assessing and placing in appropriate levels of care.

- Negotiating to ensure justice 'clients' access court-ordered treatment.

- Co-ordinating treatment requirements with justice processes.

- Imposing sanctions or incentives to prevent unnecessary or avoidable discharge from treatment or to improve treatment outcomes.

- Improving inter-system communication.

- Encouraging treatment to hold justice system referrals accountable.

- Encouraging justice responses that support effectiveness and retention of treatment.

- Providing support through transitions from prison to the community and from residential to outpatient care (*ibid.*).

Not everything is plain sailing. For example, where TASC acts as a treatment provider in addition to carrying out case management functions, there is potential for a conflict of interests. That said, the TASC programme has been established and developed over some 30 years, and federal agencies are enthusiastically supportive. The TASC programme is well researched, scientifically based and well documented. It is a comprehensive programme and it covers the whole of the justice continuum, including re-entry to the community from prison. The model has also been adopted for juvenile and civil courts. The programme is not dependent on the drug court model being employed.

It may not be necessary or advisable to transport the TASC model to Britain without seeing first how it could be introduced. A pilot pro-gramme would be needed, accompanied by an evaluation. TASC emphasises the importance of bridging the gap between criminal justice and treatment (at a conference in Perth in 2000 it was said by a representative of the Western Australian government that this was the most difficult part of their programme, yet once achieved produced enormous results). That is its strength, and it illustrates the point earlier that this was not part of the DTTO programme.

Chapter 6

Trafficking and laundering

For our purposes, trafficking is defined widely. It includes the distribution of illicit drugs by large-scale operations, which can and often do cross national boundaries. It includes also the small-scale syndicates which distribute drugs at the local level. All operations at whatever level pose questions for law enforcement, government policy or the local communities on which they have a deleterious effect. Each distribution system has its own methods and practices posing distinct problems which require different strategies.

This chapter does not examine the nature of production, although the circumstances in which drugs are produced can have an effect on distribution. The aim here is to examine some central features of trafficking. There is a large amount of information available on trafficking for South America, but less for South East Asia or elsewhere. Much less is known about the production and distribution of the precursor chemicals necessary for the manufacture of drugs such as heroin and cocaine. A great deal of the research is American, concerned with American matters, especially relating to cocaine trafficking, which has dominated American drug policy for two decades.

Trafficking – an overview

The geographical areas of production are worth listing for they show where trafficking occurs and the different types of organisations used to distribute a variety of drugs. Briefly coca leaf is produced extensively in Bolivia, Peru, Venezuela and Brazil, although for all intents and purposes

Brazil is the least important. Invariably the coca leaves are sent to Colombia in the form of coca paste to be refined into cocaine hydrochloride. 'Crack' (the base form of the salt, cocaine hydrochloride) is almost always produced in the consumption areas. Unlike other illicit drugs, which grow in a wide range of geographical regions, world coca production is limited to the Andes, with Peru (60%) and Bolivia (20%) being the major producers.

Afghanistan currently accounts for almost 75% of the world illicit opium supply (MacDonald and Mansfield 2001). Much of the remainder is from the traditional growing region of the Golden Triangle (Burma, Laos and Thailand). Significant amounts, however, are grown elsewhere, such as in Iran and Turkey. There is firm evidence that heroin production is also occurring in the Andean region, with the Colombian cartels moving away from cocaine (Drugs Intelligence Agency 1992). There, the 1970s were characterised by an increase in cannabis trafficking; in the 1980s it was cocaine and in the 1990s to the present heroin is the major concern. In 1991 and in the first quarter of 1992, Colombian authorities destroyed a total of 3,500 hectares of poppy fields and three heroin laboratories (*ibid.*). With the maximum market share of cocaine, the move is now to increase heroin production, and already high levels of purity are achieved. Whether this means a major shift in the world markets is difficult to say, but it is interesting to note that the price of heroin in Puerto Rico continues to fall – there are about 80,000 heroin addicts in Puerto Rico – giving further evidence that heroin is available in that region (DEA 1994 cited in Bean 1996).

Cannabis is produced worldwide. Estimates of cannabis production suggest that world production is increasing, in spite of intensive crop-eradication programmes. Unfortunately in countries such as Belize or Jamaica, where crop eradication has occurred, the dealers have shown a readiness to transfer to cocaine (*ibid.*). Manufactured drugs are also produced worldwide; ecstasy was until recently mainly produced in Amsterdam (Bean 1994) but local British factories are now operating. LSD is manufactured throughout the industrialised countries, and production moves as factories are closed down. The same is true for methamphetamine. However, whilst 'ice' (a distinct form of methamphetamine) is almost exclusively manufactured in North Korea and distributed through Hawaii, it is penetrating deeper into the US market and may soon appear in Britain (Bean 1991). How much has already arrived is difficult to say, but the British market is still monopolised by cocaine.

Trafficking and traffickers differ according to the drugs being smuggled, the source of production and the local distribution (Dziedzic

1989). An early important text (Cooper 1990) which concentrates on the economic forces that drive the drug trade shows that drug dealing was, at that time, worth an estimated US$500 billion per year. Moreover, Cooper shows that the traffickers are flexible and effective, especially when set against some rather ineffective and outdated forms of interdiction, especially in the Caribbean region and some parts of Europe – and that in spite of the occasional successes by law enforcement. Given the size of the drug market it would not be an exaggeration to say the drug trade is the largest and most successful form of criminal activity ever developed (*ibid.*). European research confirms this (Ruggiero and South 1995).

Once the drugs have crossed the local customs area into their final destination, such as Europe or the USA, their value increases dramatically. Table 6.1 gives the figures for cocaine. It is suspected they have not changed greatly over the last decade or so as far as the street price is concerned, but even if they had the point remains that the price in Colombia bears no relation to the price on the streets.

The figures for opium are no less impressive. The total value of opium production in Afghanistan at so-called 'farm gate' prices at harvest time was estimated at US$183 million, or about US$35 per kg. By the time it had passed through customs in the UK, it was estimated to be worth US$25,000 per kg (MacDonald and Mansfield 2001: 3). The massive increase in the price at each stage of the operation shows how the end price bears no relation to the cost of production – the distribution costs are the heaviest. Peter Reuter (2001) adds to this by calculating that a pilot who demands US$500,00 for flying a plane with 250 kg of cocaine is generating costs of about US$2,000 per kg, less than 2% of the retail price of each kg.

Moving against the drug cartels, especially in South America, involves serious economic and political costs – for governments too, as the drug industry has accumulated significant political influence (Lee 1989). The resulting concentration of wealth and coercive potential in the hands of

Table 6.1 The value of cocaine whilst en route to users (in US$ per kg)

Leaving from Guajala (Colombia) in an air drop	300
Arriving at the US border	3,000
Into the US	12,000
Distributed to users	20,000

Source: DEA (1994, cited in Bean 1996).

drug cartels, especially in Colombia, has led to a severe threat to that and some other countries' national and regional security. Whilst it is clear that the drug producers (the farmers, growers, etc.) receive only a small percentage of the vast profits, to what extent these cartels threaten Western security is not yet known, but already there are disturbing signs of their influence on smaller economies within the Caribbean. A massive inflow of drug money into economies such as the Bahamas was immensely destructive. The Bahamian government in the early 1990s had considerable difficulty meeting immense pressure from the traffickers, on the one hand, and the American government on the other, who wanted rid of the traffickers.

Damage is not restricted to the economic environment: it extends to political institutions, where the proliferation of sophisticated weaponry amongst traffickers and the ease with which they undermine democratic institutions are commonplace. This is so whether in South America, South East Asia or elsewhere, but it is in Latin America that all these factors are most often combined (Dziedzic 1989).

In Colombia the situation is almost beyond repair (MacDonald 1989), but Venezuela and Ecuador increasingly attract trafficking, and cocaine production is extensive, making them additionally vulnerable. One of the many difficulties for national governments is that traffickers have appeared to assist local industries although, of course, their assistance quickly turns out to be catastrophic. In one of the most carefully documented studies in Peru, Morales (1989) shows that coca production and the processing of its derivative alkaloids have become major Peruvian growth industries, the ramifications of which reach into the heart of Peru's political life, its law enforcement and its judicial systems. Morales (1989) says: 'the effect of this new commerce has been corrosive of traditional society and of modern institutions, has placed the country in even more onerous conditions of international dependency and has solidified new trends of social class exploitation.' In the long term Morales believes the net effect will be to create conditions producing greater levels of social and political impoverishment than hitherto. Peter Reuter (2001) is, however, more optimistic. He claims that the land under coca cultivation fell in Bolivia and Peru from 150,000 acres in 1992 to 60,000 acres in 1999 (*ibid.*: 21). Of course all figures must be estimates, but Reuter believes crop-eradication programmes have had a measure of success in parts of South America.

A study of the long-term effects of the narco industry in all societies, including Western Europe, would need to include selected political and social institutions, especially those centring around finance. It would need to determine the extent of the traffickers' current influence and then show the likely impact in the short and long term. The US experience suggests that Western European institutions are strong enough to be impervious, although to what extent they can remain so must be difficult to say. The amount of drug money available must always be a threat to institutions, however large.

Again, in his study of Peru, Morales (1990) notes the extent of dependency on the lives of peasants and workers whose livelihoods are closely linked to the production of cocaine. It was they who resisted attempts by governments to introduce alternative cash crops in the region. Peasants and workers have traditionally supported the drug producers, seeing them as providing an income higher than that expected in crop-substitution programmes. Healey (1989) found similar results in Bolivia, where support for coca leaf production came from well organised peasant unions closely tied to the national labour movement. So too in Pakistan where resistance to opium crop-eradication programmes is legendary. These studies tell us a great deal about the impact of drug production on local industries and, for that reason incidentally, could easily provide a model for a study on the impact of the drugs trade on local areas in Britain and elsewhere (i.e. of the dependency of local landlords, traders, etc., on local drug markets). There are differences, to be sure, but sufficiently isomorphic in their structure to suggest one could usefully act as a model for the other.

Generally speaking, more is known about South American traffickers than those from South East Asia or elsewhere. However, MacDonald and Mansfield (2001) report that in Afghanistan, although the agricultural conditions for growing opium are conducive, it is not grown nationwide. They say that the labour requirements are heavy so that the producing areas depend greatly on a type of share-cropping where women and young children are actively involved in weeding and harvesting. Farmers growing opium are given preferential access to credit, thereby ensuring harvesting and continuity in terms of production. Whilst the authorities in Afghanistan have passed an edict banning the use, production and sale of opium (and cannabis), implementation of this edict has been problematic (*ibid.*: 5).

Colombian trafficking operates largely in cartels which are best characterised as a federation of multiple independent groups that, when necessary, forge multiple alliances. They are not centrally organised, although some cartel members are more powerful than others and offer leadership when required. The cartels function much like legitimate businesses, with sections concerned with distribution, sales, financing, product promotion, security, etc. They tend to compartmentalise their organisations into production, transportation, distribution and money laundering. Yet unlike legitimate businesses, the cartels cannot resort to the courts or other legitimate enterprises to sort out disputes over product quality, debts or other matters. Instead they rely on bribery, extortion and violence to achieve effective and efficient production and distribution, to avoid arrest and to gain a huge profit (Florez and Boyce 1990). South East Asian heroin traffickers seem to be slightly less sophisticated in their business methods, preferring to remain more individualist, but no less reluctant to resort to extreme levels of personal violence when required (Lo and Bean 1991). In Britain, Turkish traffickers control much of the importation of heroin, with the drugs coming into Britain from Afghanistan via Turkey.

There are probably four major cartels in Colombia: the Medellin, the Cali, the Bogota and the Northern Coast cartel, although some see the North Coast and Bogata as one and the same. The Medellin cartel has had the most publicity, but the Cali cartel is larger, more efficient and certainly more businesslike, although recently unconfirmed claims have been made that the Cali cartel has been broken up. Almost all the cartel members in Colombia are known to the DEA and the FBI, as are their movements and their major business associates. By all accounts the traffickers were, or are, small-time gangsters, unsophisticated yet with an easy recourse to violence. Their lifestyles are ordinary and their tastes crude. They have a shrewd organisational sense which allows them to know whom to employ, how to obtain the best financial advice and how to enforce discipline. The DEA and FBI have developed an extensive portfolio of cartel members, and consistently and persistently apply to the Colombian government for their extradition. Rarely do they succeed (DEA pers. comm.).

Generally speaking, we can distinguish between cartel members, traffickers and dealers, although sometimes they are one and the same. Cartel members usually own the drugs, whilst the traffickers transport them, acting as middlemen between the cartels and the more local dealers. Sometimes the cartel members hand the drugs over to the traffickers, sometimes not. These high-level traffickers usually work directly with the cartels, but mostly outside national boundaries, and are responsible for transporting the drugs having purchased them from the cartels – some of whom may be cartel members in their own right. The traffickers and dealers, especially those from South East Asia, are mostly men approaching middle age or older, have excellent organisational skills, have established connections often with organised crime syndicates or are prepared to work closely with organised crime, and have capital to invest. They also have a willingness to take large business risks. Their activities exist within a highly competitive market populated by individual entrepreneurs. These traffickers change as enforcement strategies change or as they tire of the corrupt practices endemic to the illegal trade (Chaiken and Johnson 1988). Some may be intermittent traffickers, as in South East Asia, active perhaps once in every two or three years, whilst others who may not have been involved for a period of time seem to be drawn back to it. There is, it seems, some compulsive and highly attractive element about high-level trafficking, generating levels of excitement not found elsewhere (Wing and Bean 1991).

Alongside the cartel members are the financial advisers. These people mostly originated in Europe, having emigrated to Colombia before or after the Second World War. Typically, these are sophisticated professionals with a detailed knowledge of financial markets and financial institutions. Culturally and socially they have little in common with the traffickers and regard themselves as superior. Yet they are as central to the operation as the traffickers are, for money and drugs are but two sides of the same equation. Without the financial advisers there would be no trafficking, and without trafficking there would be no financial advisers – both create the profits, and without profits there would be no drugs (*ibid.*).

Cocaine is typically transported from the Guajala peninsular in Colombia or from Venezuela using at least four major methods:

1 In containers where the drugs are sent direct to selected ports.
2 By air drops to selected Caribbean locations.
3 By sea to selected Caribbean locations.
4 By small-time couriers.

Most of the earlier trafficking was done in containers. This seems to be the most successful form – at least from the perspective of the traffickers. The Port of Miami randomly selects one in every 100 of all containers passing through and subjects them to a detailed examination. This is in addition to those selected as a result of information from undercover activities, informers and the like. It takes a small team about two weeks to examine each container. Corrupt employees within the port working for the traffickers will often know in advance which containers have drugs and so remove them before they are searched. This is another example how traffickers find ways of undermining attempts to seize illicit drugs. The drugs may have travelled in a number of different containers, perhaps leaving Colombia to go round Cape Horn and by Ecuador before passing through the Panama Canal en route to Miami. The aim is the same as with money laundering: to leave no trail that can be followed.

Large amounts of drugs are sent by air to be dropped into the sea somewhere off a favoured island in the Caribbean, where they are picked up (traffickers are able to use the most sophisticated equipment, usually purchased indirectly from the US military) and stored until they can be moved to the USA, Europe or beyond. Reuter (2001) says most air drops are of 250 kg or more. Using the global positioning device, the claim is that the drugs can be dropped within six feet of the target area. Corrupt local police will be paid to look the other way, as will others, including senior politicians, who will all be paid in cocaine, and the drugs will find their way into the network as required. Air drops are probably less successful than containers as US radar is very effective in the Caribbean region.

Local fisherman using small craft are able to ship quite large quantities of drugs from Colombia to the Caribbean islands. The shortest route takes about five days. These boats are difficult to detect by traditional radar, are low slung and fast, and the local peons see drug transportation as more profitable than fishing. The aim is to avoid the patrols by the Royal Navy and others (especially from the USA), but by all accounts there is no shortage of volunteers willing to transport the drugs in what remains a hazardous exercise given the size of the boats and the distances to travel. Some go as far as Jamaica.

The fourth method of transportation is by local courier who will transport small quantities, but given the numbers operating, will, when added together, produce a large total aggregate. The major aim may have less to do with the amounts transported but to test out new routes to be evaluated later by the traffickers. Tourists, too, can be effective couriers, helping to promote new routes and new markets or seeking to sustain existing ones. Too little attention has been given to this group. Also, European nationals and former nationals returning to see relatives or coming home to Europe for other reasons (including seeking medical treatment) can help establish new networks (e.g. Suriname to Holland and so on). Again this is an under-researched area but needs closer attention. Couriers (or 'mules' as they are often called) from Nigeria or Jamaica are small-scale traffickers bringing small amounts of heroin into Britain – one of the major effects being to increase the female prison population in Britain (see Chapter 9).

Traffickers tend to sell to their own ethnic or cultural groups, believing these to be the only ones to be trusted. They will sell the drugs to Jamaica but will insist on transporting them. Accordingly and as expected, Spain is the major destination for trafficking from South America to Europe (Gillard 1993), but Jamaica is a main staging post for drugs on their way to Britain, as are some Caribbean islands, such as

St Martin for transfer into France and Holland. St Martin is an island in the Caribbean owned jointly by France and Holland. There are no customs posts between the two parts of the island and no customs posts between the island and their European counterparts. Accordingly, traffickers getting their drugs into St Martin find no difficulty in getting them into France or Holland and, once there, to send them around Europe. This is another example where political systems favour the traffickers.

Numerous methods are used to conceal the drugs and to ship them to their destination. Two famous cases involved drugs packaged as fruit. In May 1999, Interpol Madrid reported the seizure of 550 kg of cannabis concealed in tins of tomatoes. This seizure was similar to that in Essex where 2,061 kg of the drug was seized, again in tins of tomatoes (NCIS Annual Report 1999–2000). Traffickers invariably deal in specific drugs, but some high-level dealers are more generic. For example a Belgian national was intercepted driving a lorry importing drugs through Dover. In the lorry were 20 kg of ecstasy, 200 kg of base amphetamine, 2 kg of cocaine, 9 kg of herbal cannabis, and 1 kg of cannabis resin (*ibid.*: 32). Or again an operation in Nottingham resulted in the seizure of cannabis, amphetamine and ecstasy with a street value of £1.6 million (National Crime Squad Annual Report 1999–2000: 16). Traffickers and dealers will easily switch commodities depending on the profits. In Britain, large numbers of drug dealers are moving into cigarette and tobacco smuggling. The profits are as good, the operational arrangements less difficult and the likely sentence if caught much less severe – an expected sentence of three years for multi-million pound tobacco trafficking is not uncommon, whereas for a Class A or Class B drug that produces similar returns they could expect at least ten years.

It is difficult to evaluate interdiction practices. Most of the research evidence is American (Reuter 1988), and there are few comparable British studies. The American studies show that many traffickers are simply not sighted and their couriers not detected. Based on data relating to seizures, these studies invariably conclude that 'we do not have the data to support conclusions about how successful we are now, what impacts our efforts have, or what the situation might otherwise be' (Home Office 1986). It seems that the systems perform well once a trafficker is detected but, again, the data supporting this are not all that strong and many improvements are required (Reuter 1988). Reuter (2001) notes that US policies are heavily supply-side orientated: their primary aim is to restrict the availability of illegal drugs. He notes (*ibid.*: 16) that the Federal Government and other departments together spent

US$35 billion on drug control in 2000 – up from the $10 billion per year of the mid-1980s.

The general conclusion is that seizing drugs before they enter the country has little impact on drug use within the country, unless the seizure is a monopoly seizure. This was the case with Operation Julie, which was not an overseas operation but is, none the less, instructive in this respect. Operation Julie closed down a large LSD manufacturing site in Britain and, as this was a monopoly supply site, it effectively stifled LSD consumption in Britain and elsewhere for many months. A likely impact of a successful interdiction is that it will affect domestic consumption and sometimes local drug production (Reuter 1991). For example, production may be shifted to other sites, some local, some not. Those drugs having a direct substitute effect are likely to lead to shifts in production so that a successful interdiction of heroin, for example, can lead to a growth in methadone production. It is unlikely that one successful interdiction, however large and impressive, will greatly affect consumption or price. Drug production is cheap and losses can be easily restored (Bean 1995a). Indeed, Peter Reuter (1991: 22) notes that, whereas it would cost US$10,000 to ship a kilogram of cocaine from Bogota to Miami, a legitimate private company would charge only US$100 to ship the equivalent legal amount: 'It is hard not to attribute the differential to law enforcement.' This is, of course, one measure of the success of supply-side interdiction as, in a legal regime, cocaine would sell for US$5.00 per gram (*ibid.*).

Clearly, interdiction is not a complete failure and efforts should not necessarily be directed elsewhere. The best that can be expected is to disrupt and interfere seriously with trafficking so as to inconvenience the traffickers. Interdiction puts up the price and sends out an important political message that governments are not prepared to give way to trafficking and will devote extensive resources to that end.

The expansionist model of consumption asserts that the American market is almost full, and Britain (along with other Western European countries) provides the means by which the existing market can be expanded. Moreover, the amount of land area given over to cultivating coca leaf in South America has increased to such an extent that there is a need to look for new markets to take up the growth in supply (i.e. an increase in drug use as cocaine is supply led) (Stutman 1989). For other drugs, such as heroin or ecstasy, a different theory applies, which is perhaps more demand led. The expansionist model implies that trafficking to Britain will increase over the short term, which means that interdiction policies will still be required.

International co-operation

The methods of transportation and means by which drugs enter national boundaries and are transported to other countries differ widely. One means by which interdiction can be improved is through international co-operation. There is evidence to suggest that some forms of international co-operation exist and are increasing, but existing formal and informal mechanisms of co-operation need to be strengthened and developed if the investigation and prosecution of international trafficking are to be improved (House of Commons 1990; Bruno 1991; Anderson and De Boer 1992; Birch 1991, 1992). The prospects of a Europe without internal frontiers and the need for information sharing between countries are the driving forces for greater co-operation. Increasingly, high-level traffickers live in one country and direct operations in another, with the drugs imported and sold in a third.

As far as Britain is concerned, there are three main areas in which formal co-operation against trafficking takes place. This does not include the extensive co-operation between Britain and America, which takes place in the Caribbean and in other places such as Turkey and the Far East. Here, the concern is mainly with formal European co-operation.

There have been a number of developments in international co-operation. First there is the Schengen Group. Initially this included all EC countries other than Britain, Ireland and Denmark, with Greece having observer status. In 2002 the UK government decided to apply for 'partial but significant' membership of the Schengen group. Secondly, in a development described by the National Criminal Intelligence Service (NCIS) as 'significant' was the agreement of the European Convention to allow Europol to store criminal intelligence (NCIS 1999–2000: 37). Europol has no executive or operational powers and no capabilities to gather evidence: it is an intelligence-based organisation able to offer services to operational teams in the EU (*ibid.*: 39). The UK has a designated National Unit for Europol, with four officers seconded as liaison officers. Thirdly, there have been international activities, such as the International Intelligence Branch (IIB) which consists of the drugs liaison officers' (DLOs) network based at The Hague. All are seen as contributing to the increasing international nature of drug trafficking, and the annual reports of the NCIS and National Crime Squad (NCS) are full of examples where co-operation was successful. Nicholas Dorn (1993) talks of the way 'co-operation is increasingly linked through information systems, is rapidly converging in its methodologies and is becoming more slowly harmonised in terms of its general rules'.

Yet how much co-operation actually occurs is not known. Clearly some takes place, but it is uncertain how much or its level of effectiveness. One possibility is to produce larger and larger centrally directed organisations leading to 'some super Europol' (Birch 1992); another is for a more pragmatic approach which improves arrangements for co-operation between existing agencies without taking away their independence or unique role (*ibid.*). Sadly, the history of co-operation at the national and international level has not always been good. There have been some spectacular rivalries between agencies – the early years of the DEA and its rivalry with the FBI being the most dramatic – with gross inefficiencies in and between the international community. Policing at the international level has often been a hit-and-miss affair dominated by national interests which seem rarely to be transcended to allow full co-operation to occur. There is, it seems, rather more co-operation in Europe than elsewhere, with some evidence to suggest things are going quite well, but this still remains below what is or should be required as some European countries are reluctant to provide more than token assistance.

Drug dealing in Britain

The expansionist model of drug use (which sees Britain as an overflow from America) promotes a view of drug dealing in Britain as being a static triangle or pyramid, with a big Mafia-type organisation sitting at the top controlling the market. Dorn *et al.* (1992: 203) conclude otherwise: 'There is no person, no Mafia, no cartel organising the market overall. Rather a large number of small organisations operate fairly autonomously of each other in a manner that may be described as disorganised crime.' Such a view has support in Peter Reuter's seminal American study: 'The old images of highly centralised and controlled drug distribution systems have largely disappeared in face of growing evidence of competitive violence and the failure of individual organisations to endure a dominant position' (Reuter *et al.* 1990: 23).

In a later study (2001), Reuter modifies this and says: 'There are probably just a few hundred people with significant roles as importers. Roughly 400 tons of cocaine enter the US each year and since some criminal organisations handle 10 tons or more annually not a lot of importers are needed' (p. 18). Johnson *et al.* (1990) suggested that larger and more hierarchical organisations will emerge in the retail crack trade as it matures. Reuter (back in 1990) disagrees:

Two factors make this outcome unlikely. First without the ability to buy large scale corruption from law enforcement agencies, the leader of a large organisation is at risk from his employers, any of who can turn informant. Second the erratic behaviour of so many heavy drug users in the crack trade makes for a particularly difficult management problem: successful long term entrepreneurs are likely to be those able to select a small number of reliable subordinates (p. 24).

In Britain the notion of the large-scale trafficker operating within national frontiers has largely been promoted and sustained by the police. Organised trafficking, say Dorn *et al.* (1990: 203), has helped create a near consensus within the ACPO (Association of Chief Police Officers) that some degree of centralisation of policing is needed. Moreover: 'the function of the National Drugs Intelligence Unit, its role in piloting the broader National Criminal Intelligence Service (NCIS) and the elevation of the intelligence centre over local operational teams effectively bequeathed Britain a national detective agency along the lines of America's FBI' (*ibid.*). They ask: what more is needed to promote further the myths of the big trafficker?

If there is no central control organising the market, what is there? The general conclusion seems to be that there is a large number of small independent organisations:

This analysis of the returns to participation in the drug trade is not much complicated by the existence of monopolistic organisations. In most cities entry into the drug selling business seems relatively easy, requiring little capital or skill beyond that which is acquirable through familiarity with the trade and its members. Low level dealers are not apparently subject to systematic extortion by broad-based criminal syndicates (Reuter *et al.* 1990: 24).

This is so for America as for Britain. Drug markets, it seems are fluid and are made up of many diverse trafficking enterprises that change their modus operandi over time. Of course all are organised, if only to pursue strategies designed to make a profit, collect debts, sell the drugs and keep as far away from the enforcement agencies as possible. But that does not mean being organised in the sense of there being one overarching structure which controls trafficking in Britain.

I noted elsewhere that there were about 4,000 people in Britain able to move quite large quantities of drugs but not all at the same time, and that about 100 gangs were operating in London within the drugs world as reasonably high-level dealers (Bean 1995a). In the absence of any evidence to the contrary, I see no reason to revise these figures. This in contrast to the USA, which has about 200,000 people involved in cocaine retailing, some on a part-time basis (Reuter 2001: 18). Dorn *et al.* (1990) have produced a typology of trafficking firms in Britain which, they suggest, may not be able to represent the fluid nature of the British drug markets but which, they believe, has its merits none the less:

1 Trading charities are enterprises that have an ideological commitment to drugs with profit a secondary motive.
2 Mutual societies are friendship networks of user dealers who support each other and sell or exchange drugs amongst themselves.
3 Sideliners are licit business enterprises that begin to trade in drugs as a sideline.
4 Criminal diversifiers are existing criminal enterprises that diversify into drugs.
5 Opportunistic irregulars are those who get involved in a variety of activities in the irregular economy, including drugs.
6 Retail specialists are those enterprises with a manager who employs others to distribute drugs to users.
7 State-sponsored traders are those enterprises that operate as informers and that continue to trade (see Chapter 8).

Dorn *et al.* look closely at these various organisations and, *inter alia*, conclude that there are many mixed cases which are difficult to classify and that, generally speaking, the amateur trading charities have been replaced by the more overtly criminal elements (*ibid.*: xii–xiv). None the less, this is both an interesting and valuable typology which allows a greater understanding of the way dealing operates.

Whilst there is a considerable literature showing the links between trafficking and organised crime, this is rarely grounded in hard data. A great deal of this literature has been written by law enforcement officials or policy analysts who base their conclusions on an examination of official documents. Almost all that literature concludes that organised crime (including the Mafia, the triads, etc.) is deeply involved in drug trafficking. That involvement is said to be increasing and expected to increase further (European Community 1992).

Of late both the Council of Europe and the European Community have been saying within the framework of TREVI (Terrorism, Radicalism, Extremism and International Violence) that there is an urgent need for more action to deal with organised crime. They retain a strong belief that the interdependence of national economies has helped spawn the growth of multinational crime systems that are becoming difficult to identify and control (Martin and Romano 1992). Moreover, as Europe has a barrier-free style single market, the spectre of criminal organisations without frontiers looms large, and the Mafia (amongst others) is believed to have seen a golden opportunity to extend their influence – even beyond the community to the former Eastern European countries (Reuters News Agency 1993).

There is another literature that links organised crime with terrorist organisations, such as the IRA (Boyce 1987), where drug trafficking provides the money to finance these operations and the drug traffickers use the terrorists to ensure the source of their supply. The end product is social disruption (Sen 1989). One view is that, as the financial rewards of drug trafficking increase, so will drug-related terrorist activities (Langer 1986). Another is that terrorist links are constantly being redefined and new terrorist organisations are being developed. Interpol, for example (ICPO Interpol 1989), draws attention to developments in Africa where heroin from the Indian subcontinent, intended for Europe and North America, is being funnelled through Africa by Nigerian organisations – some of whom are African terrorists.

What remains unclear is how the traffickers and terrorists/organised crime syndicates interact. At what point do they work together and at what point do they part? Boyce (1987), for example, says there do not appear to be links between traffickers and terrorist groups within the USA – although there may be a measure of co-operation before the drugs enter the country. As mentioned earlier, Dorn et al. (1990) say of Britain that there is little direct organised crime linked to trafficking. In contrast, Wardlow (1988) says 'eliminating terrorist links will have little impact on the flow of drugs. Drug connections are established for practical academic reasons rather than ideological ones.' There is a shortage of data on those links. If, as Dorn et al. suggest, drug markets are fluid, then how organised crime syndicates work with terrorist groups (both of whom may also work with local distributors) is an important area for future research.

The extent of anecdotal evidence linking trafficking with organised crime is more than adequate to suggest links exist, are sustained and operate at all levels. What is less clear are the terrorist links. Terrorists avoid publicity: their world is one which thrives on secrecy, ill-informed opinion and as few contacts with law enforcement as possible. Traffickers have no great political conscience about changing the world; their aim is to change their financial position within it. Working with publicity-seeking political ideologues seems not to their liking. And yet anecdotally we are told that trafficking and dealing support terrorist organisations. If so, and there is no reason to believe otherwise given the claims made by journalists and the like, it is important to know the basis and means by which they interact and the manner in which the deals are secured. Is there a go-between and, if so, who would that be? Are contacts made directly to traffickers or are they through national dealers? These are the types of questions that need answering.

Money laundering

The recognition that drugs and money are but two sides of the same coin marked an important change in the way in which traffickers were seen and dealt with. In Britain, the Drug Trafficking Offences Act 1986 (amended by the 1994 Act) introduced detailed provisions for dealing with trafficking, including the introduction of confiscation orders (i.e. based on the older process of forfeiture – depriving traffickers of the proceeds of their crime). Mrs Thatcher, addressing her remarks to traffickers, said on 21 January 1986: 'We are after you. The pursuit will be relentless. The effort will be greater and greater until we have beaten you. The penalty will be by prosecutions. The penalty will be confiscation of everything you have ever gotten from drug smuggling' (*Parl. Debates*: col. 273).

Laundering is defined as the concealment of illicit income and its conversion to other assets so as to disguise its source or use. Laundering for the traffickers is the process used to solve the problems of large amounts of detectable cash arising from sales, which cannot at that stage be declared to the authorities. There is an extensive literature on money laundering but much less on confiscation orders.

The legislation on money laundering is complex and full of difficult moral, jurisprudential and sociological questions. Briefly, the main legislation is the Criminal Justice Act 1993, which amended the Drug Trafficking Offences Act 1986 by inserting into that Act ss. 26(b) and (c) which define the obligations to report money laundering as well as creating a new offence of 'tipping off' money launderers who are being investigated. These sections create new and drastic offences. 'Tipping off' is disclosing to any other person information or any other matter which is likely to prejudice that information (Fortson 1996). This was introduced when police officers found local bank clerks were notifying their investigations to the money launderers. As the police moved in the front door, the teller went out the back and made the phone calls. Hence it is now an offence to 'tip off'.

Section 26(b) places an obligation to report money laundering. It says a person is guilty of an offence if:

(a) he knows or suspects that another person is engaged in drug money laundering,

(b) the information or other matters on which the knowledge or suspicion is based came to the attention in the course of his trade, business, profession or employment, and,

(c) he does not disclose this information or other matter to a constable as soon as is reasonably practical after it comes to his attention.

American legislation imposes a duty on persons to report – in effect to the police – transactions and other information on the basis of suspicion held relevant to a possible contravention of the drug trafficking-legislation. That for England and Wales imposes a duty to report suspicious circumstances related to money laundering, but this applies to all persons and not just to those working in financial institutions. The amount of the transactions about which those in America must report varies, but in some states it is US$10,000 or above.

International co-operation in relation to money laundering is becoming extensive: the 1988 UN Convention against Illicit Traffic in Narcotic Drugs and Psychotropic Substances and the 1990 Council of Europe Convention on Laundering, Search, Seizure or Confiscation of the Proceeds of Crime, as well as the 1991 Council of Europe Directive on Prevention of Use of the Financial System for the Purpose of Money Laundering (Gilmore 1991). Collaboration is seen as essential, given the movement of funds and the complex processes involved in money laundering.

Assistance by way of formal treaty obligations is a major weapon to fight the traffickers. The Financial Action Task Force is a major step forward in this respect (FATF 1990). Article 3 of the UN convention against illicit drugs (1988) requires parties to establish as criminal offences, *inter alia*, the international conversions or transfer of property knowingly derived from production or trafficking for the purpose of concealing or disguising the illicit origin of the property, or assisting any person involved in production to evade the legal consequences of his or her actions. Parties to the convention are required to make laundering drug money a criminal offence. However, there are European countries who have signed but still not ratified the convention, and many Caribbean countries (amongst others) have neither signed nor ratified. Nor has the EC directive on money laundering been enacted in the domestic laws of all community states. The directive requires member states to introduce a mandatory supervision-based reporting regime applicable to all credit and financial institutions (see Gallagher 1990).

The problems about co-operation in the money laundering field are not dissimilar to those relating to policing. One view is that co-operation is largely cosmetic; another is that it is in its early stages and is developing slowly (FATF 1990). As far as providing information is concerned, one of the most important innovations in EC co-operation is the development of the commission's European Monitoring Centre for Drugs and Drug Addiction (EMCDDA). This body has comprehensive documents relating to laundering that involve the powers of the council, the commission, the European Parliament and the courts of justice concerning official discretions, decisions and even the written questions that were asked (European Commission 1993). One of the major problems relating to co-operation at the international level is that money laundering is international in scope. As the EC noted: 'Internationalism of economies and financial services are opportunities which are seized by money launderers to carry out their criminal activities, since the origin of these funds can be better disguised in an international context' (EC *Explanatory Memorandum* I (i), Document E, Chapter IV (ii): 243). The EC (through the Financial Action Task Force) goes on to say, in respect of the problems of co-operation, that:

> Many of the current difficulties in international co-operation in drug money laundering cases are directly or indirectly linked with a strict application of bank secrecy rules with the fact that in many countries money laundering is today not an offence and with insufficiencies in multilateral co-operation and legal assistance. (*ibid*.: Document B, Chapter 1: 14).

This second quotation sums up the major difficulties but, even so, substantial progress has been achieved in a relatively short period of time. Gilmore (1992: xix) argues that 'it is no exaggeration to say that in the area of drug related money laundering the landscape of international co-operation has been radically and positively transformed'.

Others would be less optimistic, pointing to the reluctance of some countries to comply (*ibid*.). By way of illustration, Levi and Osofsky (1995), speaking of the British police, say that their relationships with HM Customs are far from smooth for, among other things, they have different priorities. Customs are concerned with seizures, the police with developing informants (*ibid*.: 40–1). Herein lies the seat of the difficulty for, if co-operation cannot easily take place within national borders, it is even less likely to take place across national borders.

There are a number of bibliographies which include the major national and international declarations – one of the best is that provided by Gilmore (1992). Similarly, there are a number of collections describing the methods and nature of money laundering and the practical ways in which money launderers could be defeated (Gallagher 1990). Apart from international and national co-operation, Parlour (1994), who also includes a review of useful handbooks on the subject, suggests that the methods that seem to be recommended include the following:

1 More staff training to make staff aware of the nature and importance of money laundering.
2 The importance of staff knowing their customers and their customers' backgrounds.

There are also extensive bibliographies on money laundering – the UN in Vienna has one of the best of these.

A great deal of the literature is descriptive, setting out the ways in which money launderers operate and the environments in which laundering flourishes (e.g. poor-quality exchange controls, bank secrecy laws, unregulated casinos and money-changing bureaux, and offshore financial services) which, when combined with minimal disclosure requirements, provide a highly facilitating environment. There are also the beginnings of another literature on the role of the civil courts and what the civil courts could do to trace and recover laundered money, especially where banks are involved in involuntary laundering and the money needs to be traced (Birks 1995).

The money launderer is faced with a central question: how to return the money to the owners of the drugs in a currency that can be used. Or, if not, how to invest it in countries and forms which will produce a safe (i.e. will not be confiscated), legitimate return. Drug trafficking is cash intensive, and increasingly governments aim to confiscate that cash. Typically money laundering goes through three processes. These are placement (which also involves smurfing), layering and finally integration, although in practice there is overlap and the processes are far from discrete.

Placement

Placement involves placing the cash into the major financial institutions of the selected economy. There may be, and often is, an even earlier stage where the money is taken out of one country to be placed in another, but this does not affect the main point that the launderer is seeking to place large quantities of cash into the retail economy. The placement stage for the launderer is the weakest link in the money-laundering chain as it is the point where detection is most likely. Where, as in the USA, there are limits to the amounts of monies that can be deposited in a bank in a single deposit, 'smurfers' deliver the money in amounts of $1 below the legal amount allowed to various banks. Hence a 'smurfer' is someone who conducts financial transactions in sums below the threshold amounts. In one interesting case, a smurfer was caught with a number of caches of monies to be deposited. He told the police, correctly, that the monies did not belong to him. When the police compounded the monies, the smurfer wisely asked for a receipt. He would have to convince his immediate superiors that he had not kept the monies himself.

There are numerous ways in which placements can occur, some more sophisticated than others. The most obvious involves using a form of bank structure which produces bank deposits in such a form as to evade the threshold currency-reporting laws. This involves making numerous deposits in many different banks before bringing them all together in one central bank account. The easiest (as far as the launderer is concerned) is to place all the deposits in one bank with the complicity of a corrupt employee, who will accept the deposit without question or, better still, find a bank whose ethos is corrupt. Alternatively, the launderer could buy into the securities and commodities markets, again with the help of insider traders. Or he or she might purchase large expensive items for cash (such as precious metals, precious stones, works of art, boats or property) or play the casinos in the expectation of winning legitimate money. All these activities are the early stages of a paper trail aimed at disguising the true source of ownership.

Layering

Layering involves separating the illegal proceeds from the source by creating complex layers of financial transactions designed to disguise the audit trail. Once layered into the financial system, detection becomes increasingly difficult. The favoured method is to convert cash into monetary instruments (such as money orders, bonds and stocks) and then move them elsewhere. This allows the use of electronic funds transfers – probably the most important in the layering process as they offer the advantage of speed, distance and increasing anonymity – to move the instruments anywhere in the world. Alternatively, deposits of cash can be converted into material assets which can then be sold or exported and the proceeds held in another form.

Integration

Integration is the final stage in the process where the aim has been to create a paper trail that is increasingly impossible to follow. The methods used will involve the most sophisticated forms of financial transactions, usually through 'shell' companies which trade but which have been set up for the purpose of acting as a front. The launderer may even pay tax using bank cheques drawn on the company's account. Shell companies can also be used, say, to buy and sell property that eventually leads to a sale which appears to legitimise the company's funds. False import and export invoices are used in other transactions, where the documents overvalue the transactions. Most of all, were the launderers to get the help of a bank with secrecy laws able to protect the launderer, this bank would be the focal point of all transactions.

These are but a small number of examples of what has become a highly specialised form of criminality, yet they demonstrate the range of the laundering activities undertaken. The destructive nature of money laundering shows itself whenever a small company is taken over by launderers and converted to their aims. So imagine a small company that is trading as a boatyard, making, selling and repairing boats. This is bought up by launderers and listed as one of their companies. It then has a slow but increasing amount of laundered cash passed through its books and, on the face of it, it appears to be a wealthy company growing at an exponential rate. But in fact the lifeblood of the company has been drained away, and it has become nothing more than a route of convenience for vast sums of laundered money produced elsewhere. Here is where the impact of money laundering is important; it might not be economically destructive in the whole scheme of things – it is just one company after all – but multiply this a number of times, especially in Third World countries, and it becomes a different matter. The means by which laundering distorts economic activity is beginning to be well understood; the difficulty is to get key organisations, such as banks and professional organisations, to co-operate.

Whilst the methods involved in laundering are interesting in themselves, the implications of attempts to control money laundering are sometimes forgotten. The study by Mike Levi (1991) is a notable exception. Levi analysed the development of police–bank relationships, principally in the UK but also elsewhere within the context of money laundering. He found that we have moved from a situation of national control over bank secrecy to an emerging new international order in which most, though not all, countries are pressurised into taking greater measures to reduce bank secrecy where money laundering is suspected.

In Europe banks are being turned into an arm of the state: they are required to keep detailed records and to inform the police where they suspect, or even where they ought to suspect, that monies banked are the proceeds of crime. It is difficult not to conclude that there is a surfeit of material on how to deal with money laundering but a shortage of material such as that produced by Levi on the implications.

Confiscation orders

The literature on confiscation orders is slim by comparison, yet claiming and recovering the proceeds of drug dealing are as important as developing strategies for dealing with money laundering. Surprisingly, confiscation orders have received little attention from philosophers of punishment (Levi and Osofsky 1995). Generally speaking the justification for confiscation is cited as a way of compensating society for behaviour that is socially unacceptable (Mitchell *et al*. 1992; Bin-Salama 1996), but this cannot be the sole reason.

If conversations with high-level drug dealers are anything to go by, the confiscation order is what they fear the most. They say they can do the 'time' even if it amounts to a long sentence of eight years or more, but what they dislike the most is where, for example, their wives and children have to leave their leafy, wooded, five-bedroomed suburban houses and their children are taken from private schools and sent to comprehensive schools with the family living in local authority accommodation. If that is so, and it is said too often to suggest otherwise, we need to pay more attention to the powers and impact of confiscation orders and use them more vigorously.

However, there are important issues raised by the legislation on confiscation orders, some of which are jurisprudential and others more directly related to social science. Critics of confiscation orders point to the dangers of allowing courts to seize property without what is referred to as the 'due process of law' – for in this case the courts have considerable discretionary powers in the making of an order (Levi and Osofsky 1995). The social science questions are more about the impact of this legislation on the drug dealers, but they are also about the way in which the property is collected. For example, there is a wide discrepancy between the assets restrained by the court and the amount collected. Under the Criminal Justice Act 1988, the total assets restrained as of 31 December 1994 were £9,258,742 but the assets confiscated amounted only to £527,419. Or again, under the Drug Trafficking Act 1994, the total assets restrained as of 31 December 1995 were £3,815,707.75, but the assets confiscated were only £795,451.74 (Confiscation Statistics 1995). The figures for 2000 for England and Wales show that 334 prosecutions were made against 550 defendants. The total assets recovered on which there are restraining orders amounted to £15.5 million, whilst during that year assets totalling £10.0 million were collected.

The Drug Trafficking Act 1994 and Part VI of the Criminal Justice Act 1988 (as amended by the Powers of Criminal Courts Act 1995) give the Crown Court powers to make a confiscation order. A confiscation order is an order made against a convicted defendant ordering him or her to pay the amount of his or her benefit from crime. Unlike a forfeiture order, a confiscation order is not directed at a particular asset. It does not deprive the defendant (or anyone else to title) of the property. The legislation gives law enforcement authority to investigate, and the Drug Trafficking Offences Act 1994 gives them the tools to do it. (The Proceeds of Crime Act 1995 slightly amends the investigative process.) The Central Confiscation Bureau division of the Crown Prosecution Service (CPS) operates the system and, once an order is made, the CPS hands details over to the local financial investigation officer, usually a detective constable whose task it is to collect the assets. One of the reasons there has been an improvement in such orders is that these financial investigation officers are better trained than hitherto; earlier the task was given to a police constable, who was told simply to get on with it (Bin-Salama 1996). There is still the problem of motivating the police to be more enthusiastic. It seems the CPS loses interest once they pass the information over to the police, and the police see asset collection as another burden placed upon them. There would be an even greater incentive if the police were allowed to use the money collected for law enforcement and research purposes, as happens in America.

The number of confiscation orders in England and Wales rose from 870 in 1990 to 1,560 in 1995, but has since fallen to 840 in 2000. With a total value of about £5 million in 2000, they were made in 13% of eligible offences, half the level of that in 1995 (25%). Confiscation orders were introduced in Scotland in 1988. In 2000–1, only 12 orders were made valued at £117,300; this was compared with 17 orders made in the previous year with a value of £822,700. There were no confiscation orders in Northern Ireland until the middle of 1991. Only two orders were made in 2000 with a value of £68,000, compared with four orders in 1999 with a value of £149,359, and two orders in 1998 for a value of £94,800.

Whilst the overall trend in the number of orders was upwards (in 1990 there were 871 orders and in 1995 1,562), between 1997 and 2000 there was a substantial fall in the number and value of orders made. The amounts also varied. For example, the exceptionally high figure of £25.4

million in 1994 for England and Wales included a single order for the confiscation of £15.3 million (Corkery 2002). The important data that are missing, however, relate to the amount seized. These data are not available. It is all very well making orders, but if they are not put into practice their value diminishes. And, as said above, confiscation orders are what the drug traffickers like the least.

Under Part II of the Drug Trafficking Act 1994, a Customs or police officer can seize money that is being imported or exported where there are reasonable grounds to suspect that it is connected to drug trafficking. There were 45 such confiscation orders made with a value of £3.5 million in 2000–1. The value of drugs money forfeiture orders brought to account by Customs in 2000–1 was £3.1 million; the value of payments made against such orders in the same period was £3.9 million. The payments made may relate to orders issued up to several years previously.

Chapter 7

Policing drug markets

Policing policy

In so far as there is, or ever has been, a policy for policing drugs in Britain, that policy was derived from the Broome Report of 1985 (ACPO 1985). That report set out the structure for tackling the supply and distribution of drugs. There was to be a three-tier strategy:

1 Regional crime squads addressing the major distributions and operations at a national and sometimes international level.
2 Force drug squads targeting middle-level dealers and co-ordinating force intelligence on drugs.
3 Divisional-level officers who would encounter drug suppliers and users in the normal course of their duties.

The Advisory Council on the Misuse of Drugs (ACMD 1994) noted that, within the Broome structure, the police were responsible for deciding how drug misuse and trafficking should best be tackled, presumably within force areas and according to local conditions. At the upper level the police, working alongside HM Customs, would be concerned with international crime, the international trafficker and the high-level national dealer. Middle-level enforcement, according to Broome, was to be directed at the organisation responsible for trafficking within national boundaries. In the British case, this would be by the drug squads. Lower-level enforcement would be by uniformed street patrol officers. The former would be concerned with getting the so-called 'Mr Bigs'; the lower levels would be concerned with street dealers. The ACMD also noted that concerted action (other than at the upper level) was regarded as relatively unimportant (*ibid.*: 12).

The Broome strategy was based on the belief that drug markets operated according to a model derived from a police officer's view of the structure and importance of policing (i.e. allowing the most important traffickers to be dealt with by the most important police officers, the less important with the less important officers and so on). Clearly, the model was flawed in that there was no evidence that traffickers worked that way but, worse, it had a detrimental impact on the drug problem in Britain during its critical formative years. Street drug markets were allowed to develop and grow and, once established, are difficult to remove. The Broome model has now been discarded but not before much damage was done. It has been replaced by other models which direct attention at the low-level street markets, for these are where the drugs are sold to the consumer and where novices are recruited, whether as users or dealers.

Drug markets generally

Drug markets have certain common features. Irrespective of the size or location of the market, drugs are bought and sold like all other commodities, that is there is nothing unique or special about drugs. There are, of course, differences. Unlike most other commodities, drug markets are characterised by a high degree of immeasurable risk, by the inability to enforce contracts in a court of law and by poor information about the product (Rydell *et al.* 1996). Nevertheless, they are markets with buyers and sellers and, as with other markets, subject to the basic economic laws of supply and demand.

Within those markets dealers have to secure financial transactions in a crooked world with no one else to enforce contracts. They are always vulnerable to theft and violence by greedy business associates. Protecting their transactions takes up much of their time (Bean 1995a). Most will find it necessary to employ those who are familiar with intimidation and violence or, if not, then make themselves comfortable with the violence to collect debts and enforce discipline. In Britain, Dorn *et al.* (1992) describe how a new breed of criminal was attracted to the drugs world where violence was an essential part of their worldview. Whether this really was a new breed or simply an old breed with a previous history of violence attracted by the possibility of a share in the increasingly extensive profits is not known. Whatever the reason, the overall effect is to make drug markets violent places where those working in them become more frightened of other dealers than of the police. They operate in a Hobbesian world where no rules or guidelines exist, except those made by themselves to serve their own interests. The problem is that, once initiated into this world, it becomes difficult for them to accept any other.

The lack of skills required to enter as an entrepreneur and the ease of transportation of the high-profit commodity are likely to be attractive. In broad outline, the drug market, like all other markets, works on credit – that is, the beginner is granted credit at a certain level of interest and expected to pay back the debt within a given period of time. Failure to do so will mean certain punishment. Within this general framework there will be considerable variations in terms of the social class of the sellers, the venue and the range of credit facilities. However, the demand for repayment does not vary. Nor do the punishments for those who default.

Higher-level dealers are increasingly involved with or are part of organised crime. In Britain, this means traditional organised crime syndicates but, increasingly, includes others bound up with ethnic or local groups. For example, Turkish organised crime syndicates (who also control the major distribution networks in kebab houses) increasingly dominate the heroin trade in Britain. They have links with British nationals of Turkish origin. These organisations are difficult to penetrate as they remain part of a close-knit community trading only with others of the same nationality and background. The NCIS has a Turkish Intelligence Unit to combat heroin trafficking. This provides a co-ordination point for intelligence related to Turkish heroin trafficking in and outside the UK (NCIS Annual Report 1999–2000: 25). Triads and Mafia-type organisations are well represented amongst the high-level dealers so that, in August 1999, the Cocaine Intelligence Unit was formed by NCIS to provide an overview of cocaine trafficking within the UK (*ibid.*: 26).

There are few data on the links between these higher-level dealers and those of the streets. In America they talk of 'kingpins' who are senior local dealers who presumably make that connection. Research is needed in Britain to establish those links. It is suspected that there will be marked variations between drugs and organisations. For example, Turkish importers may also be the distributors, controlling the market at all stages. In contrast, the cocaine importers may not be concerned with distribution and hand this over to local 'kingpins'. But this is all speculation; we simply do not know.

At the lower levels dealing will differ again according to the drug, although some dealers are poly-dealers willing and able to sell anything. Cannabis is typically bought and sold from individuals who come from a broad range of backgrounds and in a wide variety of settings, from inner-city areas to middle-class institutions. Dealing tends to cover a wide range of socioeconomic groups, as it does for ecstasy, where consumption is more typically at raves or clubs (i.e. where the drugs are taken by teenagers who may be occasional rather than heavy users). Heroin, on the other hand, is very much a street drug although, as with all others, the situation changes daily so that what is typical for today is highly unusual for tomorrow. Even so, at the lowest end of the market, heroin will be bought and sold by users for whom the sale is less important as a method of generating cash than as a source for personal use. Here, the typical street seller is a user who buys an amount and uses a quantity before selling the surplus to others. Next day, he or she might well buy back that surplus, paying more for it than he or she sold it for. At the higher end the dealer will not be a user.

Cocaine sales differ again. Unlike heroin, there is a substantial middle-class demand for the drug – the income from those users coming largely from legitimate sources. The prevalence of cocaine use is growing. Heroin use remains more static even if its use increases in fits and starts. Like cannabis, cocaine is bought and sold in a variety of social settings. For example, cocaine creates a demand from some who may use relatively large quantities (*ibid.*: 17). Wealthy experienced users purchase relatively large amounts in discreet transactions, usually in London (Bean 1995a), whilst new, relatively poor users operate at street level. Cocaine has become deeply embedded into a black ethnic cultural group where its effects on the black community have been destructive. Cocaine is not, of course, confined to the black community: white users vastly outnumber black users but, from our research, its impact on the black community was particularly destructive (*ibid.*).

Cocaine is usually, but not exclusively, bought and sold where poverty and other social problems are common, and in this sense has much in common with heroin. In America, Inciardi and Pottieger (1995) found that street-level cocaine dealers were deeply involved in crime – in fact, the greater the level of crack distribution, the greater the level of other crime commission (p. 251). They concluded that 'young crack dealers commonly violate not merely drug laws but also those protecting persons and property; and the crack business appears criminogenic in ways that go beyond any potential it may have as a lure into crime' (*ibid.*: 253). This Miami study shows crack dealers as a separate and distinct group from heroin dealers; it is not certain whether this applies to Britain.

Drug markets are wider and involve more than those who buy and sell drugs. They extend into the local community where others benefit.

Rarely do the major profits remain locally. Once drug markets become organised, the profits are taken out of the area. None the less, some money is circulated locally and it is this which helps sustain the local drug community. In our research (Bean 1994) we found that one of the reasons some of the local population did not oppose the drug (cocaine) market was that it helped prop up a poor inner-city area. Derelict premises were let out to rent for use by prostitutes, poor-quality fast-food outlets remained open all hours, etc. However, the majority of the local population benefit only marginally, if at all, and any disadvantages greatly outweigh the advantages (i.e. where there is harassment from prostitutes, litter of the very worst kind and street-level dealers operating in front of young children in the neighbourhood). Drug markets are not pleasant places to have in one's neighbourhood. If and when a closer examination is made of the extent of the tentacles of drug markets, we may find they are even more embedded into the local economy than we thought. If so, we ought not to be surprised; after all, at the macro level drug money extends into all aspects of some national economies, so why not at the micro level too?

The impact of policing

Policing aimed at taking out the 'Mr Bigs' has been a major part of the strategy of law enforcement. It fits easily into the traditional notion of policing as 'chase and capture'. It was the dominant philosophy of the Broome Report, where the best police would chase and capture the best criminals, the less competent chase and capture the less competent and the least competent chase and capture the least competent. This type of strategy flourishes because capturing the 'Mr Bigs' also fits with the demands of police performance indicators, which are aimed at achieving targets based on the number of arrests. They deem it to be more worthy to arrest a dealer than to prevent a number of potential users from making a purchase.

The problem is that, when caught, the Mr Bigs are quickly replaced by other Mr Bigs waiting to take over, or the captured Mr Bigs run the operations from prison. Targeting Mr Big has less impact than the police would have us believe. In the major King's Cross project, a number of Mr Bigs were arrested. It was noted how quickly they were replaced, and how little time it took for levels of dealing to return to the same as before. Arresting key offenders may satisfy the requirements of justice but it does little to ease the drug problem, whether by assisting neighbourhood protection or reducing the amounts of drugs or numbers of drug users in the vicinity. Kleiman and Smith (1990: 84) ask: 'what essential service does Mr Big provide to the retail dealer that someone else will not supply just as well if he is made to disappear?' Their answer is that the basic financial and personnel management skills needed to run a drugs operation are not in short supply, no long apprenticeships are required and new organisations can quickly take up any supply shortages created by the loss of one Mr Big (*ibid.*: 83).

To make inroads into drug markets, we need greater investigative capabilities than are currently being used, including greater co-ordination between the investigators. The challenge may be technical but it is also about style and attitude: it is about using intelligence and combining this with high-quality research on the effectiveness of police operations. It is a salutary reminder that little research is available on the effectiveness of policing – except, of course, that related to partnerships, and even then it is small and directed at one or two high-profile operations. One of the few British studies that was conducted (by Webster *et al.* 2001) was at the request of the Metropolitan Police as part of their 'Operation Crackdown'. This was directed mainly at crack houses in the London Metropolitan District. It concluded that the impact on local drug markets appears to be limited: there was little discernible added difficulty in obtaining Class A drugs and no change in the local price. The authors go on to say: 'Several street markets were disrupted although in some cases for a relatively short period of time. Although over 80 crack houses were disrupted our best guess is that most relocated or re-opened at the same premises within a very short period of time, weeks rather than months' (*ibid.*: ii).

Perhaps a better way to start is to begin by asking: what is policing trying to achieve? Kleiman and Smith (1990: 71) say there are four main objectives to policing:

1 Limiting the number of persons who use various illicit drugs and the damage suffered as a result – psychological, physical, moral, etc.

2 Reducing the violence connected with drug dealing and the property and violent crimes committed by users, whether to obtain money for drugs or as a result of that intoxication.

3 Preventing the growth of stable, wealthy, powerful criminal organisations.

4 Protecting the civility of neighbourhoods, and thus their attractive-ness as places to work and live, from the disorder caused by drug dealing, open or otherwise.

To achieve these aims, various types of police operations are available. Three will be examined here: street sweeping, focused crackdowns and disruption with or without partnerships. This is not the complete list. Undercover work is not included and, of course, the use of informers remains central to all policing (see Chapter 8). None the less, these three provide the major models. Nor are they mutually exclusive; modern police tactics may involve all at some stage or at various points of an operation, and/or any mixture of these, plus the use of undercover, etc.

Street sweeping

Street sweeping involves what it says: a massive police presence concentrating on a specific area, ideally operating 24 hours a day. Normally, drug dealers tend not to work the same hours as most police officers. This seems such an obvious point as not to be worth making, but Kleiman and Smith say it is surprising how many police authorities seem not to notice this. Street sweeping is similar to zero tolerance policing in that, whilst the streets are being swept, all suspects are scooped up into the net. Large numbers are stopped and searched, and all laws (however small and insignificant) are enforced, with search warrants to deal with premises in which the police suspect there is drug dealing. Street sweeping, according to Kleiman and Smith, serves all the four goals of law enforcement in that it reduces drug use, reduces crime, weakens drug-dealing organisations and protects neighbourhoods.

It is, of course, not without its weaknesses. Street sweeping closely resembles an army of occupation rather than policing by consent. It produces tensions on the streets, is more expensive (police forces have to work within budgets) and raises ethical questions about being too concerned with 'victims' rather than those who are responsible for maintaining the vitality of drug markets (Dorn and Murji 1992). The tensions might be about stop and search, for which there is increasing criticism, especially following the MacPherson Report on the death of Stephen Lawrence. Stop and search is often seen as having less to do with policing and more to do with asserting a form of dominance by the police over a local population or over specific groups within that population. Street sweeping produces an enormous number of arrests, many for minor offences. However, the gains it might achieve from reducing the size of the drug market will be offset by resentment from an otherwise law-abiding population caught up in the street sweeping and prosecuted for minor offences. The police are as likely to be accused of harassment as to be thanked for their efforts. The drug market will likely reappear when the period of street sweeping ends.

Focused crackdowns

Focused crackdowns differ from street sweeping in that they concentrate on specific drugs, on specific streets or on specific features of the market, such as crack houses or clubs and pubs. Kleiman and Smith (1990: 89) say that eliminating drug dealing in one infested neighbourhood and thus creating an area where people feel safe may be more valuable than reducing drug activity by 10% in each of ten drug-infested neighbourhoods. They see focused crackdowns as providing the ideal strategy. The police move slowly from neighbourhood to neighbourhood leaving behind vigilant citizens and the minimum markets small enough to be controlled with residual enforcement efforts. Focused crackdowns can concentrate on a small area. In Nottingham, for example, there are two main areas where drug markets flourish. These could be dealt with by a focused crackdown, or the police could concentrate on one drug (say, crack), which is sold in a different part of the drug market and by different dealers. Or again they could concentrate on ecstasy, which is sold in yet a different part of the city. Focused crackdowns are likely to have stronger public support than street sweeping because the police are seen to be tackling a particular problem and a particular group rather than including everyone in their net. A focused crackdown in an area of Nottingham in the autumn of 2000 which had been plagued by firearms was given considerable public and media support. The police, after they arrested a number of dealers who had firearms, were applauded by the residents for their efforts. Operation Crackdown in the Metropolitan District is another example of a focused crackdown.

Like street sweeping, focused crackdowns are not without their problems. Dealers are likely to reappear when the crackdown is over, for they know that crackdowns do not last for ever. For them, keeping a low profile during this period is likely to be productive. Or displacement may occur: the dealers move elsewhere, again until the heat is off. Police departments have limited resources, and there are other areas to cover. It becomes a matter of attrition for the dealers and for others who wait until the police leave before they re-emerge. However, Webster *et al.* (2001) saw a positive side to this. It had an impact on community safety and, in particular, on local residents. They cite a drug agency manager as saying: 'Since the implementation of crackdown the initiative has been widely endorsed by the community. [To] a large extent Operation Crackdown is beginning to restore confidence in the police.'

Disruption, or low-level policing

Disruption, or low-level policing, is about policing street dealers and markets. The Broome Report wanted this lowest level to be policed by officers who encountered drug misusers in the normal course of their duties – that is, by ordinary beat officers with little or no experience in drug dealing. This was never likely to be successful; dealing may take place on the street but the dealers rarely carry the drugs with them, leaving it to the 'stashers' and 'runners' to make the delivery. Nor does it make the best use of one of the police's main weapons – to make life more difficult for the would-be buyers and sellers. As one chief constable said:

> The policeman's biggest weapon is inconvenience, not arresting people. Some people call it harassing. But there is no way we could do our job without occasionally having to inconvenience people. If it's just to stop and ask questions that's an inconvenience (cited in Dorn and Murji 1992: 163).

Low-level policing aims at creating 'inconvenience' by disrupting drug markets. Unless dealers and sellers are disrupted, drug markets become difficult to dislodge and, once embedded, they push the local community deeper into that world of drugs. After years of Broome there is a growing recognition that street-level policing is important and has merits in its own right. The ACPO Drugs Subcommittee, in its response to the ACMD Report (1994), talks of a 'bottoms up' approach which presumably means concentrating more resources to identify low-level dealers and traffickers. Dorn and Murji (1992: 169) in an evaluation of street-level policing, say:

> At its most positive street [low-level policing] could be an area which holds the key not to simply the ways of reducing the extent of drug trafficking and use, but also to the quality of life of many people whose daily lives are affected by the spread of drug sellers and drug users in their neighbourhoods.

Low-level policing is about making drug dealers aware of a police presence. From my experience, dealers are more frightened of other dealers than of the police, for they rarely see the police. If low-level policing means moving dealers to a different site, displacing them, then so be it. This is an advance; it means the new site is likely to be second best as far as the dealers are concerned – otherwise they would have selected it as their favoured site – and it means that it will take time to re-establish contacts. Dealing is also about creating an atmosphere of trust, which means trust in the security of the deal as well as the quality of the drug. Low-level policing helps destroy that trust and makes the drug market less secure for those operating within it. The weakness of the Broome Report is that it was too keen to chase and capture the Mr Bigs.

Another advantage of low-level policing is that it helps keep away the novice and casual user. If the drug market is unsafe, and the point at which drugs are sold is the most vulnerable for the dealer, then uncertainty will be created, and uncertainty works against the dealer. Novices expect to be guaranteed their protection; markets that are always on the move convey a measure of insecurity which makes life difficult for the dealers. No one is suggesting that these measures solve the problem, but they do offer a more coherent approach than chasing high-level dealers, busting them and then chasing their replacements. Low-level policing provides an opportunity to frustrate dealers which, in turn, puts up the costs of drugs by forcing them to incur additional overheads, and it makes their dealing more furtive and therefore less satisfying to the customer. A uniformed police presence, posted strategically in the middle of the drug market, may be all that is required. This, incidentally, is also likely to act as a reassuring sign to the local population that something is being done.

Street-level policing, at its best, would include the partnership approach. This would involve local agencies, the local community (including local government), the media (the media can, incidentally, build or quickly destroy attempts at producing partnerships) and others. Street-level policing involving partnerships is one of the most important developments in the move against drug markets and crime. Where they exist they have been shown to be successful (Home Office 1993). They challenge basic assumptions derived from the professionals' traditional view that an agency – usually their own – can have an impact on crime. In contrast, joint agency working is the key: the partnership model challenges the assumption that a single agency approach has an impact. The police can no more cope with drug dealing by arresting the dealers (others quickly take their place) than can the Probation Service by providing counselling. The way forward can only be by drawing all interested parties together although, for practical purposes, the police must always have the major input (*ibid.*).

There is little doubt that, in the development of partnerships, there exists a potent weapon against local drug markets. Partnerships, which received legal impetus from the Crime and Disorder Act 1997, remain underdeveloped and under-researched. The Home Office (*ibid.*: 1) puts it this way:

Many of the measures that contribute to prevention are not within the remit of any one agency. Prevention thus depends on action by many different agencies and this will be most effective when co-ordinated by a formal partnership. Such partnerships can share and mobilise resources, generate commitment and enable the contribution of individual agencies to be targeted to best effect. They are most successful when served by one or more dedicated staff skilled in developing proposals and implementing action.

There is clearly a need to develop the partnership approach and a need to evaluate the partnerships that are being undertaken. The difficulties are immense: getting the partnerships going, agreeing on a common approach and, above all, deciding when the project is to be ended. The starting point must be a shared agenda involving a common under-standing of the philosophies underlying the work of different agencies. For example, the police's experience and perception of drug users may not correspond to that of the local residents or traders – the police are always concerned with Mr Big and the residents with the low-level drug sellers. Moreover, probation officers see a conflict of interest between their wish to rehabilitate offenders and the public desire to move drug users out of the area. It is this lack of fit between the agencies that creates the most difficulties.

Critics of partnerships always point to the way partnerships displace drug dealing to new geographical areas and question the levels of community safety during and after the project. They question, too, the value of the changes that can be made to the nature of drug markets as a result of the partnership approach. These criticisms are predictable; whenever a crime reduction project is claimed to be successful, there will always be critics who raise the question of displacement. That should not detract from the message that the partnership approach, where it has been properly implemented, is a potent weapon against drug markets. It demonstrates that there is nothing inevitable about drug markets, that they can be controlled and that something can be done about them.

The King's Cross project (the results of which are largely unpublished) is a beacon of its kind. There, the local community drug markets were seen as disturbing and distasteful, bringing in crime (usually prosti-tution) and littering the streets with discarded syringes. King's Cross is an area in London where large populations pass through each day. It is also characterised by a vigorous local population who demanded action. The result was a programme which began with the simple but somewhat radical assumption that a partnership approach was called for, and that no single agency could deal with the problem on its own. Community responses demanded a co-ordinated effort between various bodies, leading to a partnership defined as 'an association between a number of individuals groups or agencies to pursue a common goal' (Lightfoot 1994).

Briefly, the King's Cross project involved the police, the local authority (although, in fact, there are four local authorities abutting King's Cross), a representative of the local community and voluntary associations. The police had the largest presence, but they soon found the local authorities had more powers. The local authorities could close down hotels, move bus shelters (where dealers were hiding to make the sell) and close all-night fast-food outlets. However, the biggest problem was to get agreement about policies, about which way to move forward and how to represent the interests of the local population. The tactic was to decide on a strategy, make the move, and (say) arrest all the major dealers, then watch to see how long it took to replace them. Or they could arrest the non-drug-taking, daytime prostitutes and then measure the local reaction; then move to the next strategic point and evaluate that, and so on. The result was a highly successful project, albeit an expensive one where major lessons were learnt. One of these lessons for the police officers was that a good day did not mean the 'bust' of a main dealer, but that success meant dealers were not able to sell their drugs.

Low-level policing meets the four criteria set out above: it limits the number of people using drugs, reduces the violence in the drug markets, prevents the growth of stable criminal organisations and protects the civility of the neighbourhood. Or at least these were the results from King's Cross. The problem is that our conclusions are based on one project which may not be typical, and it may not be possible to replicate it. We need more projects of this type and more evaluations to show how best to proceed.

Assessing the effectiveness of policing

In Britain, economists such as Wagstaff and Maynard (Wagstaff and Maynard 1988; Wagstaff 1989) have asked questions about the extent and the costs of resources used by the enforcement agencies devoted to drug work and the corresponding effect enforcement has on prices at each level of the illicit drug market, as well as the operation of these markets. Studies building on this type of research are to be welcomed. Reuter *et al.* (1990: 20) put it this way: 'That drug markets vary a great deal across drugs and over time points to the need for a theory of how these markets function – in particular a theory of what determines who enters the market and how much such persons earn for participation.'

Reuter and Kleiman (1986) talk of a theory based on risks, when risks affect prices. We do not know, for example, how many successful deals are completed and the risks dealers carry. It is likely that about one deal in every 80 or 100 leads to an arrest, and this irrespective of the type of drug sold. If that is so, what effect has it on dealers and prices if one in 40 deals led to an arrest, or one in 20, or even one in ten? How much extra policing would be required to change the ratio of successful deals, and would the costs be worth it? What are the effects of putting dealers in prison? Typically, the answer has been, not a lot, yet Reuter (2001) says that, paradoxically the effect on reducing demand may be greater than on reducing supply, if only because 'It's hard to replace old junkies' who consume quite large quantities of drugs.

We have learnt much from the Broome days which typified what Kleiman and Smith refer to in another context as a collection of activities in search of a strategy (1990: 104). Recent developments in London show that the Metropolitan Police have learnt the value of disruption and of low-level policing. As part of this they distribute leaflets to householders giving details of the latest arrests and explaining their tactics and the nature and extent of local policing strategies. The aim is to unsettle the dealers and not allow them to take the initiative. Policing by disruption is to be preferred to sitting back and allowing the dealers to set their pace. Kleiman and Smith (*ibid.*: 102) go on to say:

> In principle the right way to choose a drug policy for a city would be to describe the problem, invent some alternative approaches to addressing the problem, predict the costs and the likely results of each approach, and choose the least painful. Then after a while measure the results and compare them with the predictions. Unexpected results or new situations would call for changes in policy.

They added that no police force has anything resembling an accurate description of the drug problem, and nor is there a well worked out body of theory or experience to allow predictions of the likely results of alternative approaches (*ibid.*: 102). The best that can be done is to have as many data available as possible on users and sellers from the top right down to the street level. Then and only then can a measure be made of the impact of enforcement.

We know something of effect the police have in dealing with the drug problem but not much. A study of the Metropolitan Police's Operation Crackdown, which resulted in 1,600 arrests, produced some early but, albeit not too encouraging, results (Webster *et al.* 2001). In spite of the large number of arrests the impact on local drug markets appeared to be limited, with little discernible added difficulty in obtaining Class A drugs (cocaine, heroin) and no change in local price. Moreover, some police officers believed that the diversion of police officers to Operation Crackdown permitted an increase in other street robberies although, where local street robberies were directly related to local crack sales, there had been a reduction in these.

At least this crackdown showed the police as 'doing something' – not always 'being on the back foot', as it were. But more is required. Modern policing is, or should be, data led, for, without an understanding of the nature and extent of the problem, it is difficult to see how policies can be constructed. Also, without agreed definitions comparisons are difficult. In a visit to London in 2002, Mayor Guiliani said the most important lesson under his administration was the accurate appraisal of crime statistics. He said that under Compstat (a project in New York concerned with crime reduction, including drug use) he received weekly crime statistics for every precinct in the city, broken down into daily statistics. This is in sharp contrast to the Metropolitan Police Service, which publishes crime statistics only quarterly (Livingstone, cited in *The Times* 23 March 2002) (Thames Valley Police now use Compstat).

There are many reasons why the British police seem not to be 'data led' in the way they are in New York. One is the absence of an empirical tradition in British policing. Experience, intuition and an over-reliance on traditional methods remain dominant. In order to produce better models, we need better data to inform them (Kleiman and Smith 1990: 103). One way to start would be to collect more information about drug enforcement, which includes data on the number of users, the number of sellers, police operational practices, police tactics, etc. That, as Kleiman and Smith (*ibid.*: 104) say, would suggest a new seriousness about developing responses to the drug problem. It means producing a valid and reliable database. From there we could move forward.

Policing professional organisations

There are many ways in which professional organisations police their members. The most obvious is where the organisation or professional body requires its members to conform to certain professional standards. Failure to meet those standards can result in removal from the register of that professional organisation and the corresponding loss of all rights and privileges registration confers. Another method is where the government demands of professional bodies that they require their members to abide by certain rules and practices it may from time to time stipulate.

The first is the more common. For example, the General Medical Council will discipline members who take such substances as morphine or who have an alcohol problem. If such physicians prescribe for themselves or their families or over-prescribe for their patients, they could be referred to the Professional Conduct Committee of the General Medical Council who may decide to remove them or 'strike them off the register'. The activities of these physicians (though important in medical practice in general) do not greatly affect the drug problem – although over-prescribing must always be a matter of concern. Of greater importance as far as policing is concerned are the stipulations of government directed towards professional bodies.

Under the money-laundering regulations, financial institutions (including professional financial operations as in law and accountancy) are required to disclose to the police, and eventually to the Economic Crime Unit (ECU) of the National Criminal Intelligence Service (NCIS), all transactions which are suspected to involve drug trafficking. English legislation imposes a duty to report suspicious circumstances relating to money laundering, and this applies to all persons not just to those working in financial institutions. These data are analysed by NCIS and disseminated to the relevant financial investigation units. In practice this means that each police authority will be required to act on the information provided, although how and to what extent priority is given to this information is another matter. Nevertheless, although there is a duty on all persons to give the required information, in reality those at the forefront will be the professionals, lawyers, accountants, etc.

Traffickers, in addition to using the latest technology, also use – and can afford to use – the most highly paid lawyers, accountants, bankers, etc., to provide them with the appropriate expertise. These professionals give the traffickers financial advice relating to investments, the setting up of shell companies, etc. They also help traffickers avoid detection (US Treasury Department 1992). Money laundering (and all that is associated with it) is almost wholly dependent on these professional advisers. Professional privilege and confidentiality help sustain and support the activities of these professionals, with little interference if any from the appropriate professional bodies, or so it seems from the official figures.

Recruitment of these professionals into the world of trafficking seems fairly common – or, if not, then sufficient to continue to service the drug trade. Like so much else in the field, one can only speculate on matters as there is little or no research evidence upon which to draw. Recruitment of these experts is probably achieved when an able lawyer or accountant finds his or her business failing or is unable to provide for his or her own expensive lifestyle. This sort of professional becomes an easy target and, as with corrupt police officers, once recruited is unlikely to break free, at least until he or she ceases to be of value to those who recruited him or her. It probably costs the traffickers and dealers little to recruit such people: a one-off payment to remove existing debts and a foreign holiday might perhaps be sufficient. The traffickers would, of course, still pay for any subsequent professional services undertaken but their rewards would, none the less, be huge. As noted in the 1992 US Treasury Department report on money laundering: 'among law enforcement representatives, there was almost universal presumption that traffickers and cartel money launderers can usually afford to hire the best lawyers, accountants, etc., an advantage which provides them with additional sources of expertise' (*ibid.*: para 1002: 291).

Or as the former US Attorney General Meese said: 'It takes a professional – lawyer, an accountant, a banker with all the trappings of respectability – to manipulate these sophisticated schemes' (cited in Beare 1995).

'Manipulation' in this context also means defending the suspects when charged. Beare and Schneider (1990) list some of the services provided by these professionals:

- Providing a nominee function.
- Incorporating companies.
- Conducting commercial and financial transactions.
- Managing and physically handling illicit cash.
- Co-ordinating international transactions.
- Buying and selling property.

The special privileges granted to lawyers, seen as necessary to protect the lawyer–client relationship, act as a shield and barrier when they engage in criminal activities (*ibid.*: 331). Less so for accountants and bankers, but even here these professions have jealously guarded their client relationships, and attempts to intrude have met with resistance from the governing bodies. In the USA lawyers are required to notify the Revenue Service about their clients. This stipulation has been vigorously resisted, being seen as a step towards greater outside regulation of the profession which, incidentally, the lawyers claimed violated their attorney–client privileges. The US President's Commission on Organised Crime asked for more 'stings' and electronic devices to break even further through that otherwise impenetrable shield.

In comparison, professionals in Britain have escaped lightly. The major professions involved (law and accountancy) have successfully avoided outside regulation and clearly want to keep it that way. The

British government sees the solution as lying within the professions' own governing bodies: the Law Society, the Institute of Chartered Accountants and the like. These bodies have considerable powers and could exert considerable influence. In Canada, for instance, the Canadian Law Society have been particularly active in this respect and are a beacon when it comes to assisting with money-laundering regulations. In contrast their British counterparts have been reluctant to assist, and the lawyers and accountants co-operate rather less than they ought, at least if Table 7.1 is anything to go by where, over the years, the numbers of disclosure by lawyers and accountants have remained rather small.

The NCIS report for 1999–2000 shows the extent of financial disclosures over the five years 1995–9. In 1999 the Economic Crime Unit (ECU) of NCIS received about 14,500 reports of suspicious transactions. As shown in Table 7.1, the banks provided the most, accounting for about half of all financial disclosures in 1999, with rather more in 1995, but this seems a rather odd year as the amount rose to nearly 63%. The NCIS report states that there was a disparity between the number of UK authorised banks (the usual high-street banks) and the number of banking institutions making disclosures. In 1999 only 125 deposit-takers reported suspicious transactions to NCIS out of a possible 554 regulated firms. Furthermore, 78% of all disclosures from the banks were made by

Table 7.1 Disclosures by the financial sector, 1995–9 (%)

Financial sector	1995	1996	1997	1998	1999
Banks	62.84	48.40	49.5	44.05	49.91
Build societies	18.95	28.67	20.7	20.49	12.61
Bureaux	4.48	6.96	17.5	19.09	20.79
Insurance	4.57	3.03	3.7	4.50	4.11
Solicitors	1.53	2.03	1.9	1.97	1.77
IFA	1.27	2.54	3.8	3.39	2.01
Credit institutions	1.53	2.03	1.9	1.97	1.77
Gaming/betting	None	1.11	0.7	1.53	2.42
Accountants	0.31	0.51	0.3	0.74	0.58
Regulators	0.13	0.23	0.2	0.21	0.25
Others	5.46	6.59	1.7	4.02	4.43
Auction houses	None	None	None	None	0.25
Asset management	None	None	None	None	0.19
Credit cards	None	None	None	None	0.12
Securities	None	None	None	None	0.56

Source: NCIS (2000).

ten institutions. This represents 39% of all disclosures received by the ECU. The NCIS notes that: 'although high street banks might be expected to be more frequently targeted by criminals to launder their proceeds, it remains a concern that some banks make few, if any suspicious transaction reports' (*ibid.*: 21).

Solicitors and accountants produced few disclosures. Taken together, they only amount to 2.35% for 1999 – 1.77% for solicitors and 0.58% for accountants. NCIS (*ibid.*) says:

> The ECU continued to work with accountants and solicitors to raise the level and quality of financial disclosures that are received. Although the Unit is starting to see some signs of improvement in the quality of disclosures in this area the numbers received remain low. Education within these sectors will continue to remain a priority for the forthcoming year.

NCIS might be sanguine about the outcome and the likely beneficial effect of education as a means by which the numbers and quality of disclosures will be improved, but the history of professional regulation, especially when it is seen as restricting professional freedoms, suggests it will be an uphill struggle. Professions do not like this type of pressure placed on them and resist attempts at self-regulation when this involves acting against their short-term self-interests. Nor do they want to be seen as acting as a sort of state control system. At present they have a moral duty, say, to report a cheque fraud but not a legal one. Imposing a legal duty on them to report suspicious financial transactions takes them one step further along the road to becoming law enforcement agencies. Money laundering substitutes a moral for a legal duty, and this they find burdensome.

One wonders how long they can continue to use such a tactic. The estimates from the G7 countries are that the drugs trade generates more than the GDP of any European country, with about £73 billion going through the world's banking system each year. We could reasonably assume that much of this goes through important financial centres, such as the City of London. We could also reasonably assume that we have already reached the stage where there has been permanent damage to some of our social and financial institutions. Perhaps it is this which will finally persuade governments to tackle the problem. As things stand, law enforcement organisations such as NCIS have their own financial services departments or internal organisations where they investigate financial irregularities without waiting for the professional organisations to take the lead. They can and often do secure authority to examine a company's books and to seize in order to inspect any assets that may be relevant. The NCIS annual report lists some spectacular successes in this respect and, however successful this may be, it will only be a poor substitute for what might be were the professions more accommodating.

The tribunals

There is another sense in which the professions are policed, but this applies only to the medical profession and is through the tribunal system. Tribunals have a long history going back at least to 1926 to the *Rolleston Report* (for a discussion on tribunals, see Bean 1991a). The current position is that tribunals were established under the Misuse of Drugs Act 1971 and supplemented by regulations under the Drugs Tribunal Rules 1974. Briefly, the powers of the tribunals under s. 13 of the 1971 Act are concerned with irresponsible prescribing, where physicians who prescribe irresponsibly may lose their licence to prescribe. As there are links with the General Medical Council (GMC), such behaviour will almost certainly be brought before the Professional Conduct Committee and the physicians will be charged with serious professional misconduct. This carries the maximum penalty of being removed from the medical register.

The process begins as a result of routine monitoring by the Home Office Drugs Inspectorate, which has noticed irregular or overprescribing of certain drugs. This is followed by a visit from the Drugs Inspectorate. About 300 physicians are visited each year. These advisory visits usually have an immediate effect as about 90% of the physicians bring their prescribing down to acceptable levels. For the 10% (30 individuals or so) who do not, the next step involves an official written warning that they may be taken before a tribunal. This tends to reduce that 30 to about six or seven. At this point the Home Office will have clear evidence of irresponsible prescribing as prescriptions will have been analysed and patterns determined. The six or seven physicians will then be brought before a tribunal. They may be legally represented but, by then, their number will have been reduced to about three as the others will have asked that their names be taken off the medical register prior to the hearing. Tribunals can only proceed against registered practitioners. Under the regulations, those remaining physicians will almost certainly be given directions from the Home Office (i.e. have their future prescribing severely restricted, as well as having to go before the GMC).

Critics say the system is too protracted, with a built-in bias towards the professional physician. Moreover, they say the whole system is conducted in a gentlemanly way typical of assessments of middle-class deviants but quite different from the way we deal with those from the lower classes. These criticisms apart, tribunals raise other questions surrounding the rights of physicians who have little or no experience of drug users to prescribe at all. This applies equally to drugs such as Valium as for heroin. It is not just the gross over-prescriber we should worry about; it is those physicians who prescribe rather more than they ought and prescribe when there is no good reason to do so. And this includes drugs such as Prozac – the long-term effects of which are still not known.

Chapter 8

Informers and corruption

Informers are not unique to the world of drugs and trafficking but their activities throw up new questions and put others into greater relief. Definitions of informers vary. The US Drug Enforcement Agency (DEA 1982: 55) defines informers as 'any non-law enforcement person who supplies information about criminal activities to a police officer'. In Britain, the Regulation of Investigatory Powers Act 2000 (henceforth RIPA) includes informers as a 'covert human intelligence source' (henceforth CHIS), defined as someone who establishes or maintains a personal or other relationship with another for the covert purpose of:

- using that relationship to obtain information or to provide another person with access to that information; or
- disclosing information obtained by the use of that relationship or as a consequence of that relationship.

A CHIS might be an informer, an agent or an undercover operator. Here we are concerned only with the informer (and not with the so-called 'public-spirited informer' who gives information, usually on a one-off basis and who does not seek a financial reward). It is the professional informer who is of interest here, who seeks either financial rewards or a reduction in sentence in exchange for information about other offenders. The *Codes of Practice on Informant Use* (Home Office 1999) define an informer thus:

> an individual whose very existence and identity the law enforce-
> ment agencies judge it essential to keep confidential and who is

giving information about persons associated with criminal activity or public disorder. Such an individual will typically have a criminal history, habits or associates and will be giving the information freely whether or not in the expectation of a reward, financial or otherwise (para. 1.14.1).

And a participating informer is defined (*ibid*.: para. 1.14.2) as: 'An informant who is, with the approval of a designated authorising officer, permitted to participate in crime which others already intend to commit.' The first definition places emphasis on the need to protect the informer's identity as well as noting that this type of informer will usually be someone who is or was an active criminal, and who has been given approval to commit a specific crime in specific circumstances in order that others are convicted. Within the world of drugs, the participating informer is particularly useful, as possession and supply are victimless crimes with no 'victim' to make a complaint.

At a time when policing claims to be increasingly intelligence led, the value of informers cannot be doubted. Yet informers operate in that murky world where accusation and counter-accusation are commonplace, and where mistrust and deceit are the tools of the trade. John Grieve (1992) says, after years of experience as a police officer dealing with drug offenders and informers generally, he can only conclude that the drug scene is imbued with treachery. He believes there are more informers in the drug field, in aggregate and proportionate terms, than in any other area of crime. The problem for the police, according to Grieve, is how to stem the flow of information, not to acquire it, and how to use that information appropriately. Yet how do we deal with the informer who is prepared to deceive those who are his or her colleagues? And what will he or she do to those who are not his or her colleagues? Here I want to look closely at the special problem of informers in relation to the drugs field. I also look at corruption and informers, as corruption and drugs are closely linked.

Traditionally, the police have been reluctant to talk about informers. They fear that disclosing their methods and secrets will jeopardise operations. The obvious response is that outsiders do not want to know the details or have access to confidential material, but they are entitled to know that the methods fit basic legal requirements, are cost effective and are appropriate to basic standards of justice. Moreover, the more the police try to hide their activities, the more will the rest of us be suspicious and think they are up to no good. Too often the police seem to take pride in their secrets, believing this adds to that aura of being special. Giving secrets away takes away some of the mystery. It also shows up failures.

There has until recently been no guidance on how to handle informers – experience was seen to be the best way to learn. This led to some spectacular successes but to some equally disastrous failures. Under the RIPA, new procedures have been introduced aimed at reducing the risks, and matched by a new sense of openness. Both are welcome and would have not occurred a decade ago.

The legal authority for informers

As noted above, until recently there was no formal framework for the regulation of informers, although legal decisions created precedents for their use and conduct. The introduction of the Human Rights Act 1998 changed that with its demands (under Article 8 of the European Convention on Human Rights) that law enforcement be examined from the viewpoint of the citizen. Article 8, which asserts the 'right to private and family life', has led to a radical rethink of the situation. The UK government's response has been to produce a formal legal instrument to meet the demands of the Human Rights Act that allows informers to be retained. The RIPA was rushed through Parliament in time to beat the Human Rights Acts in October 2000 (Neyroud and Beckley 2001). Informers by their very nature violate their subjects' 'reasonable expectations of privacy' (Article 8 of the European Convention on Human Rights), so that when through a deceptive relationship an informer covertly uses that relationship to obtain information or covertly discloses information obtained through that relationship this is an infringement of the subject's rights (Neyroud and Beckley 2001: 166).

The RIPA provides the police with a legal framework that allows them to use informers. Informers in the RIPA are not defined on the basis of the evidence they provide but on what they do. They are called a 'covert human intelligence source' (CHIS), which places them alongside other covert operations such as undercover policing. The RIPA permits informers to operate under certain basic conditions. These are as follows:

1 *Subsidiarity*. The means of investigation should cause the minimum interference with the privacy and rights of the individual.
2 *Compulsion*. The outcome can only be achieved by the use of a specific registered source.
3 *Accountability*. The use of a registered source must be in accordance with the proper systems of accountability.
4 *Legality*. The investigatory method must not be unlawful.

5 *Proportionality.* The use of a registered source must be commensurate with the seriousness of the offence.

Points 1 and 2 are relatively straightforward. Subsidiarity means that minimum interference is required, which extends to collateral intrusion (i.e. that the privacy of other persons is also considered). Compulsion means an informer must be a registered source. The third point, accountability, has far-reaching consequences. It requires the introduction of an administrative system whereby the police must introduce checks and supervision of the informers and their handlers. The basic principles are supervision and control, which mean *inter alia* that an informer is not the property of one police officer but a resource deployed for the benefit of the law enforcement agency to which the informer reports. Point 4 is straightforward, but point 5 on proportionality requires consideration to be given to any adverse impact on the community (including the confidence of the community) which may arise as a result of the use of an informer. In practice this means a risk assessment must be made at certain key stages of the investigation, including an assessment of the overall impact of the operation. When the risk is too great, the operation must be stopped.

For the first time in Britain, formal recognition is given to the use of informers; formal procedures are to be implemented for their use and conduct, and the RIPA requires informers and handlers to comply with existing legislation. This means informers are supervised and controlled more closely than hitherto and some of the risks are removed, whether to the police, the informer or the community. No system can completely eliminate risks, and dealing with informers is always going to require skill, care, integrity and, above all, being able to anticipate the dangers, but the RIPA tries to reduce those risks as far as possible. Informers are by definition a risky business.

Protecting the informer

Protecting the informer's identity has always been paramount and must remain so. The legal authority for this is found in *Swinney & Another* v. *Chief Constable of the Northumbria Police 1999* where it was held there was a duty of care owed by the police to take reasonable care to avoid unnecessary disclosure of information an informer had given to the police. The claim was in respect of information given by a witness about a murder inquiry but which found its way into the hands of one of the suspects, resulting in threats and harassment to the witness. It was also held in an earlier case (*Hill*) that 'The public interest will not accept that good citizens should be expected to entrust information to the police without also expecting that they are entrusting their safety to the police'. Failure to provide that protection will not only compromise the informer but also deter witnesses and others from coming forward. This duty of care exists at all stages of the informer's contacts with the police. It is particularly important during the trial where there is extensive pressure to disclose the informer's identity.

The police can point to legal authority involving the granting of public interest immunity (PII), which allows them to seek from the court the right not to disclose the informer's identity nor their methods of work. These legal authorities for PII stem from three important cases: first, *Attorney General* v. *Briant 1846*; secondly, *Marks* v. *Beyfus 1890*; and, thirdly, *Hallett* v. *Others 1986*.

In the first (*Attorney General* v. *Briant 1846*) it was held that 'a witness cannot be asked such questions as will disclose the informer if he be a third person ... and we think the principle of the rule applies to the case where a witness is asked if he himself is an Informer'. In the second (*Marks* v. *Beyfus 1890*) the judge went beyond the 1846 decision and reaffirmed that the Director of Public Prosecutions is entitled to refuse to disclose the names from whom he has received information and the nature of information received. He said:

> I do not say it is a rule which can never be departed from; if upon the trial of the defendant the Judge is of the opinion that the disclosure of the name of the informant is necessary to show the prisoner's innocence, the one public policy is in conflict with another public policy, and that which says an innocent man is not to be condemned when his innocence can be proved is the policy that must prevail.

This judgment reaffirmed the earlier rulings found above. More recently in *Hallett* v. *Others* (1986), the judge said disclosing the identity of an informer to the defence is not required unless it is necessary to avoid a miscarriage of justice. The appellants appealed against their conviction for importing and being in possession of cocaine from Germany as to the court's ruling that the identity of the informer should not be disclosed to the defence.

These rulings began to be challenged by the defence claiming that protecting the identity of informers produces injustices for their clients. They asserted that an accused has the right to know and cross-examine those making the accusations. In *R.* v. *Turnball 1976* and *R.* v. *Taylor 1994*, the judgments tipped the balance back towards the defence. In *Turnball* the court ruled the identity of the informer should be revealed if it was relevant to the defence case, and added that verbatim records of the PII applications should be made available to the Court of Appeal. In the second (*Taylor*), the judge ruled that a defendant in a criminal trial has a fundamental right to see and know the identity of his or her accusers, including witnesses for the prosecution, and this right should only be denied in rare and exceptional circumstances.

There the matter rests, at least for the present, except that in *R. v. Agar* the court held that if a defence was manifestly frivolous and doomed to failure, a trial judge might conclude it must be sacrificed to the general public interest. Occasionally the defence had become involved in what were called 'fishing expeditions' aimed at identifying whether or not an informer was involved. In *Agar* the defendant appealed against his conviction for possession with intent to supply after he was arrested in a trap set by the police and an informer. The judge refused to allow details of the trap to be put to the jury. However, the judge said that, if there was a tenable defence, the rule of public policy protecting the informer was outweighed by the stronger public interest in allowing a defendant to put forward a case.

The point at which the balance is struck is always going to be difficult for it must meet the needs of the prosecution witnesses and the fairness of the trial. The pendulum is likely to swing back and forth as one judgment follows the other, the first in favour of the prosecution only to be reversed in favour of the defence. The informer's safety has to be set against the rights of the defendant.

Included, too, is the safety of witnesses, who are not informers (at least in the sense defined here), and who need guarantees of safety – otherwise they will not come forward. Informers whose identity is compromised may require witness protection (Bean 2001a). Every major trafficking operation involves an informer; for some, a witness protection scheme will be required. For how long and in what form (i.e. whether the family will need to be relocated with a new identity in another country or whether a short-term programme would be sufficient) depend on a number of matters, including the nature of the criminal organisation. It is said triads and yardies have long memories. Not all on witness protection are informers, and not all informers require witness protection – but witness protection is for those who need it and it encourages others to come forward to give information. Schemes must operate according to the highest standards of secrecy for, in the world of drugs and crime, violence is all too common and informers know they pay heavily for the information provided to the police, even if sometimes that leads to a reduction in their sentence.

Reducing the sentence

The value of informers is well recognised – by none other than the Lord Chief Justice:

> For many years it has been well recognised that the detection of crime was assisted by the use of information given to the police by members of the public. Those numbers might be either professional informers who gave information regularly in the expectation of financial or other reward, or public spirited citizens who wished to see the guilty punished for their offences. It was in the public interest that nothing should be done which was likely to encourage persons of either class from coming forward (*R.* v. *Rankine 1986*).

Not only that but, as Lord Justice Bingham said, there were rewards too, particularly when it comes to drug traffickers and dealers:

> It was particularly important that persons concerned with the importation of drugs into the UK should be encouraged by the sentencing policy of the Courts to give information to the police. An immediate confession of guilt, coupled with considerable assistance to police could therefore be marked by a substantial reduction in what would otherwise be a proper sentence (*R.* v. *Afzal*, reported in *The Times* 14 October 1989).

In this case, a sentence of 7½ years was reduced to six years. There was not, however, an expectation for a reduction in sentence just because the offender was an informer. Reductions had to be related to Index offences. In *Regina* v. *Preston and McAlery* (reported in *The Times* 14 December 1987), Mr Justice Farquharson in the Court of Appeal said that:

> What the courts should not take into account therefore as a result of this judgement is evidence of information given by an accused person which does not relate to the crime of which he now stands. The proper course to be taken was that where information is given by an accused person which does not relate to the crime of which he is charged then that is a matter which the authorities can properly take into account, but it is not a matter for the Court to consider in mitigation of the sentence passed.

Information to the court is given in what is called a 'text'. The text sets out any assistance given by an informer and details about how the informer was recruited. Here, *R. v. Taylor* is relevant where the defence claimed it had the right to know the nature of the text and, of course, the name of the informer. In an important judgment (*R. v. Piggott 1994*), the court held that it was no longer a matter of discretion by the police as to whether an informant text was issued. The defendant has the right to have all relevant information put before the court in mitigation.

In so far as a reduction in the sentence was possible, claims by the defendant had to be supported by the police. In *R. v. X 1999* it was held that a defendant's unsupported assertions were not likely to make any difference to the sentence. The courts had to rely on the completeness and accuracy of the report, and the greatest of care had to be taken in the preparation and presentation of such a text.

Informers: who are they, and how to control them?

There have been many attempts at classifying informers' motives (see Billingsley 2001b), but there is probably as wide a range of motives as there are informers. Motives are likely to include revenge, pressure from the police, an active enjoyment of the role, the associated power that comes from being an informer and fear of a heavy sentence. Those involved in drug dealing are likely to seek ways to eliminate competition and, of course, what better way to do so than through informing? Financial inducements (mainly small at about £30 for information leading to a conviction and paid only after a successful arrest) are clearly not sufficient, although of course some receive much more where the information leads to the arrest of major traffickers and dealers. Street-level dealers will be concerned with more local, mundane problems, in which case something else must drive them along and this is usually the protection and extension of their drug markets. This is what makes them dangerous.

Dunnighan (1992) provides one of the few pieces of information on the type of people who become informers. In a survey of detectives and their informers in one police force area, he found the typical informer to be male, under the age of 30, unemployed and with previous convictions (also, incidentally, the typical criminal). Dunnighan (*ibid.*) also noted that about 30% of all informers will be drug users who will also inform on a wide variety of crimes other than drug use. A more detailed study by Roger Billingsley (2001b) largely confirms these findings. He found that most informers were male, young and with criminal convictions, and over half were unemployed. Women informers constituted about 20% of his population of informers; there are no national figures on the gender ratio (Nemitz 2001b: 99).

Controlling these informers is now a much more ordered affair. Informers are allowed to operate only if they are registered and act according to defined procedures. Handlers must be trained and all contacts with the informers recorded; where payments are made to the informer, another handler must be present. Procedures are tight, largely as a result of some catastrophic blunders when informers were out of control.

Of the different types of informer described earlier in this chapter, it is the participating informer who creates the most problems, whether it be for the handler, the controller or the court – the more so in the drugs field as participating informers must know a great deal about the crimes of which they inform. The problem for the police is that the participating informer is also the most useful for he or she 'goes beyond mere observation and report' (Grieve 1992). Or, put differently, the informer needs to be 'dirty' to be useful, which, in the drugs field, means continuing to act as a trafficker or dealer where the more the informer is involved in drug dealing, the more valuable will be the information.

The problem is to decide the appropriate level at which participation should be permitted. In *R. v. Birtles 1969* it was ruled that the police are entitled to make use of information concerning an offence already 'laid on' (i.e. to be committed in any event) with a view to mitigating the consequences of the proposed offence (e.g. to protect the proposed victim). It may be perfectly proper for the police to encourage the informer to take part in the offence, but the police must never use an informer to commit an offence he or she would not otherwise commit.

Victimless crime is difficult to detect by conventional methods. Informers are therefore central to police operations and, of course, these informers will know more about dealing if they are part of that network. This means they must continue to deal, sometimes in ways that might be 'laid on' and sometimes not. The central dilemma is how to obtain information, control the informer and yet allow the participating informer the necessary leeway to continue.

In the murky world of informers, how difficult is it to know where the truth starts and ends? Some dealers claim they have a 'licence to deal' from the police, and those who do not claim they know others who have a licence. These so-called 'licences' are said to be given to informers who, in return for information, enjoy a favoured relationship with the police. The police, somewhat naturally, deny they issue 'licences' but 'licences' are mentioned so often as to suspect they do, at least in some form or another. Moreover, some dealers will say informers are able to learn about police methods and operations, thereby having an unfair advantage. In fact, some say they are placed there by higher-level dealers for that purpose. Other dealers say they take advantage of the informer's licence and use their houses to sell their own drugs, believing the informers had been granted some form of immunity. Where such claims exist and are true, the police have lost control; the informers are able to dictate their terms and the police are left to accept what is given to them. Once control has been lost it is difficult to regain it and, with a loss of control, there is also a loss of respect.

The introduction of new procedures and an emphasis on 'tasking' (i.e. requiring the informer to provide information about what the police want to know and not what the informer is prepared to give) have helped to change the ethos. Tasking produces greater control; it requires the informer to act under instructions and not to operate as a free-floating agent able to produce information the informer thinks fit to give. Those informers not producing the tasked information are deregistered, which increases their vulnerability and makes them less able to receive protected status.

Informers and drug dealing

All drug markets have informers – the police would not be able to operate without them, and are clearly grateful that informers are numerous and generous with their information. Yet how effective is the informer system, and are informers in the drug world likely to have a different impact on the overall level of drug offending from those informing in other types of criminality? Might it be that the use of informers makes the drug problem worse, when it would not, say, make armed robbery worse? (Billingsley 2001).

As a general rule we can assume that, whenever dealers provide systematic information on other dealers operating at the same level or above, those informers are extending their own dealer networks. Their aim is to extend their networks to the point where they, as dealers, are increasingly difficult to prosecute, for they will then operate at an organisational level, rarely being in possession of the drugs. Understandably, the informer system makes some people uneasy. For example, Goldstein (1960, cited in Billingsley *et al*. 2001b) gives three reasons to be wary of informers. First, he says police hesitancy to implicate informers encourages others to commit crime. Secondly he believes informers are encouraged by the police to continue to commit crime, this being especially damaging to those in the early stages of their criminal careers. Thirdly, he sees the practice of using informers as leading to widespread disrespect for the criminal law. Others doubt their effectiveness. They believe informers rarely penetrate to the high levels of trafficking organisations, this only being achieved by undercover police officers. They also believe informers increase the level of narcotic crime by making accusations against low-level dealers in order to eliminate them. This they see as particularly damaging to young offenders and others equally naïve about drug dealing because it brings them into the court system with all the deleterious impact court appearances have (*ibid.*, cited in Bean 2001b: 30).

These arguments must be taken seriously. Goldstein (among others) believes informers rarely reach the upper levels, for organised crime can be stopped only through extensive police work using undercover agents. Other critics point to the number of crimes committed by participating informers and note they inform for their own benefit rather than for that of the police. They believe that leaving horizontal informers in the system leads to trouble, which is likely to increase levels of crime rather than reduce it (*ibid.*).

In response to Goldstein and others, we may say that whilst informers may not always be able to penetrate the highest parts of the organisation, the undercover operator often needs the assistance of the informer as a means to gain entry. In fact, working alongside undercover operators might turn out to be the best combination, where the one assists the other. At street level it may be true that informers make things worse, but the solution is not to cease using them but to impose more stringent controls. At upper levels things may be different, but each case presents the opportunity of leading to deeper levels of penetration in the criminal organisation. The aim is to move beyond horizontal prosecution – the so-called 'sidewalk-level dealers' – to vertical prosecution that reaches higher-level dealers and meaningful levels of crime.

We must wait for research to help answer some of these questions but, in the meantime, we should welcome the changes introduced to establish greater measures of control over informers and the efforts made to offset some of the earlier criticisms. At the moment, however, we must expect the numbers of informers to increase, especially in the drugs field, and we should be aware that however distasteful we may find the actions of informers, the police and the courts recognise them as a necessary evil.

The special case of juveniles

We may find it distasteful for juveniles (i.e. those under 18 years of age) to become informers but many choose to do so and some choose to inform on their friends and family, including their parents. Juvenile informers come in various forms. For example, a juvenile may give information on a school friend who has enticed away her boyfriend. This is likely to be a one-off piece of information and relatively innocuous in the overall scheme of things. Alternatively, it may be the case where a parent is a burglar or a relatively important local drug dealer, in which instance the information will be of greater interest to the police. Motives will vary; it may be spite, as in the case of the young girl who has lost her boyfriend, or it may be to earn money to purchase drugs, in the case of the young person informing on his or her family. Or it may be prompted by a wish to be rid of a parent or guardian who may be persistently violent to the family. Alternatively, as Teresa Nemitz (2001b) shows, informers, especially women informers, might give information as a way of protecting themselves and their family against domestic violence; children will do likewise.

The police will be reluctant to ignore this information, especially if it comes from a source they think is reliable. Moreover, if they are to make an impact on the high rates of drug use amongst young people, they must inevitably seek information from those familiar with that world – and that means informers of the same age. The question is not about whether juveniles should be accepted as informers (although some police forces do not accept them) – the question is how to regulate their use in ways which make it more ethically acceptable.

Under the RIPA, a statutory instrument (2000, no. 2793) was laid before Parliament on 16 October 2000 and came into force on 6 November 2000. Briefly, this instrument regulates the use of juvenile informers under the age of 18 and provides special regulatory powers for those under the age of 16. In line with the language of the Act, informers are referred to as a 'source' or CHIS. For informers under the age of 18, the instrument says that a risk assessment must be made at the time the source is authorised, and the risk assessment must be by a police officer of superintendent rank. Under para. 5 (ii), that risk assessment must demonstrate that the 'nature and magnitude of any risk of psychological distress to the source arising in the course of, or as a result of, carrying out the conduct described in the authorisation have been identified and evaluated'. The risks must be justified and properly explained to the source.

For the juvenile under the age of 16, no authorisation for the conduct and use of the source may be granted if (1) the source is under the age of

16; and (2) the relationship to which the conduct or use would relate is between the source and his or her parent or any person who has parental responsibility for him or her (para. 3). Informers under the age of 16 may be authorised (i.e. registered) but an appropriate adult is required to attend any meetings with the superintendent, and an appropriate adult means a parent or guardian, any other person currently responsible for the juvenile's welfare or any other responsible person aged 18 or over.

These regulations do not stop the police from taking note of the juvenile's information against family members. What they say is that the juvenile will not be authorised (i.e. registered). In practice, however, this means they cannot proceed. For example, assume they take notice of the child and arrest the father for burglary. If the defence asks about the basis of the information that led to the arrest, the police will have to disclose their source. The defence will then say, rightly, the investigation was unlawful. That of itself is bad enough but without registration the juvenile is not given the formal protection of a duty of care (as provided by *Swinney & Another* v. *Chief Constable of the Northumbria Police* (1999)), although it would be reasonable to suppose that all juveniles would receive a duty of care from the police under any circumstances. A likely outcome, then, is the juvenile will supply the information as before but the police will not act on it. It would be unreasonable to expect them to ignore it so they may seek other ways to circumvent these regulations. Paradoxically, in order to protect the juvenile, these regulations may have the opposite effect. As noted above, sometimes that information is given to secure the juvenile's own (or other family member's) protection.

The regulations for juveniles generally (i.e. whether under 16 or not) are about providing information against those outside the family. They require a senior police officer to be present and an appropriate adult. The definition of an appropriate adult is that taken from the Police and Criminal Evidence Act (PACE). This is hardly satisfactory, including as it does 'any responsible person over the age of 18 years'. One would think some reference should be given to the suitability of the person to act as an appropriate adult: suitable in the sense of knowing what to do or say, how to respect confidentiality for all concerned, including the police, and understanding the juvenile's situation. It would seem to require a rather special sort of person trained in the art of knowing how to react to a delicate situation yet not damaging the information to be given. The lack of training of appropriate adults generally makes it likely that those used will be local authority social workers or probation officers who may be sympathetic to the child but who come from organisations rarely sympathetic to the police. If juvenile informers are to be protected yet permitted to provide information, which may after all lead to the conviction of serious offenders, suitable appropriate adults are required who are trained and who are capable of acting in ways best suited to the task in hand. Otherwise it seems again as if Britain is producing the correct procedures then emasculating them by failing to provide the levels of support necessary for them to function.

There remains another pressing ethical question that centres on payments to be made to juvenile informers. The problem is the police may reward the juvenile quite handsomely in some cases when there is every reason to believe the juvenile will use the money to buy drugs, or spend it on gambling. Some police forces have tried to get round this problem by staggering the payments (i.e. paying only small amounts at any one time); others pay for the information with food vouchers or by some other means to assist the family. This is not always acceptable to the juvenile who, say, may be a heavy drug user, homeless and have a liking for cocaine. There is little the police can do if they want the information. They would be helped if the regulations set out the conditions under which monies can be paid and if they were required to clarify this with the juvenile concerned. Presumably, the regulations would say something like this: vouchers will normally be paid and only in exceptional circumstances will money be given and then only with the approval of a senior officer of assistant chief constable rank. That may not solve all the problems but it might ease some of them.

The use of juvenile informants carries particular risks, whether to their safety or psychological development, and the police have rightly been provided with detailed rules and procedures for dealing with them. Authorising officers are required to give close attention to questions of proportionality – that is, to determine whether the use of a juvenile informer can be justified. This use must be on the basis that it is commensurate with the seriousness of the offence. The younger the informer the more pressing is the decision about proportionality. In every case, the controlling police officer must be satisfied the juvenile understands what is happening and has had the risks clearly explained. If the juvenile's identity is compromised, he or she faces additional obstacles: juveniles cannot usually move to another area and they cannot protect themselves against violent drug dealers. Carole Ballardie and Paul Iganski (2001: 113) show that most police officers in their study solved the problem of juveniles by not registering them – hardly a solution in the circumstances. The move to tasking using dedicated informer units will help reduce that practice, though it may still appear, albeit fitfully.

We may not like using juveniles as informers, might find it morally repugnant, but juveniles will keep coming forward with information. Clearly it is wrong if financial inducements or gifts are offered as inducements to give information, and so the best we can do is provide clear guidelines about how they should be handled and controlled. After all, the peak age of crime is 15 years, and the peak age group 14–17 years. If the police are expected to make inroads into levels of juvenile crime, they must expect to use informers to help them.

Corruption

Drugs are easy to transport and easy to hide, and small quantities produce massive profits. It is this message that Roy Clark (2001) graphically describes in his study of police corruption. He says corruption can be found in all organisations, including those within the criminal justice system, especially where drugs and informers are involved. He thinks the police have recognised this more than most and have unfairly been seen as the most corrupt because they have publicly displayed their anti-corruption activities. The police have also recognised where the dangers are, and Clark makes it clear that other agencies that refuse to accept that corruption exists are building up trouble for themselves by failing to turn over the stone to see what lies under it. Corruption can never be eliminated but it can be reduced. Clark (*ibid.*: 38) again:

> The risk of allowing police officers to come into regular contact with criminals under controlled conditions is therefore justified. On almost every occasion the contacts and resulting police actions are conducted according to high ethical standards. There are however rare occasions when standards fall, supervision fails and people become vulnerable to temptation. Under such circumstances the dangers of informers and police officers becoming corrupt are high.

Clark gives other examples of corruption, whether in the Crown Prosecution Service or HM Customs & Excise, and they almost all involve drug dealing. The incentive to bribe officials and engage in corrupt practices is a common and important feature of the contemporary drug trade. The large amounts of money and, from the trafficker's point of view, the need to launder that money, as well as finding better means of distributing the drugs, have meant that bribery and corruption are endemic. The bank clerk who is paid by the trafficker to look the other way or to fail to report large cash deposits, or the police officer who does not patrol a section of the coastline on selected evenings, operate at the low end of the corruption pyramid. At the upper end are the professionals, the lawyers and accountants able to promote shell companies or to engage in sophisticated trading techniques. Even higher are the corrupt politicians – some at the very top, whose practices promote and extend corruption nationally.

Some of the corrupt practices in relation to the drugs trade in the Caribbean and South American region have been documented (Paternostro 1995). For example, in 1994 the US Attorney General's office filed in excess of 15,000 criminal corruption investigations against Colombian officials, including 21 Colombian Members of Congress. Although Colombia and the USA signed a Mutual Legal Assistance Treaty in 1900, Colombia has failed to ratify the treaty and it has not entered into force (Presidential Determination 1995). It would be wrong to single out Colombia; other countries have been found to have similar levels of corruption.

Corruption is thought to be most extensive in the producing and distributing countries (e.g. in South East Asia, Pakistan, Burma, etc., the Caribbean and South America). Levels of vertical corruption are thought to be less common in non-producing countries, although the BCCI Bank proved to be a notable exception. Corruption can be defined in legal terms as 'behaviour which deviates from the formal duties of a public role or violates rules against the exercise of certain types of private practice' (Nye 1970: 566–7). It is the abuse of a position for personal gain. Accordingly, corruption damages public interest as it is dysfunctional to the workings of an organisation, whether involving the law, business or whatever.

Almost all definitions of corruption have been in functionalist terms, where corruption is viewed as dysfunctional to the workings of an organisation or national economy. There have been challenges to this legal definition (Lo 1993), where the view is that functionalist legal definitions are rarely broad enough to cover the whole spectrum of corrupt practices. Many actions lie in a grey area where corruption in the legal sense would not exist or where it is not dysfunctional but may be neutral or, at best, valuable. The handling of informers is a case in point. Skolnick (1984) argues that the enforcement pattern of 'working up the ladder' creates room for wide discretion to be given to narcotics officers who try to protect their informers by holding back information from their superiors. As a result, says Skolnick (*ibid.*: 124), opportunities are always there for corrupt practices and are always a problem. Insider trading is another grey area where corruption is always going to be near the surface, and what is and what is not a corrupt practice is open to debate. Also, the professionals such as lawyers and accountants noted below as well as bank clerks are likely to be operating in similar situations to the insider traders. If the law requires all cash deposits of £5,000 to be notified and a depositor repeatedly places £4,999, should the bank clerk ignore this?

Using a conflict perspective, Lo (1993: 153), in a study of corruption in Hong Kong and China, says corruption can be seen as more variable than that defined in moral and legal terms. It is, he says, determined by the actions of powerful political groups who are able to influence public opinion: 'If a political group succeeds in persuading the masses that a specific policy is in their interest its corrupt practices would be exonerated' (ibid.: 153). He goes on (ibid.) to say that as 'the dominant class has the capacity to mobilise the mass media and government institutions it is always in an advantageous position to articulate its own interests'. As an example he cites the Tiananmen Square massacre where the Chinese Communist Party claimed that counter-revolutionary riots had been suppressed to maintain law and order to uphold the people's interest when in fact it was the people's voice and freedom that had been suppressed (ibid.). Whether this is an example of corruption or simply of naked manipulation of power is debatable.

Clearly there is a point to be made about the way in which corruption is or is not defined by the dominant group – and the activities of some Caribbean governments illustrate this. Even so, it is not clear where such an argument takes us. If the definition of corruption varies from society to society (depending much on the political and economic structures and historical changes, as Lo would have us believe), then corruption can only be examined as another form of cultural relativism. Yet modern capitalist societies require large measures of conformity on those wanting to trade on the international market. The bank teller who takes a bribe in London is as corrupt as the bank teller taking a bribe elsewhere – hence the value of a functionalist theory. It may not be the only theory but it is likely to be the one most appropriate to drug trafficking that is, after all, about financial exploitation.

It is important to understand the structures that promote corruption. Organisations that are not corrupt or have no vertical corruption will, none the less, be prone to corruption if supervision is lax or if managers are not aware of the possibilities of corruption occurring. The poorly supervised bank clerk will not report a large cash deposit, the poorly supervised police officer will not report a cargo landing on his or her part of the beach, or the poorly supervised lawyer or accountant will accept a new client without asking too many pertinent questions. But they will report if supervision is close. On the other hand, Peter Reuter (1991: 17) sees the incentive to bribe as being not related to supervision but to the intensity of law enforcement: 'The greater the probability of long prison terms and loss of other assets, the more aggressively a dealer will seek out officials who can mitigate those risks and the more money he will be willing to offer such mitigation.' His conclusion is that active law enforcement induces corruption: 'This is one of the potential costs of more intense enforcement in raised corruption potential, particularly among the front line enforcement agencies' (*ibid*.).

Corruption and policing

Roy Clark (2001) gives the typical profile of the corrupt police officer in these terms: he (it is very rarely a woman) will be a very active police officer, usually with a reputation for being successful, having 'done a number of good jobs' and continuing to work at that pace. He will have served as a police officer for about 12 years and will have reached a reasonably high or middle rank. He will be divorced, probably paying a heavy maintenance allowance, or will have other similar monthly expenses. He will be working in one of the specialist detective units and will meet criminals who have ready access to large amounts of money.

It is difficult to believe that many police officers started their careers with the aim of becoming corrupt. More likely, they began with all the usual idealism of someone starting out in public service. What, then, goes wrong? How does an otherwise honest, hard-working police officer become corrupt? Almost certainly by gently sliding into corrupt practices beginning, first, with such matters as securing a lighter sentence in return for a relatively small payment. This is done by changing the records or finding other ways to avoid prosecution. Once involved it is easy to move to larger sums of money from more serious criminals and the point is soon reached where it is difficult (if not impossible) for him to regain his earlier reputation – and as a corrupt police officer he has lost control and becomes the employee of the offender population.

Clark (*ibid*.) describes the changes the corrupt police officer goes through from being honest and in control of the offender to being corrupt and in the offender's control. In the Metropolitan Police investigation he identified 'a new and more sinister problem' (*ibid*.: 41) with evidence that 'there was a complete reversal of the roles of the police officer and informer. The informer ... became the recipient of police intelligence whilst the police officer became the informer.' He describes it (*ibid*.) thus:

It became clear that this reversal process led to the criminals adopting many of the elements of police practices which relate to the recruitment and use of police officer informers. It was found that the criminals developed their own policy or set of standards which closely mirrored the accepted law enforcement practices. These include the active recruitment of informers, protection from exposure, the use of pseudonyms, an acknowledgement that intelligence is to be shared, the tasking of informers, the provision of more than one handler, and reward in cash commensurate with the intelligence provided.

Paradoxically, it is the informer who provides the police with information about corrupt police officers. Clark says informers have been an important source of information, introducing several lines of inquiry and adding significantly to others. He says there is no such thing as honour among thieves; rivalry, jealousy and the settling of old scores create high levels of instability within criminal circles and ensure a constant stream of information to the police. He adds (*ibid.*: 48): 'Informers are also a vital component of any strategic response to corruption.'

For the trafficker and high-level dealer, corruption comes cheap. The police officer on the Caribbean island or the bank teller in a London bank when asked to look away at the opportune moment will not expect to receive a great deal of money. Clark describes an employee from the Crown Prosecution Service who was sentenced to six years' imprisonment for giving away the identities of 33 police informers. He had received just £1,000, although the court heard he expected to receive more (*ibid.*: 45). There is no point in the bank teller receiving £1 million for that would draw attention to his or her activities and would be counterproductive. More likely, he or she will ask for enough to pay off existing debts, to buy a car and to go on holiday. And he or she will be hooked for life with no possibility of escape. In that sense corruption is a one-way street, dysfunctional to the organisation and dysfunctional to the corrupted – but highly functional and cost-effective to the corrupter.

It is reasonable to ask to what extent we should fear an extension of corrupt practices. Will corruption through the drug trade overwhelm our institutions, whether financial or otherwise? Peter Reuter (1991) is optimistic; he sees the fractionated structure of drug law enforcement as being its salvation. It means no force has exclusive criminal enforcement responsibilities (the police share much with Customs and Excise), and the often-cited lack of co-ordination between the agencies turns out to be but one aspect of the risks facing corrupt police: 'Taking money from dealers has become risky in an environment in which the individual paying the bribe has a reasonably high probability of being arrested by another agency' (*ibid.*: 18). Wing Lo (1993: 163) sees the solution in terms of changes in the dominant group so that all can contest the validity, target and purpose of the legal and moral censures of corruption.

The research evidence such as there is suggests that, in modern societies, drug dealers are unable to purchase the systemic and comprehensive protection that was available to many of their earlier bootlegging and gambling predecessors. Modern drug-dealing organisations in a country such as Britain are basically fragile and always subject to serious threats from law enforcement (Reuter *et al*. 1990: 24). Of course, whilst they operate they do considerable damage, but they are always likely to be confined and always likely to be seeking new forms of corruption. The evidence to support Reuter *et al*.'s optimistic view in the face of the growth of organised crime needs to be evaluated. A comprehensive study of corruption – how it occurs and how it can be controlled – would seem to be necessary.

If, as is often claimed, about one third of all crimes are cleared up as a result of informers and, for drug crimes, the percentage is thought to be higher, informers play a key role in any police strategy. If the trafficking cases are disaggregated and counted separately, the percentage is likely to be much higher still. There is no suggestion the use of informers will decline but every indication it will increase and, almost certainly, change to meet the contemporary demands of law enforcement. Nowadays crime generally, and drug taking in particular, has a more international dimension, where the movement of drugs and the movement of criminals require a different approach than hitherto.

Conclusion

In October 1997 the UK government published *Rights Brought Home; the Human Rights Bill* and said it intended to incorporate the EU Convention on Human Rights into UK law. The use of informers was affected by the EU convention, particularly Article 8, which provides for the right of privacy. An informer clearly violates that right. Introducing legislation in the form of the RIPA resolved some of these difficulties and provided an opportunity (through speedy amendments to other legislation) to control and supervise informers generally. The old days have gone when police officers learnt how to handle informers as they went along and then claimed an expertise in such matters that was never put to the test. In their place is a new set of rules, infinitely more bureaucratic and cumbersome but with many more safeguards for all concerned.

The link with corruption has been well established and the impact of corrupt police officers well understood. Drugs, corruption and informers seem to go together; not always found together but, when they are, they can produce the most destructive consequences. At present there is no realistic alternative to the use of informers but there is a point to be made about the way they are handled and controlled. Clark (2001) says that any form of unethical or criminal behaviour involving an informer can now be detected, and long prison sentences invariably follow for the corrupt officer. He adds (*ibid*.: 44) that if high standards are allowed to fall, the courts would lose confidence in the informer system and that the consequences of this loss in confidence to policing would be massive. Conversely, the benefits to organised crime would be vast.

Chapter 9

Women, drugs and crime

Rarely in this book has reference been made to gender or even an acknowledgement made that gender is an issue. Obviously, this is not the case – gender *is* important. For example, Table 1.4 (on p. 9) shows that, of the 40,181 people starting agency episodes in the six months ending 31 March 2001, 29,669 were men and 10,512 were women (or about 25% of them were female). The ages at which women begin drug use are similar to those of men, the peak age group being the early to mid-20s. The drugs taken are also similar – although some American studies show that women are particularly fond of cocaine. However, Edna Oppenheimer (1991: 38) notes that the ratio of women to men coming to treatment in Britain is about 1 in 3. If this reflects the numbers using drugs generally, then probably about 25% of drug takers are women.

As noted in Chapter 1, data from the British Crime Survey (BCS) show there is a gap between the male and female rates and that this gap appears to be widening. Whereas female rates remained steady at 19% in 1999, for males it increased by 5%. Women also tend to enter treatment earlier than men, and often more successfully. Yet are these differences sufficient to warrant special policies, treatment programmes, policing or whatever? Do women drug users differ in a qualitative sense from their male counterparts and, if they do, is a different approach or a different set of standards required? In trying to answer these questions we face the obvious handicaps that, paradoxically, also apply to men: there are few good research studies that provide the necessary data. If 1 in 3 or 1 in 4 of the drug-using population are women and the services provided are failing, something clearly needs to be done and adjustments made in whatever areas are appropriate. But which and how?

At one level, of course, there are no differences. As Oppenheimer (1991) points out, women who misuse drugs are subject to the same risks as men. They will experience the same forms of ill-health, will die from the same overdoses, will experience the same severe weight loss, will have the same hepatitis B and C illnesses, will suffer the same muscle wasting and will be subject to all the other diseases related to the same chaotic lifestyle and the poor and erratic nutrition as their male counterparts. Yet in other respects their medical problems are unique, the most obvious being those related to pregnancy and childbirth and the effects of drugs on the unborn child. Related to these are the social norms surrounding being a mother and the plight of children whose mothers are substance misusers.

The aim here is to look at some of the matters surrounding women and substance abuse in order to highlight certain selected features that have received attention in the literature and in Parliament. Increasingly there is a developing interest in women's issues, especially concerning the number of women drug users in prison and in the treatment facilities inside and outside the criminal justice system.

Women, health and social norms

Women who use drugs are likely to be of child-bearing age; this will create additional problems for them and the unborn child if and when they become pregnant. A number of drug users do become pregnant, but how many and how many give birth as opposed to seek a termination is not known. Sheigla Murphy and Marsha Rosenbaum (1999), in their study of pregnant women on drugs, show how, for a variety of reasons, these women did not practise birth control – one reason being that the combination of long-term drug use and erratic eating habits resulted in menstruation cessation. They did not believe they could conceive and, when they did, it was sometime before they recognised it; they often attributed morning sickness to drug withdrawal (*ibid.*: 52–3).

Generally speaking, once they have conceived there are two main sets of problems: those occurring during pregnancy and those affecting the child immediately after birth. Of the first, Oppenheimer (1991) says that while congenital abnormalities occur primarily during early pregnancy, some drugs can affect the growth of the foetus and its post-natal behaviour producing mental problems (especially where exposure to drugs occurs later in pregnancy). She says (*ibid.*: 39–40) that even after delivery maternally ingested drugs can gain entrance to the neonate through feeding on mother's milk.

Women drug users who are pregnant face additional complications to their already chaotic daily lives. If their major source of income is through prostitution, pregnancy will reduce their earning power. If they are 'busted' they will try to hide their pregnancy from the police and courts, fearing they will be remanded in custody to receive medical treatment. They know their lifestyles give cause for concern, especially if they are intravenous drug users. In the USA that concern is additionally justified. Many US states have public health laws where pregnant drug users can be detained until they give birth – and presumably a decision is also made about whether the mother may keep the child. The law operates as a form of preventative detention or preventative containment. In California (as in many other states), drug use during pregnancy can be interpreted as child abuse, and hospital staff are required by law to initiate child protection or law enforcement referrals (Murphy and Rosenbaum 1999: 107). The aim of preventative containment is to produce a 'drug-free baby', thereby reducing the complications including the health costs of a child born of a drug-using mother.

The second set of problems surrounds the mother's future contact with child-care agencies and health services. Contact with the criminal justice system is also a potential minefield. Murphy and Rosenbaum (*ibid.*: 105) say that women must choose to disclose or not disclose and, in doing so, must confront their two biggest fears: first, that their babies might be born seriously impaired and secondly that their babies might be taken away from them – 'In the long term was it better for the baby to tell or not to tell?' (*ibid.*: 133).

Sometimes the role conflict works to the woman's advantage. There are some women drug users who recognise there are conflicts between being a 'junkie' and a mother and resolve this in favour of being a mother. If this is the case they seek treatment and are likely to be successful, the more so if they want their children returned to them to reconstitute their family. Murphy and Rosenbaum (*ibid.*: 58) describe how some women who had assumed they were infertile saw their pregnancy as a cause for joy, a living proof their drug use had not impaired their reproductive capacities: 'These women viewed their pregnancies as opportunities to change their life styles, almost as if the pregnancy was a special gift to provide them with new hope and resolve.' Male counterparts rarely see parenthood as sufficiently important to choose in favour of being a father rather than a junkie. Accordingly, they have fewer demands to make them grow up. Perhaps that is why women seek treatment at an earlier stage than men (Anglin and Hser 1987a). Yet whilst a few see pregnancy as an opportunity to change for the better, many do not. Whatever advantages pregnancy brings to a small number of women, for the vast majority it brings 'seemingly never ending guilt' (*ibid.*: 7). They recognise that bringing up children in that unstable, violent world is likely to produce the same unstable, violent world for them as adults. Murphy and Rosenbaum (1999) describe – in that all too familiar way – how these pregnant mothers had been systematically abused as children and were being systematically abused as adults. They see the same prospects for their children. Yet many of the women in the Murphy and Rosenbaum study decided against an abortion. Pregnancy and motherhood offered them another chance of mending their flawed identities and of returning to a conventional role:

> For those women who had already been mothers and lost custody of their older children the decision to have another baby was another chance at being a good mother. Their decisions not to abort were often influenced by their guilt and remorse over past abortions or having failed in the past (*ibid.*: 65).

The baby offered an opportunity to do it right this time. Whether they were any more successful remains to be seen.

Women who are drug users and have young children living with them know they are at risk of having those children taken into care. Welfare workers rightly protect children, especially young children, from the dangers moral and physical of a mother who is a drug user. If she has a partner, that relationship is likely to be unstable where the demand for the drug interferes with any relationship between the adults. Each adult will believe the other is exploiting him or her by not giving them their share of the drugs – especially so where they are heroin users or are taking other addictive drugs. Fear, suspicion, distrust and violence are common to these relationships. Young children brought up in that atmosphere are bound to be damaged, psychologically at least. If as often happens the woman addict resorts to prostitution, the risk of HIV infection adds to the dangers.

Once the children have been taken away, as many are, it becomes an uphill task to get them back. How does a woman who was once a drug addict show she is reformed, has appropriate accommodation, is able to bring up children in an adequate way and convince everybody she will not return to drugs? Doesn't everyone know that 'once a junkie, always a junkie'? Increasingly it will become harder and harder to reclaim the children. American legislation requires children who have been in care for 18 months or more to be considered automatically for adoption. The days are long gone where a mother could expect a child to remain in care for a number of years and then be able to reclaim it when she was ready.

If this type of legislation is introduced into Britain it will work as in the USA – that is, reduce the mother's window of opportunity giving her less time to show she is suitable.

Oppenheimer (1994: 86) shows how the social norms surrounding the sexes differ widely so that a woman who becomes an addict violates those norms surrounding the expectations of her sex and gender roles. Or as Murphy and Rosenbaum (1999: 134, 135) say, losing her child and being regarded as unfit to reclaim it means the woman is being labelled an unfit mother. This has horrendous consequences of personal and social condemnation and social isolation. Failure to perform mothering responsibilities is tantamount to failure as a woman.

Broom and Stevens (1991), in their study of women drug dealers, say sex and gender roles and the structural position of women in society have been neglected by male researchers. Putting it more forcibly, they say research has typically failed to consider how women's lives differ from those of men. They believe one reason why drug abuse is viewed with such condemnation in women is that intoxicated women fail to perform one of their major roles – which is to act as 'God's police' by keeping men in order:

> The social expectation that intoxication is permissible for men but not for women has a long history in Australia where ... sexual stereotypes have had it that respectable women must function as 'God's Police' imposing restraint, civilisation and decorum on men who would otherwise behave in barbaric and anti-social ways (*ibid.*: 26).

That being so, presumably like all who were once beyond reproach and who acted as 'God's police', their fall will be regarded as all the more blameworthy and reprehensible. They will get little sympathy from others (men included), who will be merciless about such failings. The point is that male drug users can more easily reclaim their status; women find it harder to do so, especially where the label was that of a junkie. However, there are ways to avoid the stigma. Girl gang-members, in the study by Hunt *et al.* (2000: 350), protected their feminine status yet were able to drink more freely because they did so by:

> partying with the girls. On such occasions they did not need to worry about their drinking behaviour tainting their reputations nor did they need to worry about men taking advantage of their inebriated state. The context free from the presence of men was the only situation in which the women found themselves acting in an

environment where the wider society's double standards on female drinking did not operate.

Whilst Broom and Stevens (1991) see the problem in terms of a flawed identity, others (such as Rosenbaum 1981) see the woman drug user as trapped in a world that offers little to them, except drugs, and few ways of escape. Their world has less to do with having a flawed identity and more with the reduced number of options available to the addict as she becomes more involved with the drug world. Rosenbaum (*ibid.*), in one of the classical studies of women and drugs, describes the woman's position as the 'career of narrowing options'. She goes on to say (*ibid.*: 49):

> Heroin expands her life options in the initial stages and that is the essence of its social attraction. Yet with progressively further immersion into the heroin world the social psychological exigencies of heroin create an option 'funnel' for the woman addict. Through the funnel the addict's life options are radically reduced until she is fundamentally incarcerated in an invisible prison. Ultimately the woman addict is locked into the heroin world and locked out of the conventional world.

Rosenbaum implies that 'the career of narrowing options' applies more to women than to men. She suggests that, when women are locked out of the conventional world, they find it more difficult to return or suffer greater hardship through that isolation. They mix only with other drug users, mostly men but of the type who will exploit women as and whenever they see it is in their interests to do so, or other women in a similar condition (i.e. junkies). Whether this is always so or only for American heroin addicts is a moot point. Clearly there is a shortage of comparable data for Britain, not just for heroin addicts but for women who take other drugs such as cannabis, LSD or ecstasy. Is their status similarly flawed to the point where they are reduced to that same career of narrowing options? We do not know. There is in Britain a view that women drug users are rather more fortunate than men. They are less likely to be given severe sentences for offences than men but they are less criminal anyway, and their drug taking is explained as being promoted and sustained by men. What is needed are some sound ethnographic studies describing the women's position, showing how that may differ from their American counterparts and seeing, too, if it varies according to the drug of choice.

All of which easily leads to a note of pessimism surrounding the woman drug user, a pessimism that is often misplaced and unjustified.

The positive side is that women drug users seem to have more pressure on them to make them 'grow up' than do men, and often that is what pushes them into treatment. They can and often do break out of that 'career of narrowing options' and have a success rate in treatment that is no worse than for men and often rather better (Oppenheimer 1994). It is never going to be easy for women drug users. Many of the pregnant women in the Murphy and Rosenbaum study (1999) were recipients of violence, poor parenting and poverty: 'For these women the American dream – a nurturing family with two kids, two cars, and a house with a garden and a white picket fence – was indeed a distant dream' (*ibid.*: 17). They conclude their study (*ibid.*: 157) with the view that:

> The greatest threat to effective parenting and child survival is a system that perpetuates poverty, violence, hardship and desperation. Rather than indicting pregnant drug users for their addictions and compulsions we should do well to look at their impossible conditions in which these women and their children are forced to live their lives.

For younger women, those in the 15–21 age group, it would seem that greater possibilities exist of being able to return to more conventional roles, especially if the drug-using episode is brief with little harm (i.e. not becoming pregnant) and the drugs taken were more of the 'soft' rather than the 'hard' variety. Yet for some young girls it is already too late. In our unreported study of young prostitutes in Nottingham who are drug users, preliminary results indicate there are about 60 young girls acting as prostitutes, aged between 12 and 16, many already in care, almost all are drug users (being supplied by their 'pimps'), and some of the pimps are women. It is difficult to be other than pessimistic about their future; their identity is already permanently flawed and their hopes of achieving conventional roles remote. How does a young drug-using prostitute, perhaps no older than 15 years, in care and has been so for nearly all her life, being 'pimped' and dressing in ways that emphasise her youth in order to attract paedophiles, expect to get out of that type of world? Her future, in whatever form it comes, will almost certainly be bleak.

Women drug users, crime and prison

In a written parliamentary answer it was said that, in March 1996, there were 2,120 women prisoners in England and Wales. In March 2000 the figure had increased to 3,392 (*Hansard* 2 May 2000: col. 922). Why the increase? The answer was that it was almost all due to drug offenders. Lord Bach explained: 'That does not mean possession of drugs but the selling of drugs and sometimes the importation of drugs.' He then went on to state what feminist criminologists have railed against for years – that 'There can be some mitigation for women – they can for instance be under pressure from male partners' and added, less controversially, 'but these are serious offences which are a danger to other women and to other people in general' (ibid.: cols. 923–4).

On 31 January 1999 there were 825 women in prison for drug offences (data taken from a written answer to the House of Commons on 24 February 1999). It is interesting to compare the women drug offenders serving 12 months or more as a proportion of other sentenced women prisoners serving similar sentences. On 31 January 1999, there were 782 women drug offenders serving 12 months or more out of a total population of 825 women drug offenders (or 94%). This compares with 1,868 other women offenders who were serving 12 months or more out of a total population of 2,391 (or 78%) (ibid.: col. 308). In other words, women serving 12 months or more were more likely to be drug offenders than others – 94% compared with 78%.

Some of these women drug offenders serving 12 months or more are foreign nationals. Many are charged with unlawful importation of drugs (448 of these were serving 12 months or more). The point prevalence figures for that day in January 1999 were that 274 foreign nationals were serving sentences for drug-related offences in England and Wales. However, on 31 December 1999, some 11 months later, that figure had risen to 312, serving an average sentence of 6.7 years.

The foreign nationals serving long sentences for drug importation have been the cause of much interest and concern. In the early 1990s, these women came mostly from Nigeria but after drastic action by the Nigerian authorities the numbers dropped steadily and, by February, were down to about 20. Most are now from Jamaica. Ian Burrell (reporting in The Independent 21 February 2000) says women smugglers from Jamaica are being arrested so frequently at Heathrow and Gatwick airports that they account for 1 in 16 of the female prison population in England and Wales. He reported that there were 184 Jamaican women in jail serving ten years or more, and that those from Jamaica are over-represented and are five times greater in number than any other nationality in women's prisons. Back in Jamaica the traffickers are 'targeting mothers with no criminal records. They are targeting hospitals in the Caribbean to recruit women who need money for medical treatment' (ibid.). The money is presumably for their families as well as for themselves.

These foreign nationals distort the figures for women offenders in

England and Wales as, of course, do drug offenders generally. They accentuate the already-rising rate of female prisoners and, with so many serving long sentences, they produce a lop-sided female prison population. What sort of problems these women create for their families and children back home we can only guess. Stories abound of their naïvety and gullibility. One was of a courier or 'mule' as they are called from Nigeria who, having been told heroin was legal in Britain, declared her cargo at Heathrow and was promptly arrested. This is probably apocryphal but perhaps not too far off the mark. If, as Burrell says, the trafffickers target those women wanting medical treatment, there will always be a ready-made pool of potential recruits who are in similar desperate straits and prepared to take the risk. We do not know how many successfully deliver their drugs and return crime free.

Interestingly enough, the problem seems not to be confined to Britain. Huling (1996) reports that a high percentage of women in prison in Latin America were detained or sentenced under drug-trafficking laws. In Cuenca, Ecuador, it was 62%, in Guayaquil, Ecuador, it was 40%, in Rio de Janeiro, Brazil, it was 28%, in Caracas, Venezuela, it was 51% and in Los Teques, Venezuela it was 43%. Presumably there would be similar figures for prisons in South East Asia.

For the other prisoners (i.e. the non-drug offenders in prisons in England and Wales), many have a drug history and some have a serious drug problem. On 3 July 2000 it was reported in *Hansard* that, in 1998–99 when almost 16,000 women were screened on reception into prison by health-care staff, 3,091 completed drug detox programmes and 413 completed alcohol detox programmes. Moreover, the minister (Paul Boateng), in a reply to a written question, reported a study undertaken in 1997 that indicated that in the year before entering prison, 36% of women on remand and 39% of sentenced women reported engaging in hazardous drinking, and 54% of women on remand and 41% of sentenced women reported some degree of drug dependence (*Hansard* 3 July 2000: cols. 70W–72W). This is a considerable proportion of imprisoned offenders who require treatment whilst in prison.

There is little information to allow comparisons to be made between men and women prisoners. A study by Brook *et al.* (1998) on 995 unconvicted prisoners randomly selected from all prisons in England and Wales (750 men and 245 women) shows that, before arrest, 145 (19.3%) men were dependent on street drugs compared with 72 (29.4%) women. There were 91 men (12.1%) and 16 women (6.5%) who were solely dependent on alcohol. Seventeen men (2.3%) reported injecting drugs during the current period of imprisonment compared with four women (1.6%). Out of the 995 subjects, 235 (24%) wanted treatment whilst in prison – 172 men and 63 women. Extrapolating this figure to the prison population generally, the authors concluded that 1,905 prisoners (male and female) wanted treatment for their substance abuse whilst in prison.

The treatment of women prisoners has long stimulated interest and controversy, whether of drug offenders or not. The accusation is that women prisoners are given too much treatment and usually of the wrong sort. For example, it has been a source of concern that women prisoners generally have been over-prescribed neuroleptics and other heavy tranquillisers such as Largactil. A debate in Parliament was on the motion that:

> this House is gravely concerned at evidence of the over prescribing of damaging and addictive medicinal drugs in women's prisons … [that] neuroleptic drugs are routinely prescribed to young women prisoners who mutilate themselves, and that medicinal drugs are used as pacifiers which move prisoners from non addictive illegal drugs to highly addictive medicinal drug use (*Hansard* 22 October 1998: col. 1400).

This debate was initiated by Mr Flynn, a member who had previously taken up the cause of over-prescribing neuroleptics and tranquillisers for women prisoners. He did not get the result he required but did succeed in bringing this to public attention. In an earlier question he wanted to know how many prescriptions for Largactil or Melleril and other antipsychotic drugs were issued. The reply was that:

> The prison service recognises that many women received into custody have complex medical histories and have very often already been prescribed the types of medications cited … Efforts are being made to reduce the prescribing of major and minor tranquillisers and neuroleptic drugs except where their use is clinically essential (*Hansard, Written Answers* 14 July 1998: col. 98).

There it seems is where the matter rests – at least for the time being. It still leaves open the question: what is 'clinically essential'? How is that to be interpreted? To use terms like 'clinical judgements' walks around the problem, for they imply there is something definitive or scientific about these judgements when they could as easily represent the less than unbiased views of the physician. That prescribing and over-prescribing in women's prisons have been a long-established practice is not in doubt, and questions about that practice need to be asked. Mr Boateng again:

We believe that it is important to ensure that in prisons there is a regime that does all that it possibly can not only to keep drugs out – that is why we emphasise creating in some prisons completely drug free wings where it is possible to provide the necessary alternative to counteract offending – but to educate prisoners to come to terms with their drug misuse that led them to be there in the first place (*Hansard, Prisons and Drugs* 10 December 1998: col. 540).

This statement applies equally to men and women. It does not answer the question about prescribing in women's prisons nor, perhaps, was it intended to. That efforts are being made to reduce prescribing is to be welcomed, although many would say not before time.

Women as users and dealers

Anglin and Hser (1987b) say women tend to report first drug use at a later age than men and are frequently initiated into use by their male partners, who are often their main suppliers in the course of their addiction. They go on to say that women report a briefer transition from first drug to addiction. Anecdotally, it seems women tend to be more rapacious in their drug use, at least in the initial stages, but then for the reasons given above are more likely to see the dangers. There is also a current belief that women who see themselves involved in a mission to save their menfolk from the evils of drugs invariably finish up addicted. They also become heavier users than their men.

Distinctions need to be made between middle-class drug users and others. Middle-class women cocaine users (the drug in question is almost always cocaine and the studies almost always American) say that women use drugs for recreational reasons to add to their lives or 'just for fun' (Sterk-Elifson 1996). Cocaine is seen as the perfect lady-like drug (Greenleaf 1989). There are no unsightly injection marks and no pressure to hang around bars to obtain it. 'Also it's slimming, you're not in a stupor, you don't slur your words, and you can carry it around in your cosmetic case just like the lipstick.' Or, as one user said, 'I can feel this good and lose weight too' (*ibid.*: 12). The problem comes when the demand for the drug begins to get out of hand or when they begin to feel and recognise they are losing control. What then? Sterk-Elifson (1996) says women at this point begin to recognise they must give up the myth of using just for fun. They are then faced with a number of dilemmas: 'If their use is discovered the women might lose their jobs, their relationships, and if they are mothers the custody of their children. The women do not want to lose what they have; they want cocaine to add to their lives not destroy them' (*ibid*.: 72). The other problem is that once the drug use begins to get out of hand, women become less selective about their partners. Their decision is then based more around cocaine than the quality of any prospective relationship (*ibid*.: 70).

Outside this rather protected middle-class world, Morgan and Joe (1996) suggest that women users, with very few exceptions, are restricted to passive or victimised roles in a social world dominated by men. Their drug use is limited to their relationship with men and they rarely consider that their use was shaped by choices outside their gendered relationship. Some (a small number) become dealers, and a few are successful. In our study of drug dealing in Nottingham (Bean and Wilkinson 1988), we found a small number of women dealers who successfully operated using their boyfriends or current partners to collect debts and enforce discipline. These women changed partners regularly and the street talk was that they informed on them to remove them, either because they were not up to the task or because they were likely to take over the business. Similarly in their study of women crack users in New York, Johnson *et al.* (2000) found that crack-using women in Harlem claimed (and were so observed) to be relatively equal to male counterparts in their performance of street-level distribution roles as sellers or low-level distributors.

Morgan and Joe (1996) identified what they called the 'citizen dealer' who was mainly middle class (or aspiring middle class) and who was living in the mainstream of social life, regardless of the drug being used or the level of dealing. They also identified the 'outlaws', whose lifestyles were such as to be significantly immersed in deviant activities and who were living marginal lives. The former were either high-level dealers – in this case usually selling amphetamine that provided them with a major source of income – or part-time dealers selling to a small selective group of friends while maintaining regular employment. They felt pride in their accomplishments as dealers. Being 'able to retain or return to a measure of stability and respectability they were found to be living in good neighbourhoods. They had money, often a husband and family and sometimes a regular job' (*ibid*.: 132). In contrast, the outlaw dealer fitted more closely the view of women as operating in a passive and victimised role in which men dominated their social world. The outlaws come in one of two forms: either as victims when they are heavy users often working as prostitutes whose dealing is to make a living to furnish their own supplies or as survivors. Whether as victim or survivor, the life chances were limited, all had previous convictions and all lived marginal lives (*ibid*.: 135–42).

Most studies see women dealers as more likely to be outlaws than citizens. They support the view that the position of women in the drug world is 'parallel [to] the division in the straight society' (Broom and Stevens 1991: 27). Typically, Broom and Stevens describe women as prostitutes and couriers, whilst men occupied the high-prestige position as dealers. Johnson *et al.* (2000), in their ethnographic study of Brooklyn, reported gender and ethnic biases directed at women. They found that crack-using women were left with virtually no option other than sex work, primarily because they would not be hired as day labourers by crack-selling crews (*ibid.*: 35–6). Whilst women may resist male domination as best they can, none the less, Murphy and Arroyo (2000) argue that women are at a decided disadvantage when they try to enter and operate in the drugs markets. What they called 'ambient violence' or emotional violence (or simply physical abuse) was an all too common occurrence. They say that in the subculture of addiction, masculine values relegate women to secondary roles, making them dependent on the dominant males. Drug use, ambient violence, gender roles and inadequate retaliation capacities meant that most women did not sell for long periods of time (*ibid.*: 105).

The emphasis in the research suggests that women are in the minority when it comes to dealing: there is no suggestion they become dealers at the highest level nor that they are high-level traffickers. However, things might be changing. Dunlap and Johnson (1996) think there may be more women dealers coming forward so that, whereas women have traditionally been on the demand side of drug markets (i.e. working as prostitutes in order to purchase drugs), they may increasingly be moving into the supply side. If so, this would mark an important development.

Women in treatment

There is general agreement that drug-using women have different treatment needs from their male counterparts. How and in what form is difficult to say; too often it depends on the drugs taken, the lifestyle and their perceptions of themselves based on their life experiences. Certainly the reasons women enter treatment seem to be different from those of men – although, once in treatment, outcomes remain comparable. American research suggests that, for men, the routes into treatment are invariably through the criminal justice system whereas, for women, they are through counsellors or social workers. Grella and Joshi (1999) studied gender factors associated with having a history of drug treatment; this involved a study of 7,652 individuals admitted to the national Drug

Abuse Treatment Outcome Study (DATOS). They concluded (*ibid*.: 385–6) that:

> Prior drug treatment among men was associated with factors related to family opposition to drug use and support for treatment, whereas for women prior drug treatment was associated with anti-social personality disorder and self initiation into treatment. More-over, treatment initiatives among men appear to be facilitated by social institutions such as employment, the criminal justice system and one's family. In contrast treatment re-entry among women was associated by referral by a social worker suggesting that family service agencies can facilitate women's entry.

In other words, men were pushed into treatment by threats but women entered after counselling. If so, this supports the general view that drug-dependent women have treatment needs different from men, and that these needs should be recognised and dealt with. Too often the accusation is that they are not. At its worst, women in treatment are seen as there to assist with the treatment of men ('Would someone take the part of this man's wife/girlfriend/mother in this next role play' type of situation). Slightly better but no more helpful is the assumption that women are to receive the same therapeutic inputs as men, which may be wholly irrelevant ('All he [the therapist] keeps saying is that patients should exercise and receive more controls. It's because I had too much control from my father/husband/boyfriend that I became a drug user in the first place' type of comment). Greenleaf (1989: 7) reports that women are more passive and depressed about their situation than male drug users in treatment: 'They're just not dealing with their problems and are not assertive about how they feel about things.'

Wellisch *et al.* (1993) note the shortage of data on women drug users, especially on those women in treatment. They believe two models of treatment have emerged: the first is an empowerment model where women are encouraged to perceive themselves as actors rather than victims, able to direct their own lives. The second is more practical, aimed at providing women with coping skills that will permit them to make the desired changes to their lives. These may relate to their status as parents (single parents and otherwise) or to family planning, alongside assertiveness and vocational training. The aim is to recognise the failings of women drug users (defined as 'a combination of inadequate and maladaptive social-behavioural and cognitive skills' (cited in *ibid*.: 8)) and yet remedy these whilst, at the same time, treating the substance abuse. Wellisch *et al.* argue that all treatment programmes for women, including those for women in prison, should, irrespective of the main theoretical formulation, contain the following components:

1. Provide the means for women to maintain or re-establish contact with their children.
2. Provide vocational training and career opportunities in higher-paying fields for women.
3. Ensure women offenders receive adequate health care.

Wellisch *et al.* (*ibid.*: 23) say that many women do not understand the child-care system or how to present their case. Also, there may be shame and resentment from both mother and children, which makes it difficult to re-establish and maintain contact. Visiting their mothers in prison is never an edifying experience for children, but that will be the only way to continue the relationship so it has to be done and made the best of. However, in the last few years the climate has changed and the rights of the child are being seen as increasingly important. For whilst every effort must be made to assist the mother to provide a life for herself and her family, the onus is on her to make the necessary changes to her life. She must make the effort; she must get off drugs and stay off if she is to be allowed to have her children back. She must convince the authorities she is serious, and that her intentions are firm about accepting treatment and about staying drug free. There are limits to the amount of time children can be expected to wait for their mothers to make the decision. They, too, have a life to lead and have the right to be brought up in a drug-free environment with parents who place children above the importance of using drugs.

In the second the aim is to persuade the women drug users to think about training for higher-paid jobs and away from seeing themselves as capable of working only in the traditional low-paid industries generally reserved for women. Wellisch *et al.* (1993) say that most women are the sole providers for their children, rarely receiving help from the fathers. Worse than that, most at the time of arrest or at the end of any sentence were less equipped to earn a high wage than many men in a similar situation (*ibid.*: 23). Opportunities are available. Sometimes all that is needed is for women to have the confidence and encouragement to train and apply. Their motivation is not in question; the hurdle to be overcome is more about self-belief than anything else.

Finally, access to health care is, for obvious reasons, less of a problem in Britain than the USA, but the point needs to be made, none the less. Wellisch *et al.* (*ibid.*) say that women have special health problems, such as those relating to gynaecological care, alongside the need for mammary examinations. In addition, women dependent on drugs are likely to have sexually transmitted diseases, which may include being HIV positive and that will need special attention. They also say that, since a large number of female drug users have also been subject to sexual abuse, counselling and psychological support are also required (*ibid.*: 24).

These three components are regarded as essential in any treatment plan for women drug users. How far they are part of the programmes for treatment in Britain is not known – nor is it known the extent of support they could expect from significant others in their families or friends. There is a suggestion that little support is forthcoming; indeed, Grella and Joshi (1999) report that women should expect little support from their partners and family members. They say they will more likely receive opposition, which sometimes includes intimidation and threats. That being so, the task is greater and the level of pessimism mentioned earlier increasingly justified. Hence, Wellisch *et al.* (1993: 25) conclude that 'it is incumbent on policy makers to increase treatment availability and to the extent that current knowledge permits, optimise the effectiveness of treatment programmes'.

A note on juveniles

Helene White (1990), in her review of the literature on drug use and delinquency in adolescence, concludes that although the findings are sometimes equivocal and sometimes outright contradictory, several of the contradictions may be due to the differences in measurements and samples. Writing in 1990 she concluded (p. 240) that there are four con-vergent views that emerge from the literature:

1 In adolescence, general forms of drug use and delinquency are not causally related but are spuriously related because they are both types of deviant action in which adolescents engage.

2 Adolescents are heterogeneous in terms of their levels of substance use and delinquency, and the occurrence of both behaviours.

3 The majority of adolescents have no or only minor delinquency involvement regardless of the extent of their substance use.

4 Peer group influences are the best predictors of delinquency and drug use.

In the decade following these comments a number of changes have occurred. The so-called four convergent views no longer seem relevant, especially that which sees the relationship between drugs and crime as spurious. The links for this age group seem more pronounced. However, before looking at that in more detail, some points need to be made about juvenile offenders generally.

In Britain (as in all Western European-type countries) the peak age for delinquency is 15 and the peak age group is 15–18, followed by 18–21 and then 18–24. The peak age for boys is slightly younger than for girls. This has been so for almost as long as records have been kept, and confirmed by almost every research study. The ratio of convicted boys to girls is about 4:1; boys also tend to commit a wider range of offences than girls. The peak onset age is 13–16 while the peak desistence age is 21–25, but of course many offenders continue to commit offences after this. An early onset of offending predicts that a boy will follow a serious criminal career. The majority of offences committed by young people are property offences but most offenders are versatile: people who commit one type of offence have a significant tendency also to commit other types (e.g. violent offenders also commit non-violent offences) (see Farrington 1997).

The onset of drug abuse is a little later (i.e. delinquency often precedes drug abuse). Although some young people begin taking drugs at a very young age (12 or 13 years), the peak age of onset is 20–24 (Bean 2001a: 5). However, a sizeable number began drug taking – called a starting episode – earlier. Table 9.1 gives the age and gender of users 'starting agency episodes' in the six months ending 30 September 1998 for those classified as addicts. Thereafter the rate is reduced, and dramatically so once over the age of 34 years. In Table 9.1 the ratio of male to female drug takers is about 3:1 and remains so for all ages – incidentally, up to the age of 64+. The peak age is 20–24. Data from the British Crime Survey in 1998 show that young people aged 16–29 reported the highest level of drug misuse (Ramsey *et al.* 1999). There, some 49% indicated that they had taken a prohibited drug at some time over the last month or year. For the

Table 9.1 Age and gender of users starting agency episodes, 6 months ending 30 September 1998

Age group	Male	Female	Total
<15	175	74	249
15–19	3,353	1,517	4,870
20–24	6,845	2,570	9,415
25–29	6,788	2,190	8,978

Source: Derived from Department of Health (1999a: Table C2).

16–29 age group, this figure was 25% in the last year and 16% in the last month (*ibid.*).

Generally speaking, therefore, criminality proceeds drug use by four or five years, at least as far as is shown by the peak age for both morbidities is concerned. However, it is likely that *serious* drug abuse begins at an earlier age, as does delinquency, thereby skewing the prevalence and incidence. Research shows extensive drug use amongst juveniles: between 40% and 57% of adolescents treated for substance disorders had also committed delinquent acts. What is also alarming is the high rate of mental disorder in these populations, especially where drug use was of early onset (Nemitz 2001).

The first point made by Helene White (1990: 240) is that drug abuse and delinquency are not causally related – she says the relationship is spurious. This, however, is not supported by other research mentioned above or of the type of 'criminal career' research undertaken by David Farrington. Farrington's conclusion (1997: 399) is that offending is one element of a larger syndrome of anti-social behaviour that arises in childhood and tends to persist in adulthood with numerous differential manifestations. This is the most detailed and comprehensive research programme on juvenile delinquency. It is methodologically sound and theoretically relevant.

Farrington defines a criminal career as a longitudinal sequence of offences committed by an individual offender (*ibid.*: 361). It has a beginning (onset), an end (desistance) and a career length in between (duration). The criminal career approach operates on the basis that not all people from the same geographical area commit offences, or even those within the same family. The question, then, is: why do some and not others? The aim is to study human development over time, which means investigating how one type of behaviour facilitates or acts as a stepping stone to another. Farrington gives the example of hyperactivity – not a criminal offence – but hyperactivity at the age of two may lead to cruelty to animals the age of six, shoplifting at ten, drug abuse at 14 and violence at a later age (*ibid.*).

This type of research shows how an anti-social syndrome, of which drug taking and delinquency are but two features, is tied into a wider set of behaviour. In the Cambridge study Farrington found that some delinquents tend to be troublesome in their primary schools, tend to be aggressive and frequent liars at 12–14, and bullies at 14. By 18 they tended to be anti-social in a wide variety of respects, including heavy drinking, heavy smoking, heavy gambling, and using prohibited drugs. In addition they tend to be sexually promiscuous, often beginning sexual intercourse under the age of 15. Delinquency, of which drug taking is but one part, is dominated by crimes of dishonesty and is one element of a larger syndrome of anti-social behaviour which arises in childhood and persists until adulthood.

Desistance (which, for offending and drug taking, seems to coincide) generally takes place in their late 20s, although heavy alcohol consumption is likely to continue throughout their lives. Farrington lists a number of reasons for desistance from crime: the cost of crime (long prison sentences), the importance of intimate relationships with the opposite sex (yet many will have been divorced by the age of 30 and fail to support their children), increasing satisfaction with their jobs and becoming more settled as they grow older (*ibid*.: 374). There is little research on desistance from drugs; anecdotally it seems that by their late 20s many drug users will take 'early retirement' – drug use, it seems, is a demanding career with numerous disappointments, numerous periods in prison, high rates of depression and few prospects. (There is also a high mortality rate, estimated at about 27 times than for the age group as a whole.) Drug users talk of the 'straw that broke the camel's back' or 'turnaround time'. That means that the cumulative impact of numerous periods of imprisonment catches up with an offender: he suddenly decides to stop. How and why such changes occur at the particular time remain unclear, but 'retirement' tends to be an abrupt decision and, although there may be occasional relapses, drug taking as a lifestyle ceases. Alcohol use, however, does not.

The essential features of criminal career research are that offenders, which include drug takers, differ significantly from non-offenders in many respects, including impulsivity, intelligence, family background and socioeconomic deprivation. The most persistent chronic offenders could be predicted as early as the age of two (i.e. individuals at risk can be identified with reasonable accuracy). The precise causal connections are still not known and most of the research is confined to males.

In one important respect, the problem of juveniles is a problem of the manner in which a large proportion of substance misusers have the responsibility for the care of children. Substance misuse may not necessarily lead to problems in child care or the neglect or abuse of children (Department of Health 2002), but it often does. NTORS (Gossop *et al*. 1998) found that 47% of drug misusers entering treatment were responsible for children aged 18 or under – over 90% of females presenting for treatment were of child bearing age. The evidence suggests that parental substance abuse is associated with a higher risk of involvement of families in care proceedings, and children of substance misusers are more vulnerable to substance misuse than children of non-substance misusers (Department of Health 2002: 146).

The Department of Health (*ibid.*: 146–7) provides a catalogue of failings due to the impact on the children's physical and emotional health of substance-abusing parents. First is the birth itself:

> The foetus is at risk of harm due to substance misuse through the direct effects of drugs or alcohol: infection, lack of adequate antenatal care, poor maternal health and nutrition … Opiates and cocaine cause an increased risk of obstetric complications including low birth weight, still birth, prematurity and neonatal withdrawal.

After birth the following are likely to occur: 'Inadequate stimulation, an increased risk of Sudden Infant Death Syndrome, poor care and nutrition and exposure to domestic violence.'

In late life, school-aged children have an increasing risk of developing the following: 'behavioural problems including truancy, adjustment problems, poor academic achievement, and school exclusion.' When they are older, children of substance-abusing parents have a greater risk of developing 'mental health problems, comorbid psychiatric disorders that are a consequence of or are worsened by substance misuse [which] can have a negative impact on parenting (e.g. psychosis, depression) often making the parent emotionally "unavailable" to the child' (*ibid.*).

Children who are brought up in substance-misusing families face additional problems (local addiction units are now treating the grandchildren of methadone-maintenance users). They are likely to spend periods in care, and their physical health may also suffer. We have not taken it upon ourselves to determine the outcome of children in these substance-abusing families. Notwithstanding that, problem drug use generally often begins with children under the age of 15 years, and some of these will be problem drug users by the time they are 18. Presumably many will simply stop taking these substances and come to no harm, but some will not: hence the need for good longitudinal studies to see what the effects are on those who continue to take drugs.

As far as the criminal justice system is concerned, astonishingly the youth court system in Britain appears not to have made provisions for juvenile drug users. For example, drug use is not mentioned in the large number of provisions found in the Crime and Disorder Act 1997. There are parenting orders, orders that deal with unruly children, etc., but these are not tied into a debate about children as drug misusers. This omission is all the more noticeable when set against the conclusions reached in American drug courts – namely, that it was neither possible nor practicable to transplant drug courts on to the juvenile justice system without adjusting to the special demands of children. That is to say the treatment of juveniles is qualitatively different from that of adults. Treatment must include treatment of the child's family for without agreement and support from the parents and family members, treatment programmes are quickly undermined. Similarly, children in treatment have to be separated from their peer groups lest treatment is also undermined, albeit for different reasons. Most of all, children should not be seen as young adults but as children. Children are children. Treatment for children requires a different approach and schema that are more labour intensive than with adults and a great deal more complicated. Yet the rewards are also greater. A child treated successfully will be cost effective in terms of future criminality and be a significant success in terms of a reduction in the extent of drugs to be consumed.

In Britain, the *UK Anti-drugs Coordinator's Annual Report 1999–2000* has a section on young people and another on treatment (Cabinet Office 2000). In the first, considerable attention is given, rightly, to prevention and drug education in schools, the latter linked to primary health-care professionals. These programmes take various forms, most are imaginative and many will improve the levels of drug education and prevention. There are programmes which include targeted drug prevention focusing on young people at risk. These are important given the data which came out of the schools' survey of drug prevalence carried out by the Office for National Statistics (cited in *ibid*.: 47). The survey was carried out among more than 9,000 pupils aged 11–15 in about 340 schools in England. Results show that 7% (about 1 in 14) had used drugs in the last month prior to the survey. In 1999, of pupils aged 11–15, there were 12% who had used drugs in the last year. Cannabis was by far the most likely drug to have been used; fewer than 0.5% of 11–15-year-olds had used opiates (heroin and methadone) in the last year, but 3% had used stimulants, including cocaine, crack, ecstasy, amphetamines and poppers. This gives some indication of the extent of the problem, but which children are those who stop using drugs and which are those who will not are the key questions here.

Chapter 10

Suggestions for the way forward

If there is a general sense of gloom surrounding the drug problem in Britain, that view is misplaced. There is nothing inevitable about the current level of substance abuse; we do not have to live with high levels of abuse, any more than we have to live with high crime rates. There are a number of things we can do but most require changes, and change is not always welcome. Resistance can come from the unlikeliest quarters. For example, American judges in drug courts often say they do not believe British judges and magistrates will adopt the necessary procedural changes required to introduce drug courts generally into the UK. They may turn out to be wrong, as the Scottish and Irish examples may to some extent prove. Resistance to change may come from other quarters, such as those involved in treatment who, on the face of it, would be expected to support greater measures of treatment for offenders. Or partnerships will be unwelcome because some criminal justice organisations are reluctant to set aside their ideological differences. Change means more than making adjustments to new ideas – it means accepting changes in status and influence.

The 1960s and beyond

Writing in 1974 on the links between drug taking and crime, I remember saying that the relationship was complex and the research evidence inconclusive – at worst poor and at best able only to identify a small number of the many strands that made up the debate. Few attempts were made to establish a causal connection between the two morbidities.

Now, looking back over 30 years, it seems we have not moved very far, except perhaps we now have different pictures of the drug users – and this may not be an advance. Then, drug takers were seen as victims of social and psychological pathologies; now they are more likely seen as predatory criminals. Not entirely, but the image of the drug taker as predator would likely be dominant. Changes can be seen in small things, such as the way drug takers are encouraged to receive treatment, not for therapeutic benefits but to stop them taking drugs. The emphasis is different now.

Also, in that earlier period, few specific questions could be formulated, so wide and vast appeared the subject and so limited was our experience. It was an entirely new problem to Britain. One question that has emerged and which remains uppermost is the links with crime. Then the debate, such as existed, was dominated by the rights and wrongs of the maintenance prescribing of heroin or cocaine. Did prescribing reduce or encourage criminality? The answer then as now is that it all depends, but on what does it depend? It depends on whether the drug user is 'basically criminal' – a term derived from America in the 1930s when Commissioner Anslinger said 'it was the criminal type who became the addict'.

In Britain in the 1930s the crime figures showed drug takers were not prone to criminal activity, but this had changed by the 1960s when prescribing was at its height. Then, Ian James, the prison medical officer at Brixton Prison, found that at any one time about 200 addicts were in his prison. This represented about one quarter of all known male heroin addicts. He noted, too, that most addicts sold their prescribed drugs, later buying them back having used up their own supplies. He described most addicts as 'full time addicts whose daily routine was scoring and fixing, allowing no time for anything but casual work' (cited in Bean 1974). They had no regular employment, presumably supplementing what they had by crime. Yet, and here was the essential point, others (about half) were also prescribed heroin and cocaine, but were not criminal, whether before drug taking or later. It is this non-criminal group of drug users, especially those taking heroin or cocaine, who undermine any argument about the inevitability of the links with crime.

In the 1960s the general consensus was that about 40% of heroin addicts were 'basically criminal', defined as having criminal convictions prior to drug taking (Bean 1971). Drug takers, it seemed, came from two distinct groups: one from lower social class backgrounds, who were antecedently delinquent before drug taking, and the other from a higher social class who were not. The former saw drug taking as an extension of their deviant lifestyles, whilst the other saw drugs as an extension of a worldview influenced by writers such as Aldous Huxley, where drugs provided new forms of spiritual salvation. These two groups remain. The difference then was that the middle-class group dominated; now it is those who are 'basically criminal'. There remains, however, a sizeable middle-class group who take drugs to enhance social relationships and to produce more intense psychological experiences. For these, cocaine remains the champagne drug. These are in addition to the so-called recreational users who take ecstasy and cannabis occasionally. Nowadays, terms like 'basically criminal' or 'ideologically motivated' (the latter for the middle-class group) are not used; others are preferred, but they simply put a different label on the same product.

In the 1960s no one spoke of traffickers or thought of dealers as importing drugs into Britain to sell for profit. The world of organised crime was alien to that period – organised crime took place somewhere else, in Italy or the USA. Dealers, such as there were, bought and sold drugs from their friends or other users in Piccadilly Circus and the like. These were not the shadowy figures from overseas but locals who sold their surpluses creating a new group of users who, in turn, found their own over-prescribing doctors and received their own inflated supplies. In the mid-1970s, when prescribing was reduced (i.e. after the introduction of treatment centres and licensed doctors), the first imports of 'Chinese heroin' appeared on the streets – and with them the first traffickers and dealers in their modern form. In the 1980s the cocaine epidemic confirmed the identity of the trafficker and dealer, and the role of the organised criminal as a potent force in the British drug scene. Back in the 1960s the American position and policies were derided. Now they are hardly distinguishable from the British.

In one respect the British system remains distinct, iconoclastic almost, in that prescribing continues, even for the opiates. Controlling the prescribing habits of the medical profession remains a less than easy task that is now undertaken by the Home Office Drugs Inspectorate with the assistance of the General Medical Council, but what constitutes over-prescribing and its corollary of serious professional misconduct will always be difficult. During the 1960s the largest 'pusher' of drugs was the National Health Service (NHS) through its over-prescribing doctors. The heaviest over-prescribers were small in number but gross over-prescribers, none the less. Alongside these were another group, much larger in number, who prescribed rather more than the average. The NHS is no longer seen as an over-prescriber, but over-prescribing still exists. Whilst there may not be the gross over-prescribing of the 1960s, there remain a number of doctors who 'prescribe rather more than the average', whether to typical drug users or to the less typical, such as those receiving repeat prescriptions for such drugs as Valium and other benzodiazepines – and in large amounts. As before, the surpluses can be sold producing the same type of 'spillage' as occurred in the 1960s when over-prescribed heroin users sold their surplus supplies.

Maintenance prescribing of opiates remains, although there is probably little over-prescribing here. (This in contrast to methadone. The case for prescribing as an alternative to heroin has not, in my view, ever been adequately made but that is a different question.) Currently there are about 300 drug users in Britain receiving maintenance supplies of heroin. These are almost the forgotten users – no one mentions them and no one knows much about them – yet their numbers remain steady and they continue to receive their supplies. They raise the age-old question so dominant in the 1960s about the role of the prescribing physician, supplying addicts with the drug of their choice. What should be the place of maintenance prescribing of heroin in any system of control? Should it be permitted, should it be encouraged or should it be banished? If, as it appears, maintenance prescribing is, *inter alia*, a delinquency prevention device, can this form of medical intervention be justified or should prescribing be permitted only in exceptional circumstances and, if so, what are they? Not much thought appears to be given to these matters, so keen are we nowadays to push drug taking into criminal justice and see the drug user as a property offender funding a habit.

There is, however, a groundswell of opinion which suggests we should return to greater levels of over-prescribing, in the sense that more addicts should receive maintenance prescribing. Rarely is this view linked to the experience of the 1960s, where the system was regularly abused whether by the users or prescribers. The lesson learnt then was that maintenance prescribing must be controlled, and those undertaking the prescribing must be strictly regulated. Also, it must be understood that maintenance prescribing is not for everyone but for those who are unlikely to seek and benefit from treatment. It is for the 'end of the road' user, not the young initiate.

Again, as far as comparisons with the 1960s are concerned, we have no reliable national database; if anything the situation has deteriorated. In the 1960s there was the Home Office Addicts Index. This peculiarly British institution was scrapped in 1997, leaving mainly the British Crime Survey – hardly a database. The Home Office Index was neither reliable nor valid, but it was of some value, producing interesting socio-demographic material on selected addicts over a long period. It could have been improved had there been the political will to turn it into a large-scale national longitudinal database, but that was not forthcoming.

Its history is interesting. It began in the early 1920s in a haphazard way when a number of addicts notified the Home Office that they were drug users and said they were receiving supplies of heroin and the like from their physicians. Other addicts followed, some asking to have their names recorded on a register. The myth of the so-called 'registered' addict was born and was sustained throughout the 1960s and beyond. Being on the register produced no favours or privileges but, presumably, the addicts thought it did, or at the very least thought it protected them in some way. In fact it merely gave the Home Office information about the extent of use and the numbers on prescription (Spear 2002).

This Index illustrated the measure of trust that existed between the addict and the government in ways unrecognisable today. Losing that Index and trust has not been wise for where else in the world would this happen? Where else would drug users inform a government department responsible for their control that they had been involved in illegal activities, that they had recently used a drug illegally and wanted to change into a fully fledged, protected and lawfully supplied drug addict? There were attempts to make registration a less haphazard process. Under the Notification of Addict Regulations, selected professional groups were required to inform the Home Office of users they were treating or meeting in other areas in their professional capacity. This they seldom did and, mainly for this reason, the index fell into disrepute. Attempts to revive it have not been successful. As a result a potentially valuable research and planning instrument has been lost and will not easily be revived.

Finally, and continuing with comparisons with the 1960s, the quality of research then as now was poor. It offered little help to policy-makers and governments, the difference being that in the 1960s there was little understanding of the research agenda and more excuse for shortcomings. Government policy then, as now, was based on a set of a priori assumptions driven by political rather than pragmatic, empirical demands. In the 1960s, when drug use was rare, spoken of by only a small number of interested physicians and a few government officials such as H.B. (Bing) Spear, such research as existed was basic and of an exploratory, descriptive nature. There was no research tradition and little to go on, nationally or internationally. This has changed; there is more of a research tradition today but whether this has intruded on government policy is another question.

Earlier research was dominated by a psychiatric worldview – a fairly common phenomenon in the early stages of a new social problem. Later, as academic interest widened, other social scientists began to take an interest but, even then, the range was narrow. That problem remains; for example, there are too few economists interested in drug research and too few lawyers, but rather too many of what Bing Spear disdainfully called 'policy analysts'. We badly need research on the impact of prices on drug use, on the way confiscation orders operate, on the cost effectiveness of treatment programmes and policing, and on some of the jurisprudential questions raised by current legislation. We have a surfeit of small-scale epidemiological studies showing that drug use has increased and criminality has increased likewise, but little that sheds light on, say, the supply system or the treatment services. We have only one or two longitudinal studies able to provide data showing patterns and trends, and this is a serious failing.

We need two or three high-quality research centres with guaranteed funding undertaking a long-term research programme. Sadly, there is not the political will to push ahead with this type of programme. Instead we produce reports by committees, where the enthusiastic amateur holds sway. The journalist and the celebrity are given more credence than the researcher. It is a recipe for going nowhere except to re-examine and debate the old same questions – usually, it seems, about whether cannabis should be legalised or its penalties be reduced. There are more pressing questions than this, about the quality of life on drug-ridden housing estates or levels of violence by dealers – whether on dealers or by dealers – or on the impact of drug abuse on fragile communities. Yet as long as we continue with this type of blue-ribbon committee where members are experts in other fields, in fact in almost any other but substance abuse, we shall make few advances. The opportunities are there. We have a government strategy and public recognition that something must be done if the next generation is to be protected from the drug scourge. If we waste this opportunity now it may not easily come again.

Contributions from the drugs–crime debate

What can the drugs–crime debate offer to help promote a reduction in drug use? The answer is quite a lot. We may not know much but we know a great deal more than before, and we are beginning to know what we do not know. We are also increasingly aware that time is not on our side; the problem increases daily. In the USA, drug use is declining but largely among students and the middle classes, not in the inner cities which produce the most intractable problems. There it remains, defying all obvious and apparent solutions, wreaking havoc as before.

A comment by James Inciardi and Duane McBride (1991: 75) sums up for me the essential elements of the current position. I want to pick up some of these points throughout:

> In the final analysis drug abuse is a complicated and intractable problem that cannot be solved with quick fix approaches tended to by politically appointed boards. Deploying more patrol boats in the Caribbean or diverting additional high technology military hardware will not guarantee an end to or even a slowing of the war. Intercepting drugs at the border or cutting off illegal drugs at the source are praiseworthy goals but they are likely impossible ones. And pressurising source countries into compliance with U.S. objectives is also an elusive task, even when there is willingness.

So what then is the answer? Inciardi and McBride again:

> Thus if total elimination of the supply of drugs is impossible then more attention should be focussed on the demand side of the equation. For after all without drug users there would be no drug problem. The weapons here are treatment and education, initiatives that seem to be both working and failing – working for some but failing for others (*ibid.*).

Inciardi says we must concentrate on demand for we can expect only limited success from interdiction policies or other forms of law enforcement. John Grieve (an experienced police officer concerned with drugs in London) said a good day for the police was a day when the problem was no worse. He added that these days are few and far between (Grieve 1993: 8). Presumably he echoes Inciardi's views. We should not lose the appetite for interdiction or enforcement, but reducing the supply side of the equation cannot solve the problem. There will always be limits to what can be achieved by reducing supply although, of course, we could still do better. For example, undermining the profits by a more efficient confiscation policy would help. But the demand side is the key; reducing demand will offer the best and only long-term results.

We can begin by saying what does not work. For example, sending police officers into schools to frighten children about the effects of drugs does not work, nor does the so-called 'Scared Straight' programme work where young people on the edge of criminality (drug abuse) meet convicted offenders (addicts) who have landed up in gaol. Nor it appears do programmes such as DARE (Drug Abuse Resistance Education), where children are taught to say 'no to drugs'. These programmes come in various forms. For example, the DARE programme in Nottingham is run by the police who teach the courses in the primary schools – I would add at enormous cost, probably about £750,000 per annum – but there are others, much smaller, run by other agencies. To say these do not work is premature; rather we do not know if these programmes work as rarely have they been evaluated, except by DARE itself, which hardly gives confidence that the findings were unbiased. Some of the smaller programmes have been evaluated and, whilst early results are encouraging, long-term effects are not yet forthcoming.

We also know what does not work in the criminal justice system – that is, we know that fining drug users, placing them on probation or sending them to prison have little effect of themselves. Without a built-in treatment programme in these sentences we can expect few successes. Long-term street addicts are unsuitable for fines or for probation as, indeed, are almost all drug users. They rarely pay fines, and probation is unlikely to have sufficient impact. Everything we know about probation and the way it works says that probation cannot be the answer. As for prison, again without a built-in treatment programme prison on its own is likely only to hold back drug abuse until release. Fortunately there are some imaginative and successful treatment programmes in prison nowadays; these offset the experience of most drug users in prison that the sentence means drug use is suspended rather than treated – and often not even that as drugs are available in prisons as well as in special hospitals such as Broadmoor, Rampton and Ashworth.

In our eagerness to succeed we should avoid going down that other route which places abstinence above all else, including civil liberties. Some programmes are unacceptable if only because they infringe, violate or simply ignore civil liberties. The most common are those involving preventative treatment (sometimes called preventative containment) which are used to detain drug users *qua* drug users – that is, without there first being a conviction for an offence and without the safeguards provided by due process of the criminal law. Typically, preventative treatment permits detention in a hospital for as long as necessary to cure the addiction. The justification is that drug abuse is also a public health measure; it involves treating a disease, albeit self-inflicted, which, if left untreated, will take disproportionate amounts of health resources to the detriment of the non-addicted population. Preventative treatment is widely used in the USA, especially where the drug user is pregnant and taking heroin or cocaine. It is suggested that, if left untreated, the patient will incur extensive health-care costs, not just for herself but for her child. Better therefore to detain her early and provide treatment before it is too late (i.e. before giving birth).

Going down that route, in my view, leads to an unjustifiable loss of liberty and is certainly not acceptable on the basis of health-care costs. I am aware that certain notifiable diseases permit civil courts in Britain to detain a person until cured, but drug use would not in my judgement meet the necessary criteria for such detention. After all, why select drug abuse? Preventative treatment could as easily be used for those activities likely to incur high disproportionate health costs – riding motorbikes, for example, or skiing or playing football? One suspects that drug abuse has been selected for preventative treatment more on the basis of mere dislike than anything else, but it provides a precedent that permits measures of control far above that which are acceptable. It does so in ways that not only circumvent the safeguards provided by the criminal law but that also come dangerously close to providing a new control system based on behaviour adjudged on financial terms. To misquote Brenda Hoggett: in effect this creates a special sort of crime called 'anti-social financial disorder'. If so, should we not admit to it (Hoggett 1984: 70)?

What, then, *does* work? One route we should be going down was identified by the Carter Report (2003) when it talks of the need for integrating services. Unfortunately is says nothing about how integration should take place. Integration is more than meetings between senior organisation personnel. It requires a short and long-term effort: in the short term to get organisations to agree on an agenda; in the long term to implement it. One of the first (and best) attempts at integration was by the TASC programme, which linked treatment to the judicial process (Nolan 1998: 81). As noted in Chapter 5, TASC began in Delaware in August 1972, and those prisoners who volunteered for the TASC programme were sent to a local treatment programme where their treatment was monitored and progress reported back to the court. TASC is essentially a diversion programme aimed at taking offenders out of prison to treatment. There are about 150 TASC sites in 40 states, making it the most respected organisation of its kind (*ibid.*: 82).

The TASC programme organisers were very conscious of the philosophical differences between a traditional criminal justice perspective and a treatment one, recognising also the potential for conflict. They sought not to fuse the two operations but to act as a bridge between them. They saw the justice system's legal sanctions as reflecting community concerns for public safety and punishment, and the treatment community as recommending therapeutic interventions to change behaviour and reduce the suffering associated with substance abuse and related problems (*ibid.*). Bridging the gap has not been easy or always successful but it has been worth while, and the services provided under

TASC produce a model which is worth introducing in Britain. That bridge is ever more urgently required.

There was no better example of the need for a TASC-type programme than that which occurred during a research project conducted in Leicestershire in the mid-1990s. There it was found that offenders seeking treatment were almost always refused admission to the local statutory treatment agency if subject to a court order, or there was a direct requirement from the court to seek treatment. Those not under an order or who were prepared to enter treatment voluntarily were often given appointments two or three weeks in advance. It was not clear whether this was part of the treatment providers' policy to test motivation or assess levels of determination, or whether it was because the agency had few vacancies. Either way, by the time of the appointment the drug users had invariably appeared in court for other offences or were unable to attend, having been remanded earlier in custody. There was no drug testing. Inciardi sees the solution to the shortage of treatment as 'easily solved by a financial restructuring of the war on drugs' (Inciardi and McBride 1991: 75). Would that it were that simple. None the less 'financial restructuring' must be part of any solution, and a TASC-like programme where the case management of drug-using offenders is given priority must be the key.

Successful case management involves bridging the ideological divide between criminal justice and treatment. That is a more daunting task. There has been no grassroots movement in Britain aimed at bridging the gap. For example, there were no such preparations for the DTTO. Nor have the Drug Action Teams appear to have moved in that direction. The net result is that treatment services and criminal justice walk past each other. Taxman's 'six threats that impede the implementation of treatment services' are relevant here (cited in McBride *et al.* 2000). They include 'insufficient case management services' but notice, too, how drug testing and the need for clear crime control goals alongside clear assessment and eligibility requirements are also included – all of which have been noted elsewhere in this book:

- Lack of clear crime control goals for treatment services.
- Lack of clear assessment and eligibility requirements.
- Insufficient treatment duration to effect behavioural change.
- Lack of supervision and sanctions/rewards to reinforce treatment goals.
- Lack of objective drug testing to monitor treatment progress.
- Insufficient case management services.

The TASC model could be used for all drug offenders who are referred for treatment, irrespective of the source of referral. For example, arrest referral schemes permit the police to refer drug users to treatment programmes. As the law stands, the police cannot require treatment as a condition of bail (the Bail Act prohibits this). Changing the Bail Act would not be difficult. Or referrals could come from the courts, again as a remand condition, or more use could be made of treatment as a condition of probation. Where treatment has been imposed as a condition of probation, the results have often been less than satisfactory: either the drug users fail to attend or if, they do, they give up quickly. There is no overarching agency responsible for the treatment so that users slip through the net or, as with the Leicestershire study, they see the treatment facilities as irrelevant.

Similarly, certain groups could be targeted. An obvious group would be those heavy users who probably account for about three quarters of the total volume of drugs used in Britain, especially cocaine and heroin. This group uses a disproportionate amount and comprises persistent offenders who have served lengthy and frequent sentences. Their prognosis is poor and will remain so as long as their drug use continues. Reducing or removing their habit will have two important effects: it would reduce their criminality, which is persistent and serious, and it would reduce the overall demand for the drug. John Grieve (1993) is correct when he says we need to undermine the acquisitive base on which drug purchases are derived. The vast sums of money that fuel inter-dealer status and violence in a paranoid treacherous environment are the product of thousands of burglaries by the same criminals who are arrested again and again (ibid.: 8). This type of offender needs a treatment programme which takes account of the chronic nature of the problem, the high relapse rate and the persistent offending accompanying drug use. They present an obvious case for a TASC-type programme. TASC could act as an umbrella, dealing with all phases of referral from the criminal justice system and directing the offender to the appropriate treatment programmes.

Modern thinking behind successful programmes is based on a three-pronged approach involving treatment, mandatory drug testing and supervision. All have to be linked and the programme has to be delivered in such a manner as to demonstrate to all – patients and treatment providers alike – that integration is complete. Each feature is important but of itself cannot produce satisfactory results. It is no good producing treatment facilities or a drug-testing programme or having supervision unless the treatment facilities are underscored by testing.

Supervision can back up the programme, details of which must be agreed in advance – especially the quality of supervision. Inciardi talks of the value of treatment; if it is to be of value it must be linked to supervision and testing. It is of little use on its own.

In the USA the TASC programme was able to show that this three-pronged approach worked – and, incidentally, formed the basis for drug courts. Their impact has been dramatic. In Britain, by contrast, is the DTTO. As I said earlier, in my view this order does not work. Moreover, the government has failed to take advantage of a set of opportunities uniquely favourable to change and of a period when it was able to promote a thorough-going examination of criminal justice policies. No attempt was made at integration in the DTTO. The three main features were themselves poorly developed, reducing further the possibilities of success.

Take, first, supervision. Here the DTTO was simply added on to the Probation Service workload. Yet the Probation Service, as currently constituted, is not, in my opinion, the appropriate service to undertake such a task – nor would it be were drug courts to be introduced. Too often probation officers retain their social work value system and are antithetical to the demands of coercive treatment. As the American research shows, the longer the offender remains in the programme the better the chances of success (Anglin and Hser 1991). A 90-day treatment period is likely to be the minimum, supported by clear unequivocal guidelines. Fudging issues, accepting excuses for shortcomings and ignoring violations do not help offenders in treatment. Different rules might need to be applied to patients outside the criminal justice system, but for those within it a greater measure of certainty is required.

Nor are the drug-testing facilities adequate. They leave too many opportunities to manipulate the system and allow offenders to avoid or escape the consequences of their illicit use. Drug testing under the DTTO is an amateurish affair, falling far short of what should be expected. The report on the DTTOs describes drug testing thus:

> The frequency of urine testing varies markedly between pilot areas. Very frequent testing may not be good use of money and can be counter-productive in those who are reducing the amount of drugs they use. However testing does appear to be a valuable tool in reinforcing the motivation of those who are drug free ... We think that testing needs to be integrated fully with treatment pro-grammes, with testing regimes tailored to the objectives set for individual offenders (Turnbull *et al.* 2000: 85–6).

The drug court programme, which uses drug testing, requires more exact criteria. It starts from the premise that drug testing must be certain. Elements contributing to the reliability and validity of drug testing are, *inter alia*:

1 Direct observation of the urine sample.
2 Specific, detailed, written procedures regarding all aspects of urine sample collection, sample analysis and result reporting.
3 A documented chain of custody for each sample collected.
4 Quality control and quality assurance procedures for insuring the integrity of the process.
5 Procedures for verifying accuracy when drug-test results are contested (US Department of Justice 1997: 21–2).

Under the DTTO, these minimum procedures are rarely met. The evaluation report describes staff attitudes to treatment in ways which cast doubts about the possibility of them seeing eye to eye with the sentencers, who were more enthusiastic about the tests. They regarded them as valid, giving confidence to their decisions to make a DTTO in the first place. The treatment staff, in contrast, said:

- The tests worked well in reinforcing good progress.
- Frequent testing was expensive and pointless for those who continued to use drugs.
- The tests were very destructive to the motivation of those who were reducing drug use considerably but were continuing to test positive.
- The tests were crude instruments which did not reflect different patterns of use (Turnbull *et al.* 2000: 37).

Some of these comments illustrate a basic misunderstanding of the function of drug testing. The staff at testing and treatment centres are correct when they say drug tests do not reflect different patterns of use, but they do show which drugs had been used and that is a pattern of sorts. They are also correct to say drug tests work well in reinforcing progress. Yet, as far as being expensive and pointless for those who continued to use drugs, it would be an obvious rejoinder to say that tests provide the major source of data on these users and provide evidence as to the motivation to continue drug use. Also, when staff say tests were destructive of motivation, etc., presumably it does not occur to them to insist that offenders try harder; after all, no one ever suggested that getting off drugs would be easy. Successful programmes admit to no such compromises. That is why they are so successful and give another reason why the DTTO will fail. If the procedures are not appropriate, then enforcement will not be appropriate either, and the system will lose the respect of all concerned. It will become an unnecessary irritant that no one takes seriously, whereas it should be the linchpin of the programme providing verifiable results of the offender's progress and drug-taking practices.

Yet treatment facilities *are* better in Britain than almost anywhere else. The range is wide and the quality of treatment provided is often more than satisfactory. The defects are ideological rather than practical. For example, an attempt was made under the DTTO to produce a clear line of accountability about treatment where interagency practices differed and where conflicts and disputes could be resolved. The final evaluation report (Turnbull *et al.* 2000: 82) noted that interagency working practices were 'perhaps the single most important factor to address in establishing programmes'. The report showed that rarely had the problems been resolved. It said:

> It would be wrong to discount the difficulties encountered by the schemes [the three schemes in the pilot programme] as a function of personality clashes or deficits in skills. They are a consequence of work on a difficult joint enterprise involving organisations with big differences in working styles, traditions and values. We think they are likely to be widespread when DTTOs are rolled out nationally. (*ibid.*).

This comes as no surprise given that little or no attention was paid to this in the first place. What it shows is that developing a team approach within criminal justice is difficult and time consuming but necessary. Otherwise the programme ends up as interagency rivalry. Attempts to resolve some of the difficulties in the pilot programme involved the interchangeability of staff, where community psychiatric nurses, probation officers and drug workers all do the same work. This was not given much approval by the evaluators, who said they were sceptical about aiming for interchangeability (*ibid.*: 83) and that 'requiring criminal justice competence from CPNs [community psychiatric nurses] and medical skills from probation officers is an inefficient use of the skills of both groups' (*ibid.*: 57). The muddle we get ourselves into arises because no attempt is made to seek out information from others who had a tried-and-tested track record. Consideration of TASC would have helped.

In contrast, the American drug court programme offers that integrated approach. I have argued elsewhere that we should initially introduce a limited drug court programme in selected cities in England and Wales and evaluate this. Scotland, Ireland and Canada are in the vanguard here with their newly introduced schemes. This programme would be aimed at the more serious offenders and, if successful, could be extended to other cities and other types of offender. What is needed is the political will which, I fear, might not be there unless and until the DTTO has run its course.

There might also be the possibility of extending drug courts to the juvenile justice field, for there is no reason why youth courts should be excluded (Nemitz 2001a). Initially in the USA, drug courts were introduced into the juvenile justice system on the basis of the model of the seamless web – that is, they could be transferred to the juvenile system as there was no need to offer a different approach to juveniles. Juveniles were seen as young adults. This view had to be revised to include the child's family in the treatment programme, as well as his or her school or other educational establishment. It also had to concentrate on dissociating the child from his or her peer group. A new programme therefore had to be devised to take account of these differences. The result were juvenile and family drug courts that seek to retain all the features of adult drug courts but are adapted to the juvenile system.

Before leaving the subject of drug courts I want to clarify a point. I do not want to convey that drug courts are without blemish and should be introduced at all costs. I have said elsewhere (Bean 2001b) that they are open to criticism, not necessarily because of the type of regime they offer but because of the way they resurrect many of the earlier features of rehabilitation which were discredited in the late 1970s and beyond. I have, however, argued that the advantage we have is that we can learn from what has gone before, whether in America or elsewhere, and adapt these features to local circumstances. The DTTO will be a failure and we need to think out the next stage. Drug courts offer the possibility of moving to that stage, and do so with a track record from which to draw.

What impact could education within the drugs–crime debate have on any drug-reduction programme? Again, quite a lot. Too little is made of the point that everyone purchasing illicit drugs explicitly buys into and supports the most violent and cruel set of criminal organisations yet known. Drug markets are violent places, and purchasing the products tacitly (if not openly) gives de facto support to that level of violence. Presumably few people would buy products from legitimate organisations where employees were treated with such violent disdain, so what is different about the illegitimate? The usual answer would be that violence occurs only because the product sold *is* illegal and, by implication, legal markets would be different – that is, the illegal ones would somehow be expected to wither away.

If so, then such a position should be challenged. It fails to understand the nature of trafficking. Legalising drugs would simply permit traffickers to undercut the legal price and continue as before. They might shift their activities to other drugs when it suited them – cigarettes might be smuggled rather than cocaine – but that would depend on the economic conditions available. Traffickers do not have a problem about supply. There is no shortage of the product they wish to sell. Their problems are of distribution, of discipline within their employee network and of collecting money from sales. Their methods would not change were it likely that their product was legal. Suggesting that legality would produce a different ethos is to avoid looking at the reality.

It is also worth emphasising that drugs have a destructive effect on the social fabric of many inner cities. These areas are not pleasant places in which to live for, as the residents of King's Cross made known, young children were exposed to discarded syringes and used condoms. Inner-city areas are often inhabited by those living on the margins of social life. They are separated culturally, socially and politically from the mainstream, and all too often their adaptation to ghetto life is drug use (Inciardi and McBride 1991: 75). Young teenagers able to earn £100 a night trading in drugs are likely to taunt others with their new-found wealth. This undermines the fabric of the community as well as having a more immediate destructive effect on their families. The end product of these actions is likely to be the downfall of the local dealers. This, too, needs to be emphasised, whether it be out-of-control drug use or violence from the other dealers, for one or the other will almost certainly occur. Either way impoverishment will be the end product, whether financially or otherwise, leading to further damages to the community. That local drug markets might add to the wealth of a few absentee, high-ranking dealers merely adds to the sense of decay. It will take a long time to erase the damage.

The message needs to be conveyed that drug markets (at whatever level) undermine the democratic institutions of any society. The aim of the high-level dealers is not to empower but to extract the maximum profit from local transactions and leave with the institutions under their control. Vulnerable institutions fall easily to the traffickers, as a number of small Caribbean countries and commercial organisations have found to their cost when used by the traffickers. Falling prey to the dealers can only lead to impoverishment in the same way that it does to those who sell the drugs on the streets. If these types of messages are conveyed this might assist with other demand-reduction programmes. To repeat the point: demand reduction is the key to reducing the use of drugs and eventually to making inroads into the problem.

There are no easy solutions and, of course, a reduction in drug-related crime will not produce solutions to the crime problem. At best it will produce a significant reduction in the use of drugs and, consequently, a significant reduction in criminal behaviour, but there is no reason to suppose that ex-drug users will stop all criminality once free of drugs. This is an assumption made by drug courts and it seems unwarranted: treatment could easily turn some drug-using offenders into non-drug-using offenders. There may be a falling off in drug use after treatment but not necessarily a termination. The aims should be modest and realistic. The money spent on Drug Action Teams could be used to advantage if they saw themselves as involved in these types of programmes.

References

Advisory Council on the Misuse of Drugs (ACMD) (1994) *Drug Misusers and the Criminal Justice System. Part 2: Police, Drug Misusers and the Community.* London: HMSO.

Advisory Council on the Misuse of Drugs (ACMD) (1998) *Drug Misusers and the Environment.* London: HMSO.

Advisory Council on the Misuse of Drugs (ACMD) (2000) *Reducing Drug-related Deaths* (June). London: Home Office.

Aldridge, J., Parker, H. and Measham, F. (1999) *Drug Trying and Drug Use across Adolescence.* London: DPAS/Home Office.

Anderson, M. and de Boer, M. (eds) (1992) *European Co-operation: Proceedings of a Seminar.* Edinburgh: University of Edinburgh.

Anderson, S. and Frischer, M. (1997) *Drug Misuse in Scotland; Findings from the 1993 and 1996 Scottish Crime Surveys.* Crime and Justice Research Findings 17. Edinburgh: Scottish Office Central Research Unit.

Anglin, M.D. (1988) The efficacy of civil commitment in treating narcotic addiction. In Leukefeld, C.G. and Tims, F.H. (eds) *Compulsory Treatment of Drug Abuse; Research and Clinical Practice. NIDA Research Monograph 86.* Washington, DC: US Department of Health and Human Services.

Anglin, M.D. and Hser, Y.I. (1987a) Addicted women and crime. *Criminology* 25, 359–96.

Anglin, M.D. and Hser, Y.I. (1987b) Sex differences in addict careers. *American Journal of Drug and Alcohol Abuse* 13, 253–80.

Anglin, M.D. and Hser, Y.I. (1990) Treatment of drug abuse. In Tonry, M. and Wilson, J.Q. (eds) *Drugs and Crime.* Chicago, IL: University of Chicago Press.

Anglin, M.D. and Hser, Y.I. (1991) Criminal justice and the drug abusing offenders; policy issue of coerced treatment. *Behavioural Sciences and the Law* 9, 243–67.

Ashworth, A. (1995) *Principles of Criminal Law.* Oxford: Oxford University Press.

Association of Chief Police Officers (ACPO) (1985) Drug-related crime (the Broome Report) (mimeo).

Balenko, S. (1999) Research on drug courts; a critical review. *National Drug Court Institute Review* 2(2), 1–58.

Ballardie, C. and Iganski, P. (2001) Juvenile informers. In Billingsley, R. *et al.* (eds) *Informers: Policing, Policy, Practice.* Cullompton: Willan Publishing.

Bean, P.T. (1971) Social aspects of drug abuse. A study of a group of offenders in London magistrates courts. *Journal of Criminology, Criminal Law and Police Science* 62(1), 80–6.

Bean, P.T. (1974) *The Social Control of Drugs.* London: Martin Robertson.

Bean, P.T. (1991a) Policing the medical profession. The use of tribunals. In Whynes, D. and Bean, P.T. (eds) *Policing and Prescribing.* Basingstoke: Macmillan.

Bean, P.T. (1991b) 'Ice' in Britain. *British Medical Journal* 303(20 July), 152.

Bean, P.T. (1994) Ecstasy: supply and use. Report to Business Against Drugs (mimeo).

Bean, P.T. (1995a) Report to the Home Office on the use of crack/cocaine in Nottingham. London: Royal Society of Health (mimeo).

Bean, P.T. (1995b) Policing drug offenders and the Broome Report. In Dickerson, J.W. and Stimson, G.V. (eds) *Drugs in the City.* London: The Royal Society of Health.

Bean, P.T. (1996) Trafficking. A literature review. Report to the ESRC (mimeo).

Bean, P.T. (1998) Dual diagnosis and beyond. *Alcohol Update* 37(October), 2–3.

Bean, P.T. (2001a) Violence and substance abuse. In Pinard, G.-F. and Pagani, L. (eds) *Clinical Assessments of Dangerousness.* Cambridge: Cambridge University Press.

Bean, P.T. (2001b) Drug courts, the judge and the rehabiliative ideal. In Nolan, J. (ed.) *Drug Courts in Theory and in Practice.* New York: Aldine de Gryter..

Bean, P.T. (2001c) Informers and witness protection schemes. In Billingsley, R. *et al.* (eds) *Informers: Policing, Policy, Practice.* Cullompton: Willan Publishing.

Bean, P.T. (2002) Report to the EMCDDA. Drugs, crime and indicators (mimeo).

Bean, P.T. and Billingsley, R. (2001) Drugs, crime and informers. In Billingsley, R. *et al.* (eds) *Informers: Policing, Policy, Practice.* Cullompton: Willan Publishing.

Bean, P.T. and Nemitz, T. (2000) An examination of Crime Report Information Statistics (CRIS) to determine a model for policing drug offenders (mimeo).

Bean, P.T. and Nemitz, T. (eds) (2002) *Treatment: What Works?* London: Routledge.

Bean, P.T. and Wilkinson, C.K. (1988) Drug taking, crime and the illicit supply system. *British Journal of Addiction* 83(5), 533–9.

Beare, M.E. (1995) Money laundering: a preferred law enforcement target for the 1990s. In Albanese, J. (ed.) *Contemporary Issues in Organised Crime.* Monsey, NY: Criminal Justice Press.

Beare, M.E. and Schneider, S. (1990) *Tracing of Illicit Funds. Money Laundering in Canada* (report 1990-05). Solicitor General Canada.

Benn, R.S. and Peters, S.I. (1975) *Social Principles and the Democratic State.* London: George Allen & Unwin.

Bennett, T. (1998) *Drugs and Crime: The Results of Research, Drug Testing and Interviewing Arrestees.* Home Office Research Study 193. London: Home Office.

Bennett, T. and Sibbitt, R. (2000) *Drug Use among Arrestees. Home Office Research Findings* 119. London: Home Office.

Bewley, T., Ben-Arie and James, I. (1968) Morbidity and mortality from heroin dependence. *British Medical Journal* 1, 725–32.

Billingsley, R. (2001a) Informers. Unpublished PhD thesis, University of Loughborough.

Billingsley, R. (2001b) Informers' careers, motivations and change. In Billingsley, R. *et al.* (eds) *Informers: Policing, Policy, Practice.* Cullompton: Willan Publishing.

Billingsley, R., Nemitz, T. and Bean, P.T. (eds) (2001) *Informers: Policing, Policy, Practice.* Cullompton: Willan Publishing.

Bin-Salama, W. (1996) Confiscation orders. Unpublished PhD thesis, University of Loughborough.

Birch, R. (1992) Policing Europe. Current issues. *Home Office PRSW Bulletin* 4–6.

Birch, R. (1991) Intentional co-operation of the police. *Police Journal* 64(4), 289–98.

Birks, P. (1995) *Laundering and Tracing.* Oxford: Oxford University Press.

Boldt, R. (1998) Rehabilitation, justice and the drug court. *Washington University Law Quarterly* 76, 1205–306.

Boyce, D. (1987) Narco terrorism. *FBI Law Enforcement Bulletin* 56(11), 24–7.

Brain, K., Parker, H. and Bottomley, T. (1998) *Evolving Crack Cocaine Careers.* Home Office Research Findings 85. London: Home Office.

Brook, D., Taylor, C., Gunn, J. and Maden, A. (1998) Substance misusers remanded to prison; a treatment opportunity. *Addiction* 193(12), 1851–6.

Broom, D. and Stevens, A. (1991) Doubly deviant; women using alcohol and other drugs. *International Journal of Drug Policy* (2), 25–7.

Brown, D. (1997) *PACE Ten Years on: A Review of the Research.* Home Office Research Study 155. London: HMSO.

Brownstein, H.H. and Crossland, C. (2002) Introduction. In 'Drugs and Crime Research Forum' (mimeo).

Brownstein, H.H. and Goldstein, P.J. (1990) A typology of drug related homicides. In Weishart, R. (ed.) *Drugs, Crime and the Criminal Justice System.* Anderson.

Bruno, F. (1991) *Cocaine Today. Its Effects on the Individual and Society.* UN Inter-regional Crime and Justice Research Institute.

Bureau of Justice Statistics (1991) *Survey of Inmates in Federal Correctional Facilities and Survey of Inmates in State Correctional Facilities.* Washington, DC: US Department of Justice.

Burrows, J., Clarke, A., Davison, T., Tarling, R. and Webb, S. (2000) *The Nature and Effectiveness of Drugs Throughcare for Released Prisoners.* Home Office Research Findings 109. London: Home Office.

Cabinet Office (2000) *UK Anti-drugs Coordinator's Annual Report 1999–2000.* London: HMSO.

Carter, P. (2003) *Managing Offenders, Reducing Crime. A New Approach.* London: Strategy Unit, HM Government.

Carver, J.A. (1991) Pre-trial drug testing: an essential step in bail reform. *BYU Journal of Public Law* 5(1), 371–407.

Carver, J. (2004) Drug testing. A necessary prerequisite for treatment and for crime control. In Bean, P.T. and Nemitz, T. (eds) *Drug Treatment: What Works.* London: Routledge.

Carver, J.D., Boyer, K.R. and Hickey, R. (1995) Management information systems and drug courts: the District of Columbia approach. Paper prepared for the National Symposium on the Implementation and Operation of Drug Courts, District of Columbia Pre-trial Services Agency.

Caulkins, J. and Reuter, P. (1996) The meaning and utility of drug prices. *Addiction* 19(9), 1261–4.

CDSC and SCIEH (2003) *AIDS/HIV Quarterly Surveillance Tables; Cumulative UK Data to End June 2003* (No. 59; 03/2). Communicable Disease Surveillance Centre, Health Protection Agency and Scottish Centre for Infection and Environmental Health.

Central Drugs Co-ordination Unit (1998) *Tackling Drugs to Build a Better Britain; the Government's 10 Year Strategy for Tackling Drug Misuse* (Cm 3395). London: HMSO.

Chaiken, J.M. and Chaiken, M.R. (1990) Drugs and predatory crime. In Tonry, M. and Wilson, J.Q. (eds) *Drugs and Crime.* Chicago, IL: University of Chicago Press.

Chaiken, J.M. and Johnson, B.D. (1988) *Characteristics of Different Types of Drug Involved Offenders.* National Institute of Justice.

Charles, N. (1998) *Public Perceptions of Drug Related Crime.* Research Findings 67. London: Research and Development Statistics Directorate, Home Office.

Christophersen, O., Rooney, C. and Kelly, S. (1998) Drug related mortality; methods and trends. *Population Trends* 93, 29–37.

Clarke, R.V.G. (1980) 'Situational' crime prevention. Theory and practice. *British Journal of Criminology* 20, 136–47.

Clark, R. (2001) Informers and corruption. In Billingsley, R. *et al.* (eds) *Informers: Policing, Policy, Practice.* Cullompton: Willan Publishing.

Cloward, R. and Ohlin, L. (1960) *Delinquency and Opportunity.* Free Press.

Cloward, R. and Ohlin, L. (1961) *Delinquency and Opportunity.* London: Routledge & Kegan Paul.

Coid, J., Carvell, A., Kittler, Z., Healey, A. and Henderson, J. (2000) *The Impact of Methadone Treatment on Drug Misuse and Crime.* Home Office Research Findings 120. London: Home Office.

Cooper, M.H. (1990) *The Business of Drugs. US Congressional Quarterly.* Washington, DC: US Government Printing Office.

Corkery, J.M. (1997) *Statistics of Drug Addicts Notified to the Home Office, UK, 1996.* Home Office Statistics Bulletin 22. London: Home Office Research and Development Statistics Department.

Corkery, J.M. (1999) The nature and extent of drug misuse in the UK: official statistics, surveys and studies. Lecture given to St. George's Hospital Medical School, London (mimeo).

Corkery, J. (2000) Snowed under; is it the real thing? *Druglink*, May/June, 12–15.

Corkery, J. (2002) *Drug Seizure and Offender Statistics, United Kingdom 2000. Area Tables*. London: Home Office Research Development and Statistics Directorate.

Corkery, J. (2003) The nature and extent of drug misuse in the UK. Official statistics, surveys and studies (lecture given to St George's Hospital Medical School) (mimeo).

Corkery, J. and Airs, J. (2003) *Seizures of Drugs in the UK 2001*. Findings 202. London: Home Office Research Development and Statistics Directorate.

Cornish, D.B. (2001) The rational choice perspective. In Adler, P. (ed.) *Encyclopaedia of Criminology and Deviant Behaviour. Vol. 1*. Sheridan Books.

de Leon, G. (1998) Legal pressure in therapeutic communities. In Leukefeld, C.G. and Tims, F.H. (eds) *Compulsory Treatment of Drug Abuse; Research and Clinical Practice. NIDA Research Monograph 86*. Washington, DC: US Department of Health and Human Services.

Department of Health (1960) *Report of the Interdepartmental Committee* (first Brain Report). London: HMSO.

Department of Health (1965) *Report of the Interdepartmental Committee* (second Brain Report). London: HMSO.

Department of Health (1978) *Review of the Mental Health Act 1959* (Cmnd 7320). London: HMSO.

Department of Health (1996) *Report of an Independent Review of Drug Treatment Services in England (Task Force Report)*. London: HMSO.

Department of Health (1999a) *Drug Misuse and Dependence – Guidelines on Clinical Management*. London: HMSO.

Department of Health (1999b) *Review of the Mental Health Act 1983 (Report of the Expert Committee, December)*. London: HMSO.

Department of Health (2001) *The Government's Response to the Advisory Council on the Misuse of Drugs Report into Drug Related Deaths*. London: Department of Health.

Department of Health (2002) *Statistics from the Regional Drug Misuse Databases for 6 Months Ending March 2001*. Department of Health Statistical Bulletin 2002/07. London: Department of Health.

Ditton, J. and Hammersley, R. (1994) The typical cocaine user. *Druglink* 9, 11–12.

Dorn, N. (1993) Europe and drugs. *Criminal Justice Matters* 12, 19.

Dorn, N. and Murji, K. (1992) Low level drug enforcement. *International Journal of the Sociology of Law* 20, 159–71.

Dorn, N., Murji, K. and South, N. (1992) *Trafficking; Drug Markets and Law Enforcement*. London: Routledge.

Downes, D. and Rock, P. (1998) *Understanding Deviance* (3rd edn). Oxford: Oxford University Press.

Drug Enforcement Administration (DEA) (1982) *Narcotics Investigators' Manual.* Washington DC: Paladin.

Drugs Intelligence Agency (1992) *The Colombian Heroin Connection* (formerly *RCMP Monthly Digest of Drug Intelligence Trends*).

Duke, K. (2000) Prison drugs policy since 1980. *Drugs Education: Prevention and Policy* 7(4), 393–408.

Dunlap, E. and Johnson, B.D. (1996) Family and human resources in the development of a female crack seller's career; case study of a hidden population. *Journal of Drug Issues* 26(1), 175–98.

Dunnighan, C. (1992) Reliable sources. *Police Review* 14 August, 1496–7.

Dziedzic, M.J. (1989) The international drugs trade and regional survival. *Survival* 31(6), 533–48.

Edgar, K. and O'Donnell, I. (1998) *Mandatory Drug Testing in Prison; an Evaluation.* Home Office Research Findings 75. London: Home Office Research Development and Statistics Directorate.

European Community (1992) *Report Drawn up by the Committee of Inquiry into the Spread of Organised Crime Linked to Drug Trafficking in the Member States of the EC* (EP Document A3-0358/91), 23 April.

European Community (1993) *Inventory of Legal Texts on Drugs.* Office for Official Publications of the European Community.

Everest, J., Tunbridge, R. and Widdop, B. (1989) *The Incidence of Drugs in Road Traffic Fatalities. Research Report* RR202. TRL Ltd.

Fagan, J. (1990) Intoxication and aggression. In Tonry, M. and Wilson, J.Q. (eds) *Drugs and Crime.* Chicago, IL: University of Chicago Press.

Fagan, J. (1993) Interaction among drugs, alcohol and violence. *Health Affairs* (Winter), 65–77.

Farabee, D., Prendergast, M. and Anglin, M.D. (1998) The effectiveness of coerced treatment for drug abusing offenders. *Federal Probation* 62(1), 3–10.

Farrington, D. (1997) Human development and criminal careers. In Maguire, M. *et al.* (eds) *The Oxford Handbook of Criminology.* Oxford: Oxford University Press.

FATF (1990) *Report on Money Laundering.* Financial Action Task Force.

Florez, P. and Boyce, B. (1990) Colombian organised crime. *Police Studies* 13(2), 81–8.

Fortson, R. (1996) *The Law in the Misuse of Drugs and Drug Trafficking Offences* (3rd edn). London: Sweet & Maxwell.

Foster, J. (2000) Social exclusion, crime and drugs. *Drugs Education: Prevention and Policy* 7(4), 317–30.

Fraser, F. (2002) *Drug Misuse in Scotland; Findings from the 2000 Scottish Crime Survey.* Edinburgh: Scottish Executive Central Research Unit.

Gallagher, R. (1990) *The Report of Mr Rodney Gallagher of Coopers and Lybrand on the Survey of Offshore Finance Sections in the Caribbean in Dependent Territories* (the Gallagher Report). London: HMSO.

Gebelein, R.S. (2000) *The Rebirth of Rehabilitation. Promise and Perils of Drug Courts*. National Institute of Justice (May).

Ghodse, H. (1995) *Drugs and Addictive Behaviour. A Guide to Treatment* (2nd edn). Oxford: Blackwell.

Gillard, M. (1993) The pain in Spain; Europe's southern frontiers. *Police Review* 25 June, 28–9.

Gilmore, W. (1991) *Going after the Money. Money Laundering: the Confiscation of the Assets of Crime and International Co-operation. A System of Police Co-operation after 1992. Working Paper Series*. Edinburgh: University of Edinburgh.

Gilmore, W. (1992) *International Efforts on Money Laundering. Cambridge International Documents Series* Vol. 4. Cambridge: Grotius Publications.

Glasgow Drug Court (undated) *Guidance Handbook*.

Goldstein, P. (1985/1995) The drugs–violence nexus; a tripartite framework. *Journal of Drug Issues* 1985 (Fall), 493–506. Also in Inciardi, J. and McElrath, K. (eds) (1995) *The American Drug Scene*. Los Angeles, CA: Roxbury.

Goldstein, P., Brownstein, H. and Ryan, P. (1992) Drug related homicide in New York City 1984 and 1988. *Crime and Delinquency* 38, 459–76.

Goldstein, P., Brownstein, H., Ryan, P.J. and Rellucci, P.A. (1991) Crack and homicide in New York City, 1988; a conceptually based analysis. *Contemporary Drug Problems* 16, 651–87.

Goodman, L. (2004) Report to the Adam Smith Institute; Treatment Accountability for Safer Communities (TASC) (mimeo).

Gossop, M., Marsden, J. and Stewart, D. (1997) The National Treatment Outcome Research Study in the UK; sixth month follow up and outcomes. *Psychology of Addictive Behaviour* 11, 324–37.

Gossop, M., Marsden, J. and Stewart, D. (1998) *The National Treatment Outcome Research Study (NTORS). Changes in Substance Use, Health and Criminal Behaviour One Year after Intake*. London: Department of Health.

Greenleaf, V.D. (1989) *Women and Crime*. Lowell House.

Grella, C.E. and Joshi, V.J. (1999) Gender differences in drug treatment careers among clients in the National Abuse Treatment Outreach Study. *American Journal of Drug and Alcohol Issues* 25(3), 385–406.

Grieve, J. (1992) The police contribution to drugs education; a role for the 1990s. In Evans, R. and O'Connor, L. (eds) *Developing Educational Strategies in Partnership*. London: David Fulton.

Grieve, J. (1993) Thinking the 'unthinkable'. *Criminal Justice Matters* 12, 8.

Griffiths, C. (2003) Deaths related to drug poisoning; results for England and Wales, 1997–2001. *Health Statistics Quarterly* 17, 65–71.

Griffiths, C., Brock, A. and Mickleburgh, M. (2002) Deaths related to drug poisoning; results for England and Wales, 1994 to 2000. *Health Statistics Quarterly* 13, 76–82.

Hague, L., Willis, M. and Power, M. (2000) *Experience of Drug Misuse; Findings from the 1998 Northern Ireland Survey*. Research and Statistics Bulletin 4/2000. Belfast: Northern Ireland Statistics and Research Agency, Northern Ireland Office.

Hammersley, R., Forsyth, A., Morrison, V. and Davies, J.B. (1989) The relationship between crime and opioid use. *British Journal of Addiction* 84, 1029–43.

Haughton, G. (2001) Dublin Metropolitan District Drug Court. Address to the Scottish Seminar on Drug Courts (mimeo).

Hawton K. *et al.* (2001) Effects of legislation restricting packsizes of paracetamol and salicylate on self-poisoning in the UK before and after study. *British Medical Journal* 322, 1203.

Healey, K. (1989) Bolivia and cocaine; a developing country's dilemma. *British Journal of Addiction* 83(1), 19–23.

Hearnden, I. and Harocopos, A. (2000) *Problem Drug Use and Probation in London.* Home Office Research Findings 112. London: Home Office Research Development and Statistics Directorate.

HM Government (1995) *Tackling Drugs Together; a Strategy for England 1995–8.* London: HMSO.

HM Government (1998) *Tackling Drugs Together to Build a Better Britain; the Government's Ten Year Strategy for Tackling Drug Misuse.* London: HMSO.

Hoggett, B. (1984) *Mental Health Law.* London: Sweet & Maxwell.

Home Office (1986) The border war on drugs. London: Office of Technology Assessment (mimeo).

Home Office (1993) *A Practical Guide to Crime Prevention for Local Partnerships.* London: Home Office.

Home Office (1998a) *Drug Treatment and Testing Order; Background and Issues for Consultation.* London: Home Office.

Home Office (1998b) *Tackling Drugs in Prison; the Prison Service Strategy.* London: Home Office.

Home Office (1999) Codes of practice on informant use. London: Home Office (mimeo).

Home Office (2000) *Guidance for Practitioners Involved in Drug Treatment and Testing Order Pilots.* London: Home Office.

Home Office (2001) *Prison Statistics. England and Wales 2000* (Cm 5250). London: HMSO.

Home Office (2003) *Prison Statistics. England and Wales 2001* (Cm 5743). London: HMSO.

Hough, M. (1996) *Drug Misusers and the Criminal Justice System; a Review of the Literature. Drugs Prevention Initiative Paper* 15. London: Home Office.

House of Commons (2000) *Criminal Justice and Court Services Bill. Explanatory Notes (15 March 2000).* London: HMSO.

House of Commons (Home Affairs Committee) (1990) *Practical Police Cooperation in the European Community.* London: HMSO.

Huling, T. (1996) Prisoners of war. Women drug couriers in the US. In Green, P. (ed.) *Drug Couriers.* London: Quartet Books.

Hunt, G., Joe-Laidler, K. and Mackenzie, K. (2000) 'Chillin, being dogged and getting buzzed'; alcohol in the lives of female gang members. *Drugs Education: Prevention and Policy* 7(4), 331–53.

ICPO Interpol (1989) Heroin trafficking in Africa; its impact on Europe (General Secretariat Drug Subdivision). *International Police Review* Sept/Oct (44.420), 25–8.

Inciardi, J. (1988) Compulsory treatment in New York. A brief narrative history of misjudgement, mismanagement and misrepresentation. *Journal of Drug Issues* (28), 547–60.

Inciardi, J. (1991) *Handbook of Drug Control in the US.* Westport, CT: Greenwood.

Inciardi, J.A. and Harrison, L.D. (eds) (1998) *Heroin in the Age of Crack-Cocaine.* Thousand Oaks, CA, and London: Sage.

Inciardi, J., Lockwood, D.A. and Pottieger, A.E. (1993) *Women and Crack Cocaine.* Macmillan.

Inciardi, J. and McBride, D.C. (1991) The case against legalisation. In Inciardi, J. (ed.) *The Drug Legalisation Debate.* Thousand Oaks, CA, and London: Sage.

Inciardi, J., McBride, D.C. and Rivers, J.E. (1996) *Drug Control and the Courts. Drugs, Health and Social Policy Series* Vol. 3. Thousand Oaks, CA, and London: Sage.

Inciardi, J. and Pottieger, A.E. (1995) Kids, crack and crime. In Inciardi, J. and McElrath, K. (eds) *The American Drug Scene.* Los Angeles, CA: Roxbury.

Ingram, D., Lancaster, B. and Hope, B. (2001) *Recreational Drugs and Driving; Prevalence Survey.* Edinburgh: Scottish Executive Central Research Unit.

ISD (2002) *Drug Misuse Statistics, Scotland 2001,* Information and Statistics Division.

ISD (2003) *Drug Misuse Statistics, Scotland 2002,* Information and Statistics Division.

Johnson, B., Dunlap, E. and Tourigny, S. (2000) Crack distribution and abuse in New York. In Natarajan, M. and Hough, M. (eds) *Illegal Drug Markets; from Research to Prevention Policy.* Monsey, NY: Criminal Justice Press.

Johnson, B.D., Goldstein, P., Preble, E., Schmeidler, J., Lipton, D.S., Spunt, B. and Miller, T. (1985) *Taking Care of Business; the Economics of Crime by Heroin Users.* D.C. Heath.

Johnson, B.D., Williams, T., Dei, K.A. and Sanabria, H. (1990) Drug abuse in the inner city; impact on hard-drug users and the community. In Tonry, M. and Wilson, J.Q. (eds) *Drugs and Crime.* Chicago, IL: University of Chicago Press.

Kleiman, M.A. and Smith, K.D. (1990) State and local drug enforcement. In search of a strategy. In Tonry, M. and Wilson, J.Q. (eds) *Drugs and Crime.* Chicago, IL: University of Chicago Press.

Korf, D., Bless, R. and Nottelman, N. (1998) *Urban Drug Problems and the General Public.* Lisbon, Portugal: Intersearch and EMCDDA.

Labour Party (1996) *Breaking the Vicious Circle* (October). London: Labour Party.

Langer, J.H. (1986) Recent developments in drug trafficking; the terrorist connection. *Police Chief* 52(4), 44–51.

Lee, R.W. (1989) *The White Labyrinth; Cocaine and Political Power.* London: Transaction Books.

Leukefeld, C.G. and Tims, F.H. (eds) (1988) *Compulsory Treatment of Drug Abuse; Research and Clinical Practice. NIDA Research Monograph 86.* Washington, DC: US Department of Health and Human Services.

Levi, M. (1991) Pecunia non olet; cleansing the money launderers from the temple. *Crime, Law and Social Change* 16(3), 217–302.

Levi, M. and Osofsky, L. (1995) *Investigating Seizing and Confiscating the Proceeds of Crime.* London: Police Research Group, Home Office.

Lewis, P. (1980) *Psychiatric Probation Orders.* Cambridge: University of Cambridge, Institute of Criminology.

Lightfoot, J. (ed.) (1994) *Towards Safer Communities.* CDF/Crime Concern.

Lindesmith, A. (1965) *The Addict and the Law.* Indiana: Principia Press.

Lipton, D.S. (1995) *The Effectiveness of Treatment for Drug Abusers under Criminal Justice Supervision.* National Institute of Justice (November).

Lo, T.W. (1993) *Corruption and Politics in Hong Kong and China.* Milton Keynes: Open University Press.

Lo, T.W. and Bean, P.T. (1991) Heroin traffickers in Hong Kong. Report to the British Council (unpublished).

MacCoun, R., Kilmer, B. and Reuter, P. (2002) Research on drugs–crime linkages; the next generation. In 'Drugs and Crime Research Forum' (mimeo).

MacCoun, R. and Reuter, P. (1998) Drug control. In Tonry, M. (ed.) *The Handbook of Crime and Punishment.* Oxford: Oxford University Press.

MacDonald, D. and Mansfield, D. (2001) Drugs and Afghanistan. *Drugs Education: Prevention and Policy* 8(1), 1–16.

MacDonald, S.B. (1989) *Mountain High. White Avalanche; Cocaine and Power in Andean States and Panama.* Praeger.

MacKenzie, D.L. and Uchida, C.D. (eds) (1994) *Drugs and Crime. Evaluating Public Policy Initiatives.* Thousand Oaks, CA, and London: Sage.

Makkai, T. (2002) The emergence of drug treatment courts in Australia. In Harrison, L. *et al.* (eds) *Drug Courts: Current Issues and Future Perspectives.* Office of International Criminal Justice, Sam Houston State University.

Makkai, T. and McGregor, K. (2002) *Drug Use Monitoring in Australia. Research and Public Policy Series 41.* Australian Institute of Criminology.

Mallender, J., Roberts, E. and Seddon, T. (2002) *Evaluation of Drug Testing in the Criminal Justice System in Three Pilot Areas.* Home Office Research Findings 176. London: Home Office Research Development and Statistic Directorate.

Martin, J.M. and Romano, A.T. (1992) *Multinational Crime; Terrorism, Espionage, Drugs and Arms Trafficking.* Thousand Oaks, CA, and London: Sage.

McBride, D.C. and Swartz, J.A. (1991) Drugs and violence in the age of crack cocaine. In Weisheit, R. (ed.) *Drugs, Crime and the Criminal Justice System.* Cincinnati, Ohio: Anderson Publishing.

McBride, D.C., Vander Waal, C.J. and Terry-McElrath, Y.M. (2002) The drugs–crime wars; past, present and future directions in theory, policy and program interventions. In 'Drugs and Crime Research Forum' (mimeo).

Merton, R.K. (1957) *Social Theory and Social Structure*. New York: Free Press.

Meyers, P.H. (1991) Pre-trial drug testing: is it vulnerable to due process challenges? *BYU Journal of Public Law* 5(2), 285–340.

Ministerial Drugs Task Force (1994) *Drugs in Scotland; Meeting the Challenge. Scottish Home and Health Department*. Edinburgh: HMSO.

Mitchell, A., Hinton, M. and Taylor, S. (1992) *Confiscation*. London: Sweet & Maxwell.

Morales, E. (1989) The Peruvian case; the political economy of cocaine production. *Latin American Perspectives* 17(4), 91–109.

Morales, E. (1990) *Cocaine: the White Gold Rush Peru*. Tucson, AZ: University of Arizona Press.

Morgan, P. and Joe, K.A. (1996) The private and public lives of women in the illicit drug economy. *Journal of Drug Issues* 26(1), 125–42.

Mott, J. (1987) The relationship between alcohol and crime; a review of the literature. Paper presented at the British Society of Criminology conference.

Mott, J. (1992) *Crack and Cocaine in England and Wales*. Home Office Research and Planning Unit Paper 70. London: Home Office Research Planning Unit.

Mott, J. (1994) Drug misuse in the UK in the 1960s and the new paper Presented to the Royal College of Physicians.

Murji, K. (1998) *Policing Drugs*. Aldershot: Ashgate.

Murphy, S. and Arroyo, K. (2000) Women as judicious consumers of drug markets. In Natarajan, M. and Hough, M. (eds) *Illegal Drug Markets: from Research to Prevention Policy*. Monsey, NY: Criminal Justice Press.

Murphy, S. and Rosenbaum, M. (1999) *Pregnant Women on Drugs*. New Brunswick, NJ: Rutgers University Press.

Murray, C. (1990) *The Emerging British Underclass*. London: IEA Health and Welfare Unit.

NACD and DAIRU (2003) *Drug Use in Ireland and Northern Ireland: First Results from the 2002/2003 Drug Prevalence Survey. Drug Prevalence Survey Bulletin*. Dublin National Advisory Council on Drugs, and Belfast Drugs and Alcohol Information and Research Unit.

NACRO (1993) *Diverting Mentally Disturbed Offenders from Prosecution. Policy Paper 2*. London: NACRO.

Natarajan, M. and Hough, M. (eds) (2000) *Illegal Drug Markets; from Research to Prevention Policy*. Monsey, NY: Criminal Justice Press.

National Association of Drug Court Professionals (NADCP) (1997) *Defining Drug Courts: The Key Components*. NADCP.

National Crime Squad (NCS) (2000) *Service Authority for NCS. Annual Report 1999–2000*. NCS.

National Crime Victimisation Survey (2000) *Criminal Victimisation in the United States. 1998 Statistical Tables*. Washington, DC: US Department of Justice.

National Criminal Intelligence Agency (2000) Destroying the glamour of organised crime. *Nexus* 9, 7–9.

National Criminal Intelligence Service (NCIS) (2000) *Annual Report 1999–2000* Research and Planning Unit. NCIS.

Nee, C. and Sibbitt, R. (1993) *The Probation Response to Drug Abuse. Paper 78.* London: Home Office Research and Planning Unit.

Nemitz, T. (2001a) Report to the Youth Justice Board on the development and use of juvenile drug courts (mimeo).

Nemitz, T. (2001b) Gender issues in informer handling. In Billingsley, R. *et al.* (eds) *Informers: Policing, Policy, Practice.* Cullompton: Willan Publishing.

Neyroud, P. and Beckley, A. (2001) Regulating informers; the regulation of the Investigatory Powers Act, covert policing and human rights. In Billingsley, R. *et al.* (eds) *Informers: Policing, Policy, Practice.* Cullompton: Willan Publishing.

Nolan, J. (1998) *The Therapeutic State.* New York, NY: New York University Press.

Northern Ireland Office (1999) *Patterns of Drug Use in Northern Ireland – Some Recent Survey Findings, 1996–1997.* Research Findings 2/98. Belfast: Northern Ireland Statistics and Research Agency, Northern Ireland Office.

NTA (2002) *Models of Care for Substance Misuse Treatment.* London: Department of Health National Treatment Agency.

Nye, J.S. (1970) Corruption and political development; a cost benefit analysis. In Heidenheimer, A.J. (ed.) *Political Corruption.* London: Transaction Books.

O'Hare, T. (1996) Court ordered *v.* voluntary clients; problem differences and readiness for change. *Social Work* 41(4), 417–22.

ONS (2000a) ONS drug related deaths database. First results for England and Wales, 1993–7. *Health Statistics Quarterly* 5, 57–60.

ONS (2000b) Deaths related to drug poisoning; results for England and Wales, 1994–1998. *Health Statistics Quarterly* 7, 59-62.

ONS (2001) Deaths related to drug poisoning; results for England and Wales, 1995–1999. *Health Statistics Quarterly* 5, 70–2.

Oppenheimer, E.A. (1991) Alcohol and drug misuse among women; an overview. *British Journal of Psychiatry* 158 (Suppl. 10), 36–44.

Oppenheimer, E.A. (1994) Women drug misuse; a case for special consideration. In Strang, J. and Gossop, M. (eds) *Heroin Addiction and Drug Policy: the British System.* Oxford: Oxford University Press.

Parker, H. (1998) *Living with heroin.* Milton Keynes: Open University Press.

Parker, H. and Newcombe, R. (1987) Heroin use and acquisitive crime in an English community. *British Journal of Sociology* 38, 331–50.

Parker, R. and Auerhahn, K. (1998) Alcohol, drugs and violence. *Annual Review of Sociology* 24, 291–311.

Parlour, R. (ed.) (1994) *The International Handbook of Money Laundering and Practice.* London: Butterworths.

Paternostro, S. (1995) Mexico as a narco democracy. *World Policy Journal* 12(Spring), 41–7.

Pearson, G. (1987) *The new heroin users.* Oxford: Blackwells.

Peters, R.H. (1993) Drug treatment in jails and detention settings. In Inciardi, J. (ed.) *Drug Treatment and Criminal Justice*. Thousand Oaks, CA, and London: Sage.

Phillips, C. and Brown, D. (1998) *Entry into the Criminal Justice System*. Home Office Research Study 185. London: Home Office Research Development and Statistics Directorate.

Porter, L., Arif, A. and Curran, W.J. (1986) *The Law and the Treatment of Drug and Alcohol Dependent Persons; a Comparative Study of Existing Legislation*. WHO.

Preble, E. and Casey, J. (1969) Taking care of business; the heroin user's life on the street. *International Journal of the Addictions* 4(1), 1–24.

Presidential Determination (1995) *Confiscating Major Narcotics and Transit Countries* (no. 95-15, February). Washington, DC: US Government Printing Office.

Prison Reform Trust (1998) *Drug Use in Prison*. London: Prison Reform Trust.

Ramsay, M. and Partridge, S. (1999) *Drug Misuse Declared in 1998. Latest Results from the British Crime Survey*. Home Office Research Study 172. London: Home Office Research Development and Statistics Directorate.

Ramsay, M., Partridge, S. and Byron, C. (1999) *Drug Misuse Declared in 1998. Key Results from the British Crime Survey*. Home Office Research Findings 93. London: Home Office Research Development and Statistics Directorate.

Ramsay, M. and Percy, A. (1996) *Drug Misuse Declared. Results of the British Crime Survey*. Home Office Research Study 15. London: Home Office Research Development and Statistics Directorate.

Ramsay, M. and Percy, A. (1996) *Drug Misuse Declared. Results of the 1994 British Crime Survey*. Home Office Research Study 151. London: Home Office Research and Statistics Directorate.

Ramsay, M. and Spiller, J. (1997) *Drug Misuse Declared in 1996. Latest Results from the British Crime Survey*. Home Office Research Study 172. London: Home Office Research Development and Statistics Directorate.

Ramsay, M. *et al.* (2001) *Drug Misuse Declared in 2000; Results from the British Crime Survey*. Home Office Research Study 224. London: Home Office Research Development and Statistics Directorate.

Reiss, A.J. and Roth, J.A. (eds) (1993) *Understanding and Preventing Violence*. National Academy Press.

Release (1998) *Drugs and Dance Survey. An Insight into the Culture*. Santa Monica, California: Release.

Reuter, P. (1988) *Sealing the Borders*. Santa Monica, California: Rand.

Reuter, P. (1991) *On the Consequences of Toughness*. Santa Monica, California: Rand.

Reuter, P. (2001) *The Limits of Supply Side Drug Control*. Santa Monica, California: Rand.

Reuter, P. and Kleiman, M.A. (1986) Risks and prices. In Tonry, M. and Morris, N. (eds) *Crime and Justice. An Annual Review of Research (Vol. 7)*. Chicago, IL: University of Chicago Press.

Reuter, P., MacCoun, R. and Murphy, P. (1990) *Money from Crime; a Study of the Economics of Drug Dealing in Washington, DC*. Santa Monica, California: Rand.

Reuters News Agency (1993) Italy; Mafia look towards Europe without frontiers. *Criminal Justice Europe* 3(1), 15.

Robertson, R. (ed.) *Management of Drug Users in the Community. A Practical Handbook*. London: Arnold.

Rosenbaum, M. (1981) *Women on Heroin*. New Brunswick, NJ: Rutgers University Press.

Royal College of Psychiatrists (2000) *Drugs: Dilemmas and Choices*. London: Gaskell.

Ruggiero, V. and South, N. (1995) *Euro-drugs, Drug Use, Markets and Trafficking in Europe*. London: UCL Press.

Rydell, C.P., Caulkins, J.P. and Everingham, S.S. (1996) Enforcement or treatment? Modelling the relative efficacy of alternatives for controlling cocaine. *Operations Research* 44(5), 687–95.

Satel, S. (2000) Drug treatment; the case for coercion. *National Drug Court Institute Review* 3, 1–56.

Schifano, F. *et al*. (2003a) Review of deaths related to taking ecstasy, England and Wales, 1997–2000. *British Medical Journal* 326, 80–1.

Schifano, F. *et al*. (2003b) Death rates from ecstasy (MDMA, MDA) and poly-drug use in England and Wales, 1996–2002. *Human Psychopharmacology* 18(7), 519–24.

Seaman, S.R., Brettle, R.P. and Gore, S.M. (1998) Mortality from overdose among injecting drug users recently released from prison: database linkage study. *British Medical Journal* 316, 426–8.

Seivewright, N. (2000) *Community Treatment of Drug Misuse; More than Methadone*. Cambridge: Cambridge University Press.

Sen, S. (1989) Narco terrorism. *Police Journal* 62, 297–302.

Singleton, N. *et al*. (1998) *Psychiatric Morbidity among Prisoners in England and Wales*. London: HMSO.

Singleton, N., Pendry, E., Taylor, C., Farrell, M. and Marsden, J. (2003) *Drug-related Mortality among Newly-released Offenders*. Home Office Online Report 16/03 (report by the Social Survey Division, ONS and National Addiction Centre, Institute of Psychiatry). London: Home Office Research Development and Statistics Directorate (available at http://www.homeoffice.gov.uk/rds/pdf2/rdsolr1603.pdf).

Skolnick, J. (1967) *Justice Without Trial*. New York: Wiley.

Skolnick, J. (1984) The limits of narcotics law enforcement. *Journal of Psychoactive Drugs* 16(2), 119–27.

Skousen, R.C. (1991) A special needs exception to the warrant and probable cause requirements for mandatory and uniform pre-arraignment drug testing in the wake of *Skinner v. Railway Labour Executives Association* and *National Treasury Employees Union v. von Raab*. *BYU Journal of Public Law* 5(1), 409–348.

Sondhi, A., O'Shea, J. and Williams, T. (2002) *Statistics from the Arrest Referral Monitoring Programme for October 2000 to September 2001. Arrest Referral Update*. London: Home Office Research Development and Statistics Directorate.

South, N. (ed.) (1995) *Drugs, Crime and Criminal Justice*. Aldershot: Dartmouth.

Spear, H.B. (2002) *Heroin Addiction Care and Control* (ed. J. Mott). London: Drugscope.

SPS (2001) *Fourth Prison Survey: The Prisoners' Results*. Research Bulletin Issue 6. Edinburgh: Research and Evaluation Services, Scottish Prison Service.

SPS (2002) *Fifth Prison Survey: The Prisoners' Results*. Research Bulletin Issue 9. Edinburgh: Research and Evaluation Services, Scottish Prison Service.

Sterk-Elifson, C. (1996) Just for fun? Cocaine use among middle class women. *Journal of Drug Issues* 26(1), 63–76.

Stutman, R. (1989) Crack stories from the states. *Druglink* 4(5), 6–7.

Swanson, J. *et al.* (1994) Mental disorder, substance abuse and community violence. In Monahan, J. and Steadman, H. (eds) *Violence and Mental Disorder*. Chicago: Chicago Press.

Swartz, J. (1993) TASC – the next 20 years; extending, refining and assessing the model. In Inciardi, J. (ed.) *Drug Treatment and Criminal Justice*. Thousand Oaks, CA, and London: Sage.

Tonry, M. and Wilson, J.Q. (1990) *Drugs and Crime*. Chicago, IL: University of Chicago Press.

Tunbridge, R., Keigan, M. and Jones, F. (2001) *The Incidence of Drugs and Alcohol in Road Traffic Fatalities. Report* 495. TRL Ltd.

Turnbull, P.J., McSweeney, T., Webster, R., Edmunds, M. and Hough, M. (2000) *Drug Treatment and Testing Orders: Final Evaluation Report*. Home Office Research Study 212. London: Home Office Research Development and Statistics Directorate.

US Department of Health and Human Services (1998) *Continuity of Offender Treatment for Substance Use Disorder from Institutions to the Community*. Washington, DC: US Government Printing Office.

US Department of Justice (1997) *Defining Drug Courts; the Key Components*. Washington, DC: Drug Courts Program Office.

US Department of Justice (1999) *I-ADAM in Eight Countries*. Washington, DC: US Department of Justice.

US General Accounting Office (1990) *Drug Control; how the Drug Consuming Nations are Organized for the War on Drugs*. Washington, DC: Committee of Government Affairs, US Senate.

US Treasury Department (Financial Crimes Enforcement Network) (1992) *An Assessment of Narcotics Related Money Laundering*. Washington, DC: US Government Printing Office.

Verdun-Jones, S. (1997) *Criminal Law in Canada* (2nd edn). Toronto: Harcourt Brace.

Visher, C. and McFadden, K. (1991) *A Comparison of Urinalyses Technologies for Drug Testing in Criminal Justices.* Washington, DC: US Department of Justice.

Wagstaff, A. (1989) Economic aspects of illicit drug markets and drug enforcement policies. *British Journal of Addiction* 84(10), 1173–82.

Wagstaff, A. and Maynard, A. (1988) *Economic Aspects of Illicit Drug Enforcement Policies in the UK.* Home Office Research Study 95. London: HMSO.

Wardlow, G. (1988) Linkages between the illegal drugs traffic and terrorism. *Conflict Quarterly* (Summer), 5–26.

Webster, R., Hough, M. and Clancy, A. (2001) An evaluation of the impact of Operation Crackdown (mimeo).

Weinman, B.A. and Lockwood, D. (1993) Inmate drug treatment programming in the Federal Bureau of Prisons. In Inciardi, J. (ed.) *Drug Treatment and Criminal Justice.* Thousand Oaks, CA, and London: Sage.

Wellisch, J., Anglin, M.D. and Prendergast, M.L. (1993) Treatment strategies for drug abusing women. In Inciardi, J. (ed.) *Drug Treatment and Criminal Justice.* Thousand Oaks, CA, and London: Sage.

Welsh Office (1998) *Forward Together: a Strategy to Combat Drug and Alcohol Misuse in Wales.* London: HMSO.

White, H. (1990) The drug use connection in adolescence. In Weisheit, R. (ed.) *Drugs, Crime and the Criminal Justice System.* Cincinnati, Ohio: Anderson.

White, H. and Gorman, D. (2000) Dynamics of the drug–crime relationship. In *The Nature of Crime; Community and Change. Criminal Justice 2000.* Washington, DC: US Department of Justice.

Wilson, J. and Kelling, G. (1982) Broken windows. *Atlantic Monthly* 29–38.

Wish, E.D. (1988) Identifying drug abusing criminals. In Leukefeld, C.G. and Tims, F.M. (eds) *Compulsory Treatment of Drug Abuse: Research and Clinical Practice. NIDA Research Monograph* 86.

Wish, E.D. and Gropper, B.A. (1990) Drug treatment in the criminal justice system. In Tonry, M. and Wilson, J.Q. (eds) *Drugs and Crime.* Chicago, IL: University of Chicago Press.

Wozniak, E., Dyson, G. and Carnie, J. (1998) *The Third Prison Survey. Scottish Prison Service Occasional Paper* 3 Edinburgh: Research and Evaluation Services, Scottish Prison Service.

Young, J. (1971) *The drug takers.* Washington DC: Paladin.

Subject index

Name index